Dominic Canty was born in London, where he still lives and works, and regularly writes for local newspapers and magazines. After a number of years on the music and stand-up comedy circuits, he turned his focus to fiction and studied creative writing. He is a passionate scuba diver, an aficionado of the marine world and its inhabitants – in particular the Great White Shark – and is an active conservationist.

Dead Men Should Know Better is his first novel.

To find out more, please visit
www.dominiccanty.com

DEAD MEN SHOULD KNOW BETTER

Dominic Canty

ANCON HILL
PUBLISHING

First published in the United Kingdom in 2012 by Ancon Hill Publishing

This paperback edition published 2016

Copyright © Dominic Canty 2016

Illustrations & Images © Dominic Canty 2016

Ancon Hill Publishing Limited
PO Box 68828
London SE26 9BP
www.anconhill.co.uk

A CIP catalogue record for this book is available from the British Library

Print Book ISBN 978 0 9574783 1 2
eBook Kindle ISBN 978 0 9574783 2 9
ePub ISBN 978 0 9574783 3 6

Typeset by Hewer Text UK Ltd, Edinburgh
Printed and bound in Great Britain by Clays Ltd, St Ives plc

MIX
Paper from
responsible sources
FSC® C018072
www.fsc.org

To Jill, Patrick and Francesca

I

Whatever You Do, Don't…

THE LADY WAS DRESSED to kill – literally. The trademark off-the-shoulder blood-red dress, the knife-shaped clutch bag, the silver hair that hung like scrolls of barbed wire. And on the inside of her left wrist, the two-inch dagger tattoo entwined with thistles – the symbol of the infamous Wolves of River Plate crime syndicate.

Bristo Trabant was in no doubt. This was Azara Pampita Rázzon, the Vixen of the Pampas, Argentina's premier importer of all missiles and machine guns bound for the gangland streets of Buenos Aires and Córdoba.

He eased back inside the main entrance to Le Club Maritime du Soleil, hid behind a large rubber plant, retrieved his mobile telephone and typed '523' – the recognition code for MI6's Priority Surveillance Unit. Next: '014', the allocated ID number for Rázzon, then 'AAA' to confirm she had three bodyguards here with her in Cannes. Trabant pressed 'Send', watched the message go through, then held his breath as the lady breezed past.

Yes, Azara Pampita Rázzon was scary beyond belief. But what frightened him more was that, in the grand scheme of things, she was only the small fry.

'Quick, quick!' said Henri, the banqueting manager, to his staff. 'Señor Gunboat will be here any moment. Get ready to bow, and remember – agree with everything he says!'

The waiters hurried into position, but this was no royal visit. The foyer of Le Club Maritime du Soleil was laced with danger, the kind that drips from the ceiling then runs down the back of your neck in icy-cold globules of sweat.

It was 10.28 p.m.

Bristo Trabant retreated into the alcove beneath the stuffed moose head, retrieved *The Beginner's Guide To Being A Secret Agent* from his pocket, hurried to Chapter 9, Sub-Section 12, Appendix 98 and read as if his life depended on it, because it most probably did.

> If you find yourself in a dark, alien
> environment, where the beast you stalk
> begins to snarl – remain strong, my
> friend. If it doesn't know your true
> identity, then it has no reason to
> bite. Keep calm. Breathe deeply. Refer
> to protocol.

The sound of voices drew his attention. Trabant looked up to see the main entrance doors being opened, and then, there he was – the beast himself, the whole reason Trabant was there – 'Gunboat' Charlie Chávez, the face of the illicit arms trade, standing in the entrance, revelling in the hush.

Gunboat stood five six tall, and wide, and industrial-gauge shoulders supported his oil-barrel neck and boulder-grade head, itself capped with short, black hair. His skin was dark brown, and thick eyebrows formed a perma-scowl, beneath which

2

coal-black eyes darted with a chill of intent. His nose was wide and powerful, his ears small and piggy, and a downturned moustache ran all the way south to meet the short beard, circumnavigating the jaw-line as ominously as a passage around Cape Horn.

'Señor Gunboat, it has been too long,' said Henri, embracing the yacht club's most infamous member.

Gunboat smiled, but his mouth bore not a ripple of warmth, and on its bottom lip an extra-thick Cuban cigar balanced precariously, defying the laws of gravity.

Trabant shuddered. No MI6 photos could do justice to the human battering ram now standing before him. Yet the finishing touches came from the contours revealed through the crisp white shirt; contours of a fearsome power, a chilling potential, and the subtlest but most definite signs – of man-boobs.

'Here, have a fresh cigar… and champagne!' gushed Henri.

'Muchas… (puff)… gracias.'

'And your meeting room is ready.'

Gunboat sipped the golden liquid then nodded his approval. 'Okay, first I do my business, then we start the charity auction and make lotsa money, huh?'

'That would be wonderful, thank you.'

Gunboat dragged hard on his cigar, blew out a plume of smoke then began walking across the oak-panelled floor, flanked by his two enormous heavies.

Trabant breathed a huge sigh of relief, extracted his mobile telephone, typed '523-001-AA' and pressed 'Send'. Now all he had to do was confirm everyone else Gunboat was meeting. But how many would that be? Twenty? Thirt—

'Pardon, Monsieur. Vous voulez un vol-au-vent? I can offer mushroom, cheese, or—'

'Er, n-no, merci,' replied Trabant, looking beyond the waiter's tray of puff pastries to Gunboat's swirl of evil, as it continued down the corridor towards the main function room. 'But please remind me, w-what time does the charity auction begin?'

'Refuse one of señor Gunboat's vol-au-vents, and for you it may not begin at all.'

'Really!?!'

The waiter nodded. 'I must report all decliners.'

'In that case, I'll g-go for the cheese.'

'A wise choice, Monsieur. The auction begins at 11 p.m. sharp.'

'T-thank you.'

It was 10.34 p.m. Twenty-six minutes of gut-churning hell to endure, after which, if he'd relayed enough intelligence, he might just be able to slip away.

As soon as the waiter was out of sight, Trabant discarded his vol-au-vent and made for an open window. But he longed for more than fresh air and a wonderful view. In honesty he just wanted to be back home, where he felt safe. Never in a million years was he the right man for MI6 surveillance work, let alone as part of their elite Priority Surveillance Unit.

He allowed his eyes to wander past the rustling palm trees, across the promenade and down to the beach, where an army of sun-loungers now stood at ease. To the right lay Vieux Port, the Old Port, with its cool ripples of inky black water and armada of million-pound yachts. Beyond that stretched the densely packed hill of the Old Quarter, bathed in a yellowy street-lamp wash, and under the watchful eye of the ancient fort, itself well grounded in conflict, but right now offering not a morsel of advice.

Never before had he felt so lonely.

A flash of light drew his attention – a camera flash – from somewhere to the right, near Place du Général de Gaulle. Cannes was alive with the pomp and spectacle of the Film Festival, as starlets posed on the endless rolls of red carpet, and

4

congratulation and adulation resonated from every bar and restaurant. But here, in the French Riviera's swankiest yacht club, at this private event, he could only feel the chill – the chill of the darker shadows, of the parallel world into which he should never have been thrown.

'Monsieur, it is time to adjourn,' said Henri, gesturing towards the inner sanctum of the yacht club.

Trabant reluctantly eased himself into the procession of dazzling women and well-groomed men heading into the function room. So these were the beautiful people, the likes of whom he'd only ever seen in *Hello* magazine. Radiant, sophisticated; their bronzed, glitzy sheen procured from an unbending dedication to Ra, God of the Sun, and an access-all-areas lifestyle simply beyond the wildest dreams of his nine-to-five desk job.

The scene inside was equally spectacular; of brilliant white walls and nautical portraits; of ships' bells and clusters of balloons. The floor was covered by a sumptuously thick-pile carpet, and dead ahead was the stage. To its left, a curious doorway. To its right, a long marble bar, beyond which awaited a balcony.

Trabant opted for the adjacent mirror, and rechecked himself for the hundredth time. His suit – his only suit – dark blue and single-breasted, bore not the remotest comparison to the reams of tailored silk and satin flowing all around him. He knew he stood out like a sore thumb, but worse still, a sore thumb in a cheap suit, and—

'Very handsome,' said the hostess, as she glided past.

'Who?'

'You, Monsieur!'

Trabant went to contest her remark but was too late; she'd already disappeared into the crowd. Still unconvinced, he returned to his reflection. Handsome? Never! His six-foot frame was thin and ungainly, with blue eyes that looked weary and a crest of black hair that hadn't sat straight in over thirty years. But that was the fault of his ears, who'd always had a mind of their own.

'Incredible!'

'Hmmm?' Trabant turned to see a weaselly old man, dressed in a smoking jacket and monocle, now at his side. 'W-what is?'

'Her – the hostess who just spoke to you. Look! Body contoured like an alpine ski pass. Olive skin sun-kissed as the fields of the Loire Valley. Lips red and full as a London bus at rush hour.'

Trabant followed the weasel's eyes until she came back into view, now circling the far side of the room like an exotic bird of paradise. He'd spoken to her before, or at least he thought it was her, on both previous evenings when she'd served in the restaurant, though he'd been almost too nervous to lift his eyes from his food. And now he tried again to look away, but this time his eyes refused. They lingered on her voluptuous curves that ebbed and flowed within the body-hugging black velvet dress, that hung perfectly upon her six-foot, hour-glass frame. And her jet-black hair, which was coiled into a tight bun, revealed a neckline of delicious feminine purity.

'See what I mean!' beamed the weasel.

'Yes, she's…' Trabant turned in search of the right word, but the weasel had gone, summoned back by the disapproving glare of his wife. And now the hostess was approaching once more, this time capturing him with her eyes. And how he wanted to dive into those dark pools of milk chocolate and never resurface. But he couldn't, he shouldn't. Oh, my! The girls simply weren't like this back home in Chipping Sodbury.

'Drink, sir?' she asked.

'Y-yes, please. Apple juice?'

'Straight?'

'No, on the rocks.'

'Coming up.'

The weasel had been right. She *was* incredible, earth-shudderingly so. In fact, surely the most beautiful woman in the world? Trabant pondered that thought a moment longer, then returned to the same conclusion, that it wouldn't be necessary to meet every other woman in the world to compare, for he instinctively knew that to him she would still be – the most beautiful woman in the world.

'Voilà! One apple juice.'

His heart raced like a bullet train.

'My name's Eva.'

'I'm B–Bristo.'

'I know. But please be careful, Monsieur Bristo. It is a beautiful evening, but the sharks are beginning to circle.'

Trabant watched her disappear then turned back to gather his thoughts. Sharks? In the Mediterranean? Yes, the room was full of them. And he immediately recognised another. '523-016-AAA' – Nedho 'the Hook' Hamsho, the Istanbul Confession Extractor.

Trabant typed the recognition code, pressed 'Send', then quickly moved on around the perimeter of the room, weaving through the hum of conversation until about two metres from the curious doorway. It was now guarded by Gunboat's two henchmen, both of whom had shaven heads and flattened noses – the standard requirements to excel in the fright game. And their complexions were identical too – pockmarked and grazed, as if someone had forgotten to sand properly between coats. Yes, their presence scared him rigid, but the door they guarded was half-open. He *had* to look inside.

A cluster of guests provided excellent cover. He edged closer, feigning a loss of bearings until finally able to peek into the deep, dark room. Inside, beneath a cloud of cigar smoke, stood a long, polished table littered with drinks and open briefcases. And at the far end, talking machine-gun Spanish, sat Gunboat Charlie Chávez.

Trabant checked the other faces around the table. Some he recognised from the MI6 database, while others—

'Eh, what you doing?' asked one of Gunboat's heavies, stepping forward to block Trabant's view.

'J-just looking for the, er... balcony. Honest!'

'This room's none of your business. Get lost!'

iii

The Mediterranean Sea looked cool and moody, just like the other guests on the balcony. Trabant made his way to its farthest corner, took a lungful of air and tried to regain some composure. But a quick glance back through the window confirmed the heavies were in deep consultation. They *must* be on to him. Hell! And now they were glaring right back at him! There was only one thing to do – phone HQ.

At last the line answered. 'Vauxhall Cross Plumbers, how can we help?'

'It's me, the plumber,' whispered Trabant, behind a cupped hand. 'I think I'm blown!'

'Please confirm number, location and status.'

'Er... Number 218869. Location: 247. Job status: getting really dangerous. Please, this is urgent! Is the apprentice on his way?'

'Negative. Apprentice delayed. I repeat – apprentice delayed.'

'But you said—'

'Deep breaths, 218869. The first job's always the hardest. We've received your SMS reports so far. Good work, but are there other unreported leaks in the area?'

'Yes, lots!'

'Then you must complete the evaluation.'

'But I…'

The line went dead.

Bang! Whiiiiizzzzz!

Trabant jumped out of his skin, as a firework illuminated the bay in a brilliant spread of green and red. The whole of Cannes seemed to gasp in wonder, but he could spare no time for frivolity. He had to relay the names of those in the deep, dark room with Gunboat.

The first he'd remembered was '523-021-AAA' – Paolo Varienga, the Brazilian underworld financier. Then '523-019-AAAAA' – Solomon 'Double Tap' Hurunguru, the Central African Republic warlord, nicknamed after his favoured double-shot execution technique.

He texted both their details, then tried to recall more. Ooh, yes, the Russian, number 018, or was it 025? Er… Maybe he could just text his name. Yes, but how to spell it? Hell! Was it Sergei Miskachailov, or Mischatanov, or…?

'Pardon, Monsieur. Vous voulez une crêpe suzette?' asked the waiter.

'Oh, yes, I'd better. And while you're here, could you please remind me – the Russian gentleman in the room with Monsieur Chávez; how do you spell his surname?'

The world stopped, and the waiter blinked then instantly hurried inside, towards the large cauliflower ears of Gunboat's heavy. And in that split second, in that moment of irretrievable foolishness, Trabant knew – it was the question he should never have asked. Every other guest in the yacht club seemed to know it too, as the atmosphere turned like an assassin's blade, and the heavy charged out onto the balcony to seize its quarry.

'Hey! What the—'

'Come with me!'

'No, I…'

Trabant was frogmarched back inside, past the guests and into the meeting room, where he was dumped unceremoniously into a chair at the opposite end of the table to Gunboat.

'But please, I…'

Gunboat exhaled a long, jagged plume of cigar smoke. 'What's your name?'

'B-Bristo Trabant.'

'Trabant? What, as in the—'

'C-car? Yes.'

Gunboat turned to the heavy stood behind. 'Ha! Another gringo loco, eh, Raúl?'

'Sí, Boss.'

'My men say you been snoopying around and asking questions,' continued Gunboat. 'Who you work for?'

'N-no one.'

'Oh, so you gatecrasher, huh?'

'No. I was invited. I'm a journalist, for the, er… *Pimlico & District Chronicle*.'

Gunboat leant closer. 'Not a plumber?'

Eek! 'N-n-n-no… a film critic, here for the festival. Honest! Please, you've got to believe—'

'I no got to do nothing. But I do want to know which intelligence agency you work for. MI6? CIA?'

'*P-Pimlico & District*—'

'THAT RUBBISH!'

'It's actually highly regarded.'

Gunboat sank back in his chair. 'Newspapers no mean no thing to me. And neither, señor Trabant, do you. You lying to me, so I ask again – who you spy for?'

'I wasn't!'

'Then why you so interest in my amigo, Sergei Mischailov?'

'I'm not.'

'Ah, but you ask the waiter about him. Why?'

'I just thought Mr Mischail might be a famous, er… film director?'

'He been on plenty news clips, but he no make no movies. I think you a spy.'

'But I—'

'NO INTERRUPT!' shouted Gunboat. 'You stumble in wrong place at very wrong time.'

Sergei Mischailov now spoke up. 'I agree, señor Gunboat. This man is obviously a spy. So kill him.'

'Yes, and a spy with impossibly large ears!' added Azara Pampita Rázzon, inspecting Trabant as if he were some repulsive specimen. 'Señor, did you have them made, or were you raised by a herd of elephants?'

The room erupted with laughter.

'Must have been a difficult birth,' she continued.

'Eh, perhaps the doctor pull him out by his ears, huh?' joked Gunboat.

'It was the midwife, actually,' replied Trabant. 'S-she delivered me.'

'SHUT UP!' shouted Gunboat, slamming his fist down on the table. 'I DELIVER YOU TO UNDERTAKER IF YOU NO TELL ME WHO YOU ARE!'

'I also think you should kill him,' said Rázzon.

'Hear, hear,' added Double Tap. 'Our business is done. Now it's time for the entertainment.'

'Sure is, Gunboat,' beamed another man, wearing a Texan ten-gallon hat. 'Remember Montenegro last year, when you challenged that fool to a game of cards; when you lost and then shot him to pieces? That was such great fun. P-l-e-a-s-e can we see that again.'

'Your drinks, messieurs,' cut in Eva, expanding her cleavage to divert their attention. 'Champagne for señor Gunboat, and for you, Monsieur Trabant,' she continued, walking quickly to

11

the opposite end of the table, 'apple juice on the rocks, just as you like it.'

'T-thank you.'

'My pleasure,' she replied, looking back up the table. 'Señor Gunboat, you know it is against the law in France to force someone to play games against their will.'

'Perhaps, but I no a law-abiding citizen. No ever have been. Which is why the British Secret Service is here tonight, to watch me. Isn't that right, señor Trans-Am?'

Trabant could feel the word 'Guilty!' flashing above his head like a hazard warning light. Did Gunboat really know he worked for MI6's Priority Surveillance Unit, albeit only in an IT support capacity? And if so, then how? And if he did know, he should also know he was only here by default, as every other field operative in the department was either allocated, or incapacitated with chickenpox.

'Monsieur Trabant is a renowned film journalist,' continued Eva, as she collected empty glasses from the table.

'Am I?'

'Most definitely. Ladies and Gentlemen, I have read many of his articles, and they are all exemplary. And surely someone of your intellect, señor Gunboat, would have done precisely the same?'

'Hmmm… As I say, I no read papers, but I read this gringo's mind. He here for trouble.' Gunboat turned to his nearer heavy. 'Raúl – tell Henri to prepare the gaming table.'

'Sí, Boss.'

'No!' protested Eva. 'That is wholly unnecessary.'

'The only thing necessary,' replied Gunboat, 'is for señor Sergei to continue with tradition.'

Mischailov smiled, jotted down the names of three card games on a piece of paper, then walked over to Trabant. 'Pick one.'

'D-do I have to?'

'YES!' shouted Gunboat. 'But no dare say your choice out loud, or I kill you right here.'

Trabant hastily tapped option two.

'Bravo! No so difficult, eh? Now, Ramón – take the spy to his seat.'

'But, señor Gunboat,' continued Eva, 'this is a terrible mistake!'

'Señorita, you a good hostess, but you interfere *way* too much. The gringo should know better. Now shoo! I have game of cards to play.'

iv

A large circular table had been covered with a green cloth and placed on the stage, with two antique chairs set opposite each other. Bristo Trabant sat on one.

Eva pushed her way through the hastily assembling crowd, trying to catch Trabant's eye, to warn him. She knew that if he did beat Gunboat he would pay with his life. Gunboat was the worst loser ever, but refusal to play him also carried the same life-terminating consequences. Bristo just had to play badly and let Gunboat win, as countless others had done over the years, and then – just maybe – he would escape with his life. It was the only hope.

The room fell deadly silent. Gunboat was now taking his seat, revelling in the hush, bathing in the horror etched upon Trabant's face.

'Señor, no look so worried,' he said, leaning forward.

'Really?' replied Trabant, clutching the glimmer of hope. 'W-why's that?'

'Simple. When you're a dead man, you have nothing left to lose.'

Trabant's world stopped again.

The croupier placed a pack in front of each player. 'As Monsieur Trabant is the challenger, he shall go first.'

'Wait!' shouted Eva, reappearing from the far side of the room. 'Fresh drinks!' As she placed the glasses down, she looked deep into Trabant's eyes and shook her head in warning.

'Right, out the way,' said the croupier. 'Let's get this game underway.'

As the crowd inched closer, Trabant reached forward and took a deep slug of apple juice. He could already feel the intensity of Gunboat's stare, squeezing droplets of sweat from his forehead like a wine press.

'Monsieur, if you please…'

Trabant nervously turned his first card.

Queen of Hearts.

Gunboat laid his first card beside it.

Ace of Clubs.

Trabant followed, and the game quickly gained a breakneck momentum.

Seven of Diamonds.

Four of Clubs.

The crowd stepped closer still, primed with the juicy anticipation of Gunboat's murderous reaction.

Six of Hearts.

Ten of Spades.

Tension rose higher still, now clawing at the ceiling, desperate for release, until finally Gunboat laid down his remaining card. But no winners this time.

Conversation returned to the room, tinged with a wolf-pack frustration at being robbed of the kill. As the croupier gathered the scattered cards into a pile, Trabant eased back in his chair, exhaled his own bluster of tension, and replaced it with a long slug of juice. Hmmm… delicious! Freshly squeezed apples and crushed ice always hit the spot.

'Whatever you do, don't play him at cards.'

14

The head of MI6 had been most clear. But another long slug and Bravinger's warning became further diluted.

Trabant began to look around with renewed confidence. He was still alive, he'd survived the test, and his sense of relief was such that it overruled any possible notions of something else going wrong. And so, why shouldn't he play again at cards? After all, it was only a game, and despite his gruff manner, perhaps Gunboat Charlie wasn't as bad as everyone made out. Trabant looked across to Eva as the second sets of cards were placed in front of each contestant. She wore another don't-beat-him-just-get-out-of-there expression on her face, which Trabant decided to interpret as a go-on-you-can-do-it look. He winked back. Eva closed her eyes.

Gunboat surveyed Trabant with increasing suspicion then nodded to his two heavies, who instantly moved into position – one by the room's entrance, the other directly behind Trabant.

'Mesdames et messieurs, let the second game commence,' announced the croupier.

Deathly silence reclaimed the room.

Four of Clubs – thrown down aggressively by Gunboat.

Six of Diamonds. Trabant was warming up. He'd surely impress Eva by winning the game, and become hero of the night.

Six of Spades.

Nine of Hearts.

Two of Spades.

The cards were thrown down faster and faster. Gunboat bit harder onto his cigar, emitting toxic mumblings under his Panamanian breath, tensing up as he felt the game slipping away. Trabant – stone-cold sober – felt sharp.

Gunboat threw down the *Nine of Diamonds*. As the card slid across the previous one, Trabant quickly released his next. It whistled through the air in slow motion, eventually landing on

15

the table before him. Gunboat's reactions were slow, distracted by a momentary glance to check his men were in place. His eyes returned to the table in horror. The card Trabant had thrown down had barely settled, yet matched his own card exactly. He went to mouth the word but was too late; Trabant was already there – shouting the word that would change history, the course of world affairs, and the word that would start the countdown on his very existence.

The word was final.

The word was cutting.

The word was…

'Snap!'

2

A Modicum of Self-Control

THE WORD HUNG IN the air like a hand grenade.

Henri and the croupier dived for cover, yelling for the circle of guests to do the same, to seek shelter from the impending explosion once the word detonated within the fragile confines of Gunboat's mind. Some took heed while others moved closer still, their eyes wide in joyous anticipation.

Only Trabant remained oblivious, lost upon the waves of elation that carried him away to pastures new. Victory had always been a stranger – during school days, academically, even into adult life, but at last, against the odds, it had arrived, and boy was he going to enjoy it. Once more he punched the air, then turned with open arms to milk the adoration of the awestruck room. But there was none to receive, only a scene of suspended animation.

What was wrong? Why no standing ovation? He'd played by the rules, and the best man had won, so what was the problem? No harm done, and after all, it was only a...

'Oh!'

The penny dropped, and from great altitude, smashing into a thousand tiny pieces to give all the answers he could ever need.

'*Whatever you do, don't play him at cards.*'

Now he recalled Bravinger's warning, and the fateful advice he really should have taken.

Against his better judgement, Trabant looked across the table and read Gunboat's expression like an environmental health warning. The coal-black eyes remained transfixed by the two matching cards before him, refusing to believe what had just happened, until disbelief ran out of alternatives and drew its final conclusion.

'Grrrrrrrrrrrrrrrrrr…..'

The smouldering volcano of Gunboat Charlie Chávez began to shake, and the well-drilled waiting staff took their positions, holding down the fixtures and fittings, praying to the gods of yacht club preservation for the minimum amount of damage.

Plop. Fizzzzzzz…

Gunboat's cigar teetered over the edge and fell directly into his glass of champagne. His podgy sausage-fingers curled to form wrecking-ball fists, and his head and body began to boil, like a kettle beside itself with fury. Onlookers feared for their lives as the tremors became worse, as Gunboat's eyes bulged and danced with evil spirits intent on exacting only the most violent of revenges; until finally, uncontrollably, the red-hot lava of anger rose to the surface and erupted.

'AAAAAAARRRRRRGGGGGGHHHHHH!'

With agility defying his bulk, Gunboat launched himself across the table, reaching for Trabant's throat with outstretched grasping hands. Drinks and cards flew in every direction. Trabant threw himself backwards, narrowly evading the clutches but in the process toppling over his chair to land flat on the floor. Gunboat, now spread-eagled on the table like a beached whale, scrambled across the green-cloth surface, screaming incoherently.

Raúl, still positioned behind, swung an open paw to scoop up the perpetrator, but Trabant was quicker, rolling left then diving headfirst for a gap in the crowd, the other side of which led to the doorway, and freedom, and a chance to—

The heavy seized Trabant's collar with such force that it almost ripped his head clean off. But his legs continued upwards, as if scaling an imaginary wall, until running out of momentum – pausing – then crashing back down to join the rest of his body in a crumpled, jarred heap upon the thick-pile carpet.

The crowd gasped, but the heavy wasted not a moment, tightening his grip further to haul Trabant back across the room. And the sheer power of that grip transformed his collar from neckline fashion statement into makeshift garrotte, cutting so deep it almost severed his windpipe… starving him of air… dragging him down a darkening, star-spattered tunnel from which there would be no return. Trabant fought for breath, kicking and flailing with all his might, but his strength was fading, he could barely—

'Ow!'

The heavy clattered him into one of the broad table legs, then took the chance to adjust his grip. But the momentary release was enough. Trabant hoovered up a lungful of air and began to wriggle, until finally able to free his arms from his jacket sleeves. Another few twists and he was away, and before the heavy knew it, three wobbly paces back towards the exit.

Ten metres, five metres…

Ducking and dodging between the astonished guests, his head began to clear. To the left was an open window. Should he dive through and take his chances amongst the hedgerows and shrubbery? No, the door! That was the easiest option, and nearly there, just a few more—

'Oof…'

The second heavy's foot tripped and sent him tumbling back to the thick-pile carpet, his momentum terminating at the disapproving feet of the banqueting manager.

'I shall charge you for any damages,' hissed Henri.

'But I…'

The doorway was now full of guests and staff from the foyer, drawn closer by the commotion.

'What on earth is he doing down there?' asked one.

'Je ne sais pas!' replied another.

'Few too many beers,' scoffed a third.

'P-please help me!' wheezed Trabant, stretching his fingers for a human lifeline. But no one offered, not when they saw the heavy *and* Gunboat approaching, seething with anger.

Trabant made a final dive for the gaps between their legs, but it was all too late. The door closed before him with a soft, decisive click, and the heavy's enormous hand began to drag him once more, like a fallen horseman with a foot caught in the stirrup, back across the floor.

'Hector, that horrible man on the floor knocked over my club soda!' sneered an elderly, walnut-skinned lady. '*Do* something!'

'It's okay, Véronique. Señor Chávez will exact a far more violent revenge than I. Come, let us follow him and enjoy the execution.'

In no time, Trabant was back in the centre of the room. And in one efficient movement, the heavy hauled him to his feet, locked his arms behind his head in a full-nelson wrestling hold, then lifted him a clear six inches off the sumptuous carpet. The second heavy soon joined them, smiled, then punched Trabant hard in the stomach.

The room winced in unison.

'What's that gurgling sound remind you of, Ramón?' mocked the heavy, retrieving his fist from the envelope of Trabant's stomach.

'Bath water, Raúl,' replied his brother. 'You know, when it squeeze through the plughole.'

'Sí, I agree. Guess the tide's out for this gringo, eh?'

'The tide's out! That a good one, that is,' laughed Ramón, before dropping his victim to the floor like a dead weight.

The room winced again. Trabant cradled his battered stomach, fighting the swell of nausea best he could.

'*When you're a dead man, you have nothing left to lose… to lose… to lose.*' And he had nothing left.

Gunboat moved closer, crushing the delicate strands of carpet beneath his own immense shoes, until he stood overhead. His massive frame rose and fell with each deep, hoarse breath that produced a growl all of its own; and his eyes blazed down with loathsome, despising contempt. Slowly he reached inside his jacket.

'No… p-please…' whimpered Trabant.

'Shut up!' snarled Gunboat.

The room fell deathly quiet, as the outline of a large bulky metallic weapon broke the surface and came to point directly at Trabant's head.

'He gonna use the Colt Python .357 Magnum,' whispered Raúl approvingly, as if complimenting a golfer on his choice of club.

'Wonderful!' replied Ramón, picturing the neat hole the revolver would punch, first through the victim's skull, then on through the floor, the foundations, and several layers of the earth's crust.

House lights sparkled off its nickel-plated housing, as Gunboat narrowed his eyes, adjusted his aim, then slowly began to squeeze the trigger.

'NOT HERE!'

'What?' snapped Gunboat, furious at the interruption.

'I SAID – NOT HERE!' repeated the voice, forcing its way through the crowd. 'Take him somewhere else.'

The voice was strong, commanding and decisive. And Trabant immediately recognised its underlying textures of French honey.

'But I wanna kill him – right here!' protested Gunboat.

'There are too many witnesses,' continued Eva, with maximum assurance. 'Take him to our security room. Leave him there until the crowd has gone, then do as you will.'

21

Gunboat gave her a long, hard look. 'And who the hell are you?'

'The hostess who's been serving your drinks all night.' Her words were deliberately sharp, to divert the attention. 'Come on, quickly! You know it makes sense.'

The Magnum remained pointed, while Gunboat's eyes drilled deep into Eva's soul, searching for her ulterior motive. She stared back with equal intensity, sending every telepathic vibe she could muster, to assure him it was the right thing to do. He chewed his bottom lip in deeper contemplation, desperate to just blow the Englishman's head clean off and be done with it, yet somehow her voice of reason was making an exceptional case.

'She has a point, Boss,' stated Raúl.

'I know,' grumbled Gunboat, reluctantly. 'I know.'

A modicum of self-control returned, warmed by the prospect of an evening's torture. Gunboat returned the gun to its holster, straightened his jacket then clicked the short podgy fingers of his left hand. Within seconds a new thick Cuban cigar was inserted and lit by Henri, and once Gunboat had reappeared from the smoke cloud large enough to conceal a light aircraft, he narrowed his eyes and turned towards Eva.

'Okay, señorita. I come back in one hour then do as I please.'

'No problem at all, señor Gunboat. What do you have in mind?'

'I make him wish he no ever been born.'

'I already d-do,' spluttered Trabant.

The crowd pined for blood, as did Gunboat's clients.

'P-l-e-a-s-e don't stop now!' begged the man wearing the Texan ten-gallon hat. 'It's my favourite part of the evening.'

'And I have just ordered a round of vodka shots to celebrate this wonderful happening!' added Sergei Mischailov.

But the decision had been made.

'No worry, I no let you all down. We have private execution later.'

Gunboat turned and walked out of the room, with Ramón following close behind. Raúl lifted Trabant by scruff of neck and belt of trousers, and followed Eva out through the lobby and beyond the reception desk, until they stopped outside a small door concealed from view by a twelve-foot-tall headless and armless sculpture.

'Place him in here!' said Eva, unlocking the door.

Raúl lined up with the open doorway, then released Trabant on the fourth swing.

Crash!

'I be back in one hour.'

'No problem,' replied Eva, hastily relocking the door. 'The prisoner will be here for when you return.'

Raúl leant closer and growled. 'He better be.'

3

Self-Clipped Wings

THE BROOM CUPBOARD OFFERED not a speck of light, not even a distant beam from around the doorframe or air vent, just a smothering black canvas upon which imaginary shapes ran riot.

Bristo Trabant stirred and became acutely aware of just how bad he felt. Yet the pain could have been worse, if the heavy's aim had been true, if he had hit the wall square on. Instead, his right shoulder had taken the brunt, and despite a very deep and dull aching, felt remarkably intact. Perhaps French yacht club broom cupboards were lined with rubber? Perhaps the full wave of excruciation had stopped en route for coffee and croissants? Either way, he was thankful to still be alive.

Wearily he got to his feet, waited for his head to stop spinning then began to feel his way back along the shelves, wading through the scattered debris until finally he reached the door. Despite an extensive search, there was no light-switch to be found. He ran his hands further down and felt for the door handle, then frantically turned the cold metallic lever up and down with all his might. But the door, of course, was locked.

Hope somehow remained, in the form of his mobile telephone, deep inside his trouser pocket. But as he hastily retrieved the number for Vauxhall Cross Plumbers, his fears were realised – he had absolutely no signal at all.

Hope now abandoned ship, leaving his body little option but to slide back down to the floor, and count its final breaths until the moment came. And how long would that be – forty minutes? Maybe less if the Grim Reaper had a busy schedule.

'*Whatever you do, don't play him at cards.*'

Why hadn't he listened? Why hadn't he just stayed at home?

Trabant shook his head in despair. He hadn't joined MI6 to get beaten up, thrown into broom cupboards and executed. His field was IT – safe, predictable, and with a career path that guaranteed zero contact with *any* international arms dealers, no matter where they were from. And what of Eva? How stupid had he been to believe she was on his side? Monumentally! Her beauty had clouded his judgement, and now the reality was clear – his imprisonment inside this dark cell was all her idea. Hardly the work of a good Samaritan.

The graze to his right elbow throbbed in agreement. Trabant gently touched it, winced, then slowly exhaled the pain through gritted teeth. His shirt and trousers were ripped too, but at least his suit jacket would be okay, because it—

Hey, where *was* his jacket?

Oh, no!

Oh, please no!

Panic swept like a bush fire. He shifted his legs and began to crawl, ignoring the pain to search the floor.

Please be here… please be here!

He continued scrabbling beneath the bottles and papers, his desperation building with every blind fumble.

Where the hell was…?

'Oh, no!' he cried, with sudden realisation. His jacket, jettisoned during attempts to escape, would be back in the function room, trampled underfoot and now a battered relic of a once happier time. But it wasn't the damage or separation that frosted his soul. It was the fact that it would surely have been retrieved and searched, which would inevitably lead to the discovery of the piece of paper that lay wedged between the pages of *The Beginner's Guide To Being A Secret Agent*.

Trabant scrunched his eyes in torment. The loss of that piece of paper was momentous, for it contained all the MI6 telephone numbers and security access codes. And further still, it was the piece of paper Bravinger had specifically ordered him to destroy. He shuddered at the implications, and the second valid reason why his life was no longer worth living.

ii

The last six months had gone surprising well. He'd finally plucked up the courage to take the job in London, and had moved into the spare room of Aunt Rose's townhouse in Pimlico, a delightful oasis of tranquillity (as she lovingly described it) sandwiched between Victoria train station and the River Thames.

Though at first the pace of the capital had taken him aback, and greeted him every morning like an angry bear, the intensity and relentless charge slowly became the norm. And rather than struggle against the never-ending tide of people cocooned in an iPod world, he'd learnt to relax, go with the flow and ease his way through the daily battle for survival. Yes, he'd acclimatised, made peace with the angry bear, and in his own quiet way even become one of its disciples.

Thankfully the job was great, and every morning he walked to work with a glowing sense of pride that the imposing green-and-sand-coloured building, situated just across Vauxhall Bridge, was where he belonged. Yes, the headquarters of MI6 simply oozed stature and presence, and with each day he became more convinced the only thing missing from its summit was a huge flag with the word 'Lego' emblazoned across it.

He had his own desk and mug; his colleagues were nice; he'd made new friends, and Rita, who worked in the canteen, had taken a shine to him – not in a romantic way, but more as a surrogate mother would. On the day her car wouldn't start she'd been taken aback by his offer to fix it. He'd duly devoted his lunch hour to removing the battery, express-ordering a new one, and having the car back on the road by the end of Rita's working day. Tinkering with cars was one of his favourite pastimes, especially his beloved 1978 Trabant 601, which never missed a beat, and in which he never missed an opportunity to head out to the countryside with friends. Yes, Rita's smile of gratitude was more than enough reward. Yet from then on, she always gave him an extra dollop of custard on his dessert, which made the relocation from Cotswold market town to bustling metropolis that little bit smoother. Yep, everything had seemed rosy – until the call came.

'Trabant?' the internal telephone had barked.

'Yes, how can I help?'

'You're wanted – right now! Take the lift to the top floor. Someone will be waiting for you.'

Top floor! Where Bravinger, the head of MI6, perched! Whatever could the top man want with him? Had he made some terrible error, or—

Bing!

The lift allowed little time to think, transporting him to the summit of Legoland at double speed. The doors slid open to reveal a tall lady dressed in black, already beckoning him to follow her along a corridor towards a large oak door.

Knock. Knock.

'Enter.'

'Bristo Trabant for you, sir,' she said, ushering him through like a traffic cop.

'Ah, yes. Thank you.'

The door closed swiftly behind.

'Take a seat,' ordered Bravinger.

Trabant walked across the pale-blue carpet that led to the large desk of Lord Almighty himself – Colonel Archibald

Bravinger, formerly of the British Army, before trotting the globe as MI6 Station Chief in every glamorous location he could engineer, before finally settling in, all too comfortably many would say, as head of MI6.

At first appearance, he appeared to be more barn owl than human being. Fluffy white hair and beard dominated his face, with the remainder of his body squeezed into a dark-grey, double-breasted tweed suit, complete with matching old-school tie and breast-pocket handkerchief. His eyes were dark and beady, and peering through horn-rimmed bifocals at the thick file open upon the desk. And sitting opposite was Hardcastle – Trabant's boss and head of the Priority Surveillance Unit.

Hell! What on earth was…?

'Hello, Bristo,' said Hardcastle, passing a sheet of paper to Trabant. 'Remember this?'

THE PRIORITY SURVEILLANCE UNIT

With the ever-increasing demands placed on MI6 and its field operatives, it has become necessary to create a dedicated fast-response support capability, with the purpose of not only maintaining, but also increasing surveillance on the highest-calibre targets whose activities are classified as a CATEGORY ONE NATIONAL SECURITY THREAT.

To address this necessity – and with immediate effect – the Priority Surveillance Unit (PSU) has been set up. It will comprise of two divisions:

1) Standby Field Operatives – who will be 'floating' around the world, and can be rapidly deployed to the place of necessity should the above-mentioned targets:
    a. Suddenly/unexpectedly appear on the radar
    b. Become especially active
    or also to...
    c. Step in if pre-existing surveillance measures have, for whatever reason, broken down.

2) The Hub – the main coordination centre, situated on the fifth floor of MI6 Headquarters, Vauxhall Cross, London. It will consist of a team of thirty Intelligence Coordinators providing round-the-clock monitoring of 'live' operations from all over the world.

These Intelligence Coordinators will be underpinned by their own dedicated team of IT Support Officers, working to ensure system continuity, but with no direct input into operations themselves.

Trabant looked up from the page. There was nothing new there. It was the document he had signed together with the Official Secrets Act when he'd joined MI6, but the suddenly proffered reminder told him something awful was in the offing.

'So, Trabant,' said Bravinger, looking up over his bifocals. 'Am I correct in saying you are one of those dedicated IT Support Officers?'

'Er, yes, sir.'

'Good. Well, it's time to show a bit more dedication. Ever heard of a man named Gunboat Charlie Chávez?'

'Only in p-passing, sir.'

Bravinger cast an eye over Trabant. 'How much do you weigh?'

'About twelve stone, sir. Why?'

'Are you fit?'

'Not particularly.'

'Done any martial arts?'

'No, sir.'

'How about boxing?'

'Only at Sainsbury's. Part-time, two evenings a week, and not bad money considering the—'

'No, no, no. I mean Queensberry Rules. You know, with gloves. The noble art of self-defence. Frank Bruno. Rocky Balboa. Ring a bell, if you'll excuse the pun?'

'Oh sorry, sir. No, I haven't. Why?'

'Because this assignment could cut up rough.'

Trabant's body tensed. 'W–what assignment?'

Bravinger took off his glasses. 'We need you to watch Gunboat. Only for a few days until Bentley, our Southern France field operative, is back.'

'Back from where, sir?'

'The pox.'

'Where's that, sir?'

'Where's what?'

'The pox.'

'Chickenpox, you fool!' exclaimed Bravinger. 'It's disabled both him and our department at the very moment Gunboat is to become very active indeed. That's where you come in.'

Trabant froze. A target? Under surveillance? Never in a million years was he the right man for the job. How could they possibly consider him for—

'I've seen your file. You had chickenpox when you were five, which is why you haven't caught it this time. Because you're immune, right?'

'Yes, sir. But—'

'And you once did voluntary work for the RSPB, so you're good at watching things through binoculars.'

'It was only data entry, in the school holidays, when I was fourteen.'

'Don't argue, Trabant. Africa is burning. The Middle East is raging. And of all the other field agents on our books, none have a dog's chance of getting to the South of France by tonight. So you're to go. There *is* no one else.'

'But, sir…'

'The PSU is my creation,' continued Bravinger. 'I personally got it up and running, and I won't let it fail. Neither will you.'

'But, sir, I honestly don't know anything about surveillance.'

'Do you watch television?'

'Y-yes.'

'Find your eyes glued to the screen at the most interesting moment?'

Trabant nodded.

'Good, then you'll be fine. Surveillance is just the same, all about keeping your eyes glued to the action. And with ears the size of yours, you won't miss a whisper. Got the gist?'

'Er...' No, he hadn't got it, and furthermore he didn't *want* to get it. Surveillance meant danger, and stepping far out of his comfort zone.

'Come on, man. Try to look enthusiastic,' continued the head of MI6. 'Where's your self-confidence?'

'I haven't got much of that, sir.' And he hadn't, and he knew where he'd lost it – school. The teasing he'd endured as a ten-year-old child trying to settle into a new country, with an unusual name, unusual accent and yes, unusually large ears, had made his life a misery. Only back at home was he able to feel good about himself, back beneath the shower of love his mother always bestowed, where he could feel special again, until the next day when it was time to return to school. But he never let on. He didn't want to worry his mother. Yet the jokes and the teasing – every word of every line – hurt deeply, and remained with him to this—

'TRABANT!' shouted Bravinger. 'Wake up! You look miles away.'

'Oh... sorry, sir. I was just—'

'I see from your file that your grandfather flew Hurricanes for the RAF in the Battle of Britain?'

'Yes, sir. He did.'

'So that's the spirit you want to show.'

'Y-yes, sir.'

'Still alive, is he?'

'Yes, sir. He's ninety-two.'

'And where does he live now?'

'In the bookies, mainly.'

'I mean, which town?'

'Oh, Chipping Sodbury, in the Cotswolds, sir.'

'I see. And that's where you used to work for Sodbury Town Council?'

'Yes, sir.'

'Doing what? Computer stuff?'

'Yes. Systems Support and Integration was my job title, until I was made redundant.'

'After which you applied for work at GCHQ – the Government Communications Headquarters – in Cheltenham, correct?'

'Yes, sir.'

'To do what? Computers again?'

'Yes, but that's all. Nothing whatsoever to do with national security issues.'

'I see. So they offered you a job, but the posting was here in London, as an IT Support Officer for the newly formed Priority Surveillance Unit.'

'Yes, sir.'

'And how *are* you enjoying the bright lights?'

Trabant pondered the question. For him, the bright lights were more like a Club 18 – 30s holiday, full of drinking games and debauchery, when in honesty he was far happier at home with his dinner on a tray and the latest issue of *Classic Car Weekly*. Mother Nature clearly hadn't intended him to be a hell-raiser, and so he'd made a life choice, to stick to the things that made him feel safe and happy. His tropical fish only asked for a daily sprinkle of food and an occasional clean-out. The church choir had no objections to his modest contributions, and his beloved Trabant car always waited patiently for their next outing, without the slightest murmur of discontent. No, he wasn't hurting anyone or letting anyone down. He was a home-bird with self-clipped wings, who longed for security and a stress-free existence. He knew his limitations, and that suited him just fine.

'I'm a home-bird, sir,' he continued. 'With self-clipped—'

'Ouch! Sounds painful,' winced Bravinger. 'Well, perhaps a trip overseas will do you the world of good. So, down to business. Gunboat Charlie Chávez: Panamanian national and huge international arms trafficker – both geographically *and* physically.'

Bravinger pushed the thick brown folder across the desk. Trabant reluctantly began flicking through the intelligence reports and official documentation. There were photographs of the man at various locations: eating in restaurants; smoking cigars on luxury yachts; shaking hands with bullet-belt-strewn soldiers of varying nationalities.

'Top priority target for us and every other intelligence agency on this planet,' mused Bravinger. 'Has a global delivery infrastructure like you wouldn't believe. Right now, as we speak, his cargo planes will be creaking and groaning their way along the runways of the world, laden to the rafters with weapons, climbing to the skies like pregnant ducks, and flying straight through the gaping loopholes of international law en route to the countless conflict zones around the world. Arms embargoes are disregarded with contempt; false end-user certificates created with great hilarity. Know what they are?'

'N-no, sir?'

'Documents to certify that the buyer is the final recipient, and is not planning to sell on the arms to a third party, which of course they are.'

'Oh!'

'Gunboat has more fingers in more rotten pies than you or I could imagine. Thing is, it is *he* who chooses *all* the ingredients, leaving everyone else – including us – with no choice but to say "Mmmm, how delicious," and put up with the bitter aftertaste. But I guess that's modern-day political cuisine for you, eh, Trabant?'

'Is it, sir?'

'Yes – it is!'

Bravinger flopped back in his chair. 'Pick a war, any war, and you can be certain he's involved, supplying both sides probably, then selling the spoils on to the next uprising or political coup. And have a look at these…' he continued, tossing yet more photographs across the desk. 'Ever seen such a collection of cut-throats in all your life?'

'No, sir, I haven't,' replied Trabant. 'Who are they?'

'Rebel leaders fighting deep in the Congo, the Central African Republic… the list goes on. Gunboat is supplying them with a cornucopia of weapons. Assault rifles, rocket-propelled grenade launchers, surface-to-air missiles. You name it, he'll get it. Not only are we struggling to stem the flow, we also have no idea when the next shipment is due, let alone where the weapons originate from.'

Hardcastle spoke up. 'Bristo, I appreciate this is all new to you, but we need you to confirm precisely who Gunboat is meeting. The UK's commitment to peacekeeping in Africa is huge, not to mention our oil fields that needed protecting. If they fall into the wrong hands, it will be disastrous.'

'Yes, sir. I see.'

'If we can identify who he talks with,' continued Hardcastle, 'we can identify a pattern of movements. Your mission is just to observe Gunboat until Bentley – our top man – is over the pox and able to replace you.'

'Have you met Bentley yet?' asked Bravinger.

'No, sir.'

'Well, you will. He's the finest we have – lean, mean and fearless, and always gets the job done. Don't know *how* he does it. And he's as good with his money as he is with his fists. Anyway, I digress. Do exactly as Hardcastle says: observe and report back who Gunboat is meeting. Understand?'

Trabant nodded.

'Good. It's all quite simple. Just relay that information in code back to HQ via mobile telephone text-message, and stay undetected until you are replaced. Then you can return to whatever it is you IT boys do. Okay?'

'Sir.'

'Any questions?'

'Er, yes. W-where precisely do I have to go?'

'Cannes, South of France. Gunboat is holding a charity fund-raising event at Le Club Maritime du Soleil, a very upmarket yacht club. Truth is – the event is just a distraction. He's really there to do business with many of his regular clients. You're already booked in at L'Hôtel Louis Figaro, which is directly opposite, under the name of Trabant, for three nights.'

'Three nights!'

'You have a problem with that?' glared Bravinger.

'No, sir. It's just that—'

'Your cover will be as a film critic. We thought it most appropriate, seeing as his meeting specifically coincides with the Cannes Film Festival. Or do you disagree with that as well?'

The barn owl was getting tetchy.

'No, sir. What I meant was I don't know much about—'

'Tough! Buy some magazines at the airport and get with it.' Bravinger leant forward and handed Trabant a piece of paper. 'If you need to phone HQ, dial the number for Vauxhall Cross Plumbers. Introduce yourself as "the plumber" and only speak using the coded phrases detailed. Got it?'

'But I thought I was a film critic?'

'You are, except in emergencies. It's a secondary cover to confuse the enemy.'

'Er… '

'Finally, at the bottom you will see a series of numbered code sequences and passwords. When relayed to the operator, they will give you Priority Surveillance Unit Level Five security clearance, *and* access to Bentley's whereabouts, should you need to locate him. As you can appreciate, that information is of the highest national security. Memorise everything on that piece of paper then destroy it – immediately! That's an order.'

'Yes, sir.'

'Don't worry about your normal work. I've squared it with Captain Hardcastle here.'

'Oh, I see. And when do I leave?'

'Right now! Go straight to personnel and collect your flight ticket and guide book.'

'G-guide book… to Cannes, sir?' asked Trabant.

'No – *The Beginner's Guide To Being A Secret Agent*,' replied Bravinger. 'It's a manual I wrote, to bed in all new recruits as quickly as possible. Anyway, that's all. Off you go.'

Trabant stood, and turned to leave.

'Oh, one last thing,' added Bravinger, catching Trabant as he reached the door. 'And most important of all. When I said "just observe", I meant precisely that. Whatever you do, don't get into conversation with Gunboat. Got it?'

'Yes, sir.'

'And finally, above anything else…'

'Yes, sir?'

'Whatever you do, don't play him at cards.'

4

Shelter from the Storm

THE SOUND OF FOOTSTEPS grew louder. Bristo Trabant shuffled as far away from the door as possible, an instinctive retreat within the smothering blackness of the broom cupboard. He prayed they would continue on by, but instead they grew louder and faster, until finally stopping, right outside the door.

Keys began to jangle, followed by their dull metallic clank in the lock. And then, slowly, the door began to open. Light entered, at first just a vertical beam moving along the wall, then as a total blaze, like a shattered dam of illumination flooding the room.

'Please – no!' whimpered Trabant, raising his hands to protect his body. And through the gaps in his fingers he could make out the human outline, and the extended arm now reaching towards him.

'NO!'

'Ssssshhhh… Quick! Come with me!'

The words didn't register until she said them again.

'Eva?'

'Yes. Take my hand, we must hurry.'

'But…?'

'I've come to rescue you, not kill you. And my car is parked outside. So let's get going, unless of course you'd rather wait?'

The twelve-foot headless and armless sculpture provided excellent cover. Eva peered round, waiting for a gap in the human traffic like a driver at a busy road junction. There were no staff in sight, but a group of men still loitered outside the function room. And another man soon joined them, with arms open wide in champagne-fuelled over-exuberance – the required distraction.

'Okay, now!' she whispered, leading Trabant by the hand.

They slipped unnoticed past the reception desk and continued along a corridor that led to the service lift. Down two floors, they stepped out into the basement, ran past a line of steel cages full of dirty linen, through three sets of double-doors and finally out into warm, night air.

'It's so nice to be outside,' said Trabant. 'Honestly, that broom cupboard was...'

He suddenly tensed. Two men were positioned just to the right – men he hadn't seen before, and of the nightclub bouncer variety who were clearly keeping guard. And their eyes swelled at the sound of his voice. And now they were running towards them.

'Eva, your car – where's your car?' he screamed, but she'd already diverted to confront the thugs head-on, kicking her heels off in the process. Trabant froze in the moment, wishing he were stronger, and capable, and not so afraid.

The first man threw a punch. In one lightning movement, Eva blocked it, drove the open heel of her right hand up beneath his chin, then as his head snapped back she instantly followed through with a left knee into his groin. The man fell amid screams of agony, but now man number two was upon her, grabbing her from behind in a bear-hug.

'Eva!' cried Trabant.

Her arms were locked but her legs and fists weren't. Still within range, she kicked out hard to finish off man number one, then began punching relentlessly to the second man's groin. The man yelped in pain, and quickly slackened his grip – enough for Eva to shift position, drive her left elbow deep into his solar plexus, then hard into his face. He stumbled backwards, but didn't get the chance to fall. Eva grabbed his right arm, stepped in closer, twisted, threw him up and over, then slammed him back down onto the unforgiving concrete.

It was all over within seconds.

'Pa!' she cursed. 'Dresses are so bad for fighting in!'

Trabant stood gobsmacked – by her explosion of violence, her economy of movement, and by the crumpled heap of groaning men, against whom he wouldn't have stood a chance. Yet it was they who hadn't stood a chance, and he almost felt sorry for them. Almost.

'Okay, this way,' she said, stooping to collect her shoes, but with her eyes still alert, checking for other threats.

'Y-yes,' replied Trabant. 'I'm with you!'

iii

The car park was full. Eva led them around the perimeter, avoiding the gaze of the security cameras as best she could, then over to the far corner where a beautiful white Alfa Romeo Spider awaited.

'No, the other side,' she said. 'Left-hand drive, remember?'

'Oh, yes. Sorry,' replied Trabant, diverting then waiting as Eva climbed in, leant across and opened his door.

'Now, stay down until we're out of town.'

The car-park barrier lifted slowly, like a watchman reluctantly allowing passage against his better judgement. Eva began to weave the little Alfa through the twisty, rising backstreets of

Cannes. Tall four-storey buildings with balconies and shutters loomed overhead, and a fleeting glimpse to the right revealed once more the opulence of the marina, where the resort-sized yachts still posed and postured upon the inky-black water.

The Alfa's exhaust reverberated, as if sounding its own war cry, and Eva drove on, unbelievably quickly. Left again, and the road narrowed further still, forcing the evening revellers to part and let them through, until finally they reached the brow and a huge green sign that pointed right for Antibes. Eva followed it, accelerating hard along the two-lane highway, negotiating a waterfall-encrusted roundabout with barely a lift of the throttle, and onwards again, passing another sign that revealed the road's name to be D6007.

'You can relax now,' smiled Eva. 'I think we made it.'

'Where are we heading to?' asked Trabant, tentatively peering out of the window.

'My friend's house, twenty minutes away. We can hide there and decide what to do next.'

Trabant studied Eva's face, searching for the motives of the woman he still knew nothing about. 'T-those men. How did you...?'

'It was them or us. I prefer us.' Eva reached across and squeezed his hand, knowing full well the violence had shocked him to the core. 'I'm sorry you had to see that.'

'But there were two of them, and...'

'And?' she smiled.

'I just don't understand,' he asked. 'Why *are* you helping me, when it was you who—'

'What? Got you thrown into that broom cupboard?'

'Yes.'

'I had to buy time, to get you away.'

'But why would you do that?'

'Maybe I just like you.'

Her words warmed him like a bowl of steaming porridge on

a cold winter's morning. Whatever her agenda, she *had* kept him alive, and right now that was all that really mattered.

'Hey, do you like my car?'

'I *love* your car.'

'She's a classic, in the truest sense of the word; in immaculate condition, sleek, stylish and with amazing bodywork.'

Just like its owner, thought Trabant.

'I bought her only last year,' continued Eva, full of pride. 'She's been fully restored.'

'She's a beauty, and the Duetto is my favourite Alfa Romeo.' He knew his cars well. Ever since he was a young boy he'd bury himself in classic car magazines, resurfacing only at meal times and Christmas. 'This model is so much nicer than the later Series Two, with that cut-off tail and rubber bumpers. I much prefer your chromed variety.'

Eva glanced across, holding his eyes, feeling a connection. 'You have good taste, Monsieur.' She smiled again, reached up, unclipped and then dropped the black soft-top down behind their heads. In another effortless manoeuvre she undid her hair, and shook it free to dance in the overhead turbulence. 'Let us start to enjoy the evening.'

Trabant began to tingle with a swirl of elation, confusion and excitement. It was impossible to believe in his change of fortune. He stole another glance at his saviour, unsure how to react to this wonderful free spirit of a woman. Her zest for life was infectious; her face phosphorescent with intelligence; her defiance of death seemingly unbreakable. Yet now she seemed playful, and her hands were relaxed, guiding rather than gripping the steering wheel as his would have been. And neither third finger showed any sign of an engagement or wedding ring. Perhaps she was unattainable, as free as the wind that now also ruffled his hair and ears. She smiled once more, as if reading his mind, but for the moment he didn't care. While living on borrowed time, he knew he could be in no better company.

41

The coastal road was open and blustery. Eva scanned ahead, picked her next braking point then, in one fluid movement, she blipped the throttle, shifted gear and masterfully attacked the apex of the next tight corner. The little Alfa came alive in her hands, at one with its mistress, singing a delightful melody as it charged deeper into the night.

'Are you okay?' she asked, seeing Trabant gripping his seat. 'I don't usually drive this fast, but under the circumstances…'

'Yes, I'm fine. Honestly.' And he was. Her driving was totally controlled, and it was a pleasure to witness the little Italian thoroughbred being worked to its full potential.

He eased back to let the warm evening breeze massage his face, and allowed his eyes to roam. To the left, the imposing mountains of the Southern Alps cut an ominous outline, like a disapproving big brother. To the right, from the white line of surf he could make out the water's edge, and across the bay lights twinkled up on the rugged headland. More lights were visible out to sea, perhaps belonging to a tanker or container ship, hardly moving yet seemingly a world away from… the perilous situation he had temporarily forgotten about!

He jolted as the anguish returned – the anguish Eva had so commendably tried to dispel. And the words of the MI6 file's horror story began to taunt and mock. For it warned of Gunboat's relentless pursuit of anyone who beat him at cards; a pursuit that would only end in death. Trabant shook his head. How on earth had he overlooked such a vital point? And now, no matter how fast or far Eva drove, his life could never be the same again, for as long as it lasted.

He rubbed his arms, in an attempt to banish the icy chill.

'The wind is picking up,' said Eva, flicking her eyes towards the heavens. 'I think it is the Mistral.'

'What's that?'

'The strong north-westerly wind. They said it was coming.'

Trabant looked up to see the moon seeking refuge behind a cluster of black clouds. The weather was indeed stirring, as if from nowhere, and with an ominous momentum. He lowered his chin to his chest and scrunched his eyes tight, battening down the hatches against the impending doom. Eva was right. A storm *was* brewing, and in more senses than one.

'If you are cold, put on your jacket,' she said. 'It is behind the seat.'

Trabant's head spun round in a flash.

'I retrieved it from the floor, after the crowds had left.'

'But how did you know it was mine?' he said, pulling it onto his lap.

'From your name-tag inside the collar,' she giggled. 'Only joking! I checked the pockets. Your name was written inside *The Beginner's Guide To Being A Secret Agent*. Interesting title. So you want to become a spy?'

Eva measured his reaction. His silence spoke volumes. Trabant pulled out the book and began hunting through the pages, praying with all his might that the piece of paper detailing HQ's contact numbers, passwords and numbered code sequences was still wedged inside.

It was not.

'I don't suppose you found anything inside?' he asked, trying to suppress his desperation. 'A piece of paper, perhaps?'

'No. It is exactly as I found it. Why?'

Eva glanced across and tried to read his silence. 'What is wrong? What was written on it?'

He shook his head slowly. 'Information I should never have lost; that I can't believe I—'

Eva interrupted, quickly and deliberately. 'Bristo, everything is going to be okay.'

'But how can you know that?'

'Haven't you heard? Women are *always* right.'

'But…'

Another cheeky smile sealed the moment, and she'd done it again – doused the flames of another crisis before it had any chance of taking hold.

'Thank you,' he said, swaying left to right as the little Alfa negotiated another bend.

'For what?' she replied, pleasantly impressed. Manners in the face of adversity – there was more to this man than first met the eye.

'For helping me; for being my friend; for saving my life.'

'I think you have a life worth saving.'

'But you hardly know me.'

'I know enough. The eyes are the windows of the soul, Monsieur Bristo Trabant. I guess I just like what I see.'

Trabant froze, again unsure how to respond. The most beautiful woman in the world had just paid him a compliment, yet even in a two-seater car his natural instinct was to look over his shoulder for the intended recipient.

V

About fifteen minutes outside Cannes, Eva turned inland then followed the D4 and signs for Biot. A huge marine park flicked by on the right, eerily resplendent through the overhanging trees that lined the dark road. Then an intermittent line of stone walls took over, each bedecked with ivy, that shielded houses with large patios and brightly coloured shutters.

'It's so quiet,' said Trabant.

'Yes, I love it here,' she replied, but with a hint of hesitation.

Trabant instantly detected it, and turned to see her eyes fixed on the rear-view mirror. 'What's wrong?'

'Not sure, so hold on tight.'

With that she changed down two gears and accelerated hard round the next bend, turned off the lights then flung the little Alfa sharply to the left down an unmade track, hidden by a row of tall trees that ran parallel. Without touching the brake lights, she allowed the Alfa to roll to a standstill.

The sudden blackness washed over them, as did the chorus of cicadas.

'There were lights behind us,' she whispered, peering intently back to the main road. 'I'm checking we haven't been followed.'

Sure enough, a pair of headlights were soon lighting up the road, sweeping right to left as they rounded the same bend. The car's windows were open, its radio loud and the voices inside full of youthful exuberance and early-summer cheer.

'Probably two young couples driving home after a day at the beach,' she said, checking her watch. 'But let's be sure.'

After a few minutes she eased the little Alfa into gear, switched its lights back on, then returned to the road.

'That's where we're going,' she said, pointing through the trees to the twinkle of lights upon the hilltop. 'Biot. It's the most beautiful medieval village. You will love it.'

'I'm sure I will.'

The road soon became a corkscrew hill, and with a double change of gear the little Alfa made the final ascent. At the brow, Eva turned right beneath a huge arch of ivy, and continued along a sleepy little street lined with village shops, restaurants, and on the right, an open square where a few people still sat drinking.

Another right turn then a final left brought them into a narrow mews, completely hidden from the main road. As she turned the little Alfa back round, the brake lights painted the surrounding walls an intermittent red, as if to remind them of the dangers still lurking.

'Will we be safe here?' asked Trabant, taking heed.

'As safe as anywhere.' Eva smiled, killed the engine then pointed to the end house. 'That's home for tonight.'

The house was white, three storeys high and finished with large pale-blue shutters and long trails of ivy from the window boxes. Trabant surveyed the scene a moment longer, then turned back to see Eva hoist up her skirt and retrieve a small handgun from the garter on her right thigh.

'Wait here a moment, just in case,' she said.

'C-can I help you?'

'Thank you, but no.'

'But what if there are people, you know… inside?'

'Then I will take them down. If you hear gunfire and I'm not back out within ten seconds – run!'

'Where to?'

'As far as my beloved little Alfa will take you,' she continued, handing Trabant the keys. 'But be gentle with her. She is shy with strangers.'

'I'm not a stranger, not anymore.'

'Very true, Monsieur. Okay, I won't be long.'

Eva slowly climbed the stairs to the front door, unlocked and then softly pushed it open – waited – then disappeared inside. Once again, her movements were calculated and efficient. And for a woman so unflustered by danger, it seemed only natural for her to carry a gun. Perhaps serving tables in the South of France was more dangerous than he'd imagined? The little Alfa's cooling engine began to tick, as if in agreement, and Trabant braced himself for the eruption of gunfire. But peace remained, and after what seemed an eternity, the lights flicked on and Eva reappeared in the doorway to beckon him inside.

The house was small, minimalist, and the picture of normality. A simple white sofa sat beneath the window, a single wicker chair faced the wide-screen television, and the yellow walls boasted framed pictures of harvest meadows and chickens

46

posing on farmyard machinery. There was also a vase of artificial sunflowers on the kitchen table.

'Perhaps you could make us both a drink,' said Eva, while checking the contents of the fridge. 'I think we deserve one.'

'Yes, of course. Where's the—'

'Over there,' she replied, pointing to the cabinet in the alcove. 'It's the best-stocked utility in this place. I'll have whatever you're having.'

'Er… Scotch?'

'Wonderful!' She smiled and extracted two glasses from the overhead cupboard. 'Here – use these, and don't be shy.'

Trabant poured, chinked Eva's glass then submerged his anxieties within the fiery dark-brown liquid.

'Mmmm, that's better,' beamed Eva.

'Yes… (cough)… I agree.'

'So, you like this place?'

'Yes, it's lovely,' he replied, looking around.

'My friend has owned it for years,' added Eva, with almost deliberate insistence. 'She lets me use it whenever I want.'

'Sounds like a nice friend.'

'She is. So, Monsieur, how about we eat then work out what to do next?'

'Sounds good to me. Thank you.'

'And we should shower too. Would you like to go first?'

'No, please – ladies first.'

Eva's eyes became busy with the risk-assessment. She returned to the front door, double-checked the locks were secure, drew the lounge curtains tight then put out all the lights.

'Okay, I will be quick, but you must take this,' she said, beckoning Trabant into the wash of moonlight still visible, handing him the gun and studying his reaction closely. 'Never used one before, huh?'

'No. Always been afraid of hurting someone.'

'Well, you might have to tonight if you want to stay alive.'

Eva's statement secured his full attention. 'Okay, if you need to fire, firstly take off the safety catch – like this.'

Trabant nodded.

'Then, hold the grip with both hands, like this; stand with legs comfortably apart and arms slightly bent.'

'U-huh.'

'Aim for the chest – the biggest target – and keep firing until the target falls. Okay?'

His eyes widened.

'Just stand, aim and fire. The gun will do the rest. And how many times will you shoot?'

'As many as it takes.'

'Good. And if you run out of bullets, press here, let the clip fall to the floor, insert this new one,' she continued, passing him a slim, rectangular magazine, 'and immediately continue firing. Okay?'

'I guess so.'

'Excellent. So now I will take my shower, and return scented like a field of summer flowers. In the meantime, while you're making the acquaintance of my Glock 26 semi-automatic pistol, please help yourself to more Scotch.'

'Thank you,' replied Trabant, with dread. 'I think I'm going to need it.'

5

El Cañonero

VENUS, GODDESS OF LOVE, beauty and fertility walked back into the lounge, towel-drying her hair; the outline of her curves tantalisingly enhanced by the wrap of her pink fluffy bathrobe.

'Is the coast clear?' she asked, seeing Trabant hovering beside the curtain.

'Seems to be.'

'Good,' she replied, switching on a small, shaded table lamp. 'Then I would like to propose a toast – to still being alive.'

'I'll drink to that.' Trabant chinked her glass then took another delicious sip.

'How are your bumps and bruises?' she asked.

'Pretty bumpy really.'

'Ooh, I can help you with that.'

'Really?'

'Yes.' She stepped closer, took his glass and placed it down with hers on the cabinet. 'Now – close your eyes.' She then placed her hands on his shoulders, leant forward and kissed him tenderly on the lips. 'There…' she whispered. 'Is that better?'

Trabant hung spellbound... transported to a place where suffering and anxiety could no longer reach.

'Better?' she enquired again.

'Infinitely…'

Slowly he reopened his eyes, and basked in the warmth of her smile, the sparkle in her eyes. Beautiful women usually intimidated him, yet somehow she put him at ease. And a kiss like that could surely cure all the world's ills. The question was – why kiss him? She could have any man she wanted, so why choose him – boring, unsophisticated lemonade, when stylish, delectable champagne would doubtless be on the menu too, *and* in abundance. The answer was, of course, obvious. She was simply being kind, in the same way people fuss over someone else's new puppy. And the quicker he realised that the—

'What is it?' she asked, detecting his contemplation.

'N-nothing. Why?'

'There's a lot going on in those eyes of yours.'

Trabant looked away. 'Maybe it's the Scotch, you know, going to my head.'

'I must confess,' she replied, swirling the last drops in her glass, 'I don't often drink it, or champagne. Most varieties seem too swept up in their own importance. I much prefer a nice glass of lemonade. A lady knows where she stands with a nice glass of—'

'Pppffffffff… (cough, splutter)…'

'Bristo, are you okay?'

'Y-e-s-s-s… (cough)… just a mouthful… down the wrong… I'll be fine.'

'Perhaps you'd like a shower too?' she continued, dabbing him with her towel. 'There's plenty of hot water, and clean towels and a bathrobe inside the door. When you're finished we'll eat. Is penne pollo Avante okay for you?'

'What's that?'

'Chicken pasta – Eva Avante style.'

'Sounds perfect.'

ii

The bathroom was small, square, and white-tiled floor to ceiling. A small rectangular window resided high above the toilet, with moonlight jagged upon its frosted glass. Trabant closed the door gently behind him, stepped forward and started to undress, pausing briefly to inspect himself in the mirror above the sink. His reflection did not lie – he looked gaunt, stressed and beaten. And there was no smile returned from the looking glass, but then again, do dead men ever smile?

The silver taps released jets of water from the chrome shower-head. Trabant stripped off his last few garments, adjusted the temperature and stepped inside. The water streamed down his body, across his battered shoulder and stomach, before finally locating and stinging the countless claw marks he'd accumulated, particularly those around his left ankle where the heavy's fingers had dug in like talons. His elbows were raw too, and his fingers, from where he'd been dragged across the yacht club's carpet.

He chose the least feminine-coloured bottle of shampoo, then allowed his thoughts to drift within the rising cloud of steam. Would the gods of fortune show mercy? Could they somehow get him through this terrible ordeal? And would he too have to wear a pink fluffy bathrobe?

iii

'All clean and refreshed?'

'Yes, much better, thank you,' replied Trabant, reappearing in the entrance of the kitchen, donning a bathrobe of equal fluffiness, though thankfully coloured white. The light was on, which gave confidence that the coast may finally be clearing. He looked to the two saucepans bubbling on the stove, and the neat piles of ingredients lined up like paratroopers awaiting the green light before jumping in. 'Smells good.'

'Oh, it's nothing much. Just chicken, bacon, mushrooms, onion, courgette, red pepper, salt, black pepper, garlic – not too much of that I hope,' she winked, 'er, basil, thyme, peas, carrots, healthy splash of wine, fresh tomato sauce… I think that's it; and all served upon a bed of penne rigate pasta.'

'Sounds wonderful.'

'I hope you like it.' Eva handed him a glass of wine, and gestured towards the table. 'Take a seat and relax. It's almost ready.'

The table had been delightfully laid. And a small vase of peonies now shared centre stage with a half-full bottle of pink wine. Trabant sat and read the label. Appellation Côtes de Provence Controlée Rosé Grenache. He lifted his glass, savoured the strawberry aroma then took a sip. Heavenly!

'So tell me,' said Eva, from behind the bubbling pans. 'Your surname, is it the same as—'

'The car? Yes. It's a sort of nickname.'

'What's the connection?'

'My parents owned one. And for a while they both worked in the factory in Zwickau, in the former German Democratic Republic.'

'Really?'

'Yes. My mother in the paint-shop, my father building the engines, before they moved to East Berlin, before my father was…'

Eva immediately sensed his sadness. 'Bad memories?'

Trabant didn't answer.

'Well, I think Trabant is a great name. One to be very proud of.'

'I am. And I still drive their car. Wouldn't swap it for anything.'

'It's a very sexy name too,' she added.

'It's okay, you don't have to say that, just to make me feel better.'

'I'm not,' she replied, slightly taken aback.

'I'm sorry. I guess I'm just a little tired.'

'Well, you've had quite an evening. Top-up?' she asked, gesturing towards the wine bottle.

'Yes, please. So, what about your family?'

'No cars bear my name, which is Avante. I do, however, have a family tree of wine makers and musicians, which always makes for a great party.' Eva poured then returned to the kitchen. 'Well, I think you played it pretty cool tonight, Monsieur Trabant.'

He shook his head. 'I don't think so. I'm not very good at being cool, or anything else, come to think of it.'

'I disagree,' she replied, retrieving two hot plates from the oven. 'And you are definitely excellent at snap.'

'Snap? I even got that wrong. HQ specifically told me not to play Gunboat at—' His body suddenly stiffened, as he realised he'd said too much.

'Ah, so you *are* a secret agent?'

Trabant closed his eyes. 'Not so secret anymore.'

Eva quickly dished up then brought the food to the table. 'Voilà!'

'Thank you so much, it looks amazing.'

'Let's hope it tastes as good. Parmesan?'

'Yes, please.'

'There we are. So, bon appetit!'

'Yes, bon app… er?'

'Tee.'

'Thank you.'

'You're welcome,' she replied, watching intently as Trabant loaded then shovelled in his first mouthful. 'Is it okay?' she asked nervously. 'I can add more pepper or tomato if you—'

'Eva, it's absolutely delicious. Thank you.'

She smiled in relief then began assembling her own mound of pasta. 'So, please, carry on. You were on a mission to watch Gunboat Charlie, only you went too far, broke the golden rule, and now you have to pay with your life?'

He looked up to plead his case. 'I'm only a stand-in while the rest of the unit recovers from chickenpox. I never asked for any of this.'

'An MI6 surveillance unit?'

'Yes, the Priority Surveillance Unit.'

Eva chose her next words carefully. 'So what does *The Beginner's Guide To Being A Secret Agent* advise you do next?'

'Phone HQ.'

'Sounds like a plan to me. So, let's eat up while it's hot, then I'll clear the table and you can make your call. But use the landline – it's safe. Your mobile phone may no longer be.'

iv

'Vauxhall Cross Plumbers, how can we help?'

'H-hello, it's the plumber,' said Trabant. 'The pipe is blown. I repeat, the pipe is blown. Request instructions as to what to do now.'

'How badly is the pipe blown?' came the urgent reply.

'As badly as possible.'

After a long pause came the question he dreaded. 'Was the blow caused by failure to follow instructions?'

'Er… y-yes.'

Trabant lowered his head in shame, clung to every instruction given, then dejectedly placed the receiver back in its cradle.

'What did they say?' asked Eva.

'That the mission is aborted, and that an immediate return to London is too dangerous. So I'm to fly directly to Vienna instead, where the local MI6 team will meet me, at 9 a.m. sharp, then hide me.'

'Meet you where?'

'In the city centre. I'm booked on the 6 a.m. flight. Thankfully I still have my passport, which I always keep in my back pocket.'

'I'll take you to the airport.'

'But I've been enough trouble already.'

'No trouble at all. Airport check-in will be from 5, so we should leave at 4.30, which, yikes – gives us an hour and a bit.' Eva poured the last of the wine. 'So tell me, Monsieur Secret Agent, what *are* you good at?'

'As I said – not much really.'

'There must be something.'

Trabant thought long and hard. 'Perhaps there *is* one thing...'

'Ooh – please tell.'

'Probably not for me to say.'

'Oh go on, don't tease!'

'Okay. Well, apparently I make a pretty mean steak and kidney pie.'

Eva laughed. 'Ah, the way to every woman's heart.'

Trabant looked puzzled.

'It's okay. I'm only playing.' But she saw the tiredness in his eyes, and knew he was in need of what little sleep he could grasp, and regrettably nothing else. 'We really must try to rest. You can either sleep here on the sofa, or join me in bed. I'll do my best to keep my hands off you, I promise.'

V

From under the sheets, Eva's body resembled the undulating outline of an amusement park roller-coaster.

'Are you sure there's room?' asked Trabant, standing in the doorway.

'Positive. So climb in, it's warmer with two.'

Trabant untied his bathrobe and hurried beneath the covers.

'That's better,' said Eva, cuddling up close behind. 'Now tell me – your Rupert Bear boxer shorts; are they personal choice or standard field issue for all British Secret Agents?'

Trabant crumbled with embarrassment. 'No, they're all mine. A Christmas present from my aunt.'

'They're cute.'

'And you're a good liar,' he replied, light-heartedly. 'But on a serious note, could you tell me, you know… how Gunboat usually does it?'

'What – wears boxer shorts?'

'No – how he kills people.'

'It is not important. Try to sleep.'

'Please tell me.'

'It'll keep you awake.'

'Please!'

'Well, if you insist,' sighed Eva. 'As he didn't shoot you, then most probably he will feed you to the sharks.'

'SHARKS!'

Eva held him closer still. 'You will not be fed to anything, I promise.'

'But why is Gunboat so violent?'

'Some people are like that. You are nice and gentle. He is just the opposite.'

Trabant turned to face Eva. 'But all I did was beat him at cards.'

'Sadly there's much more to it than that. Your victory is a direct challenge to his authority, and the first crack he fears will bring his empire crashing down.'

'But it was only a—'

Eva shook her head. 'He thinks defeat will make people question his ability to supply arms.'

'That's crazy!'

'It's an interesting case study. This is a man who dominates and commands, yet deep down he fears it could all be taken away in the blink of an eye, thus returning him to the slums where his life began. The absurdity is his clients couldn't care less if he won, lost or drew, as long as they still get their weapons. But Gunboat can't grasp that, and so killing you is the only way he can begin to alleviate those fears.'

'It's absurd!'

Eva nodded in sympathy. 'Absolutely, but even murderous tyrants have their insecurities. Gunboat just takes it one step further. And failing to kill you in Cannes will make him twice as angry.'

'But what if he *can't* find me? He'll have to give up, right?'

'Do not underestimate the intensity of his pursuit. He will shake the world like a toy until you fall out and down at his feet.'

Trabant scrunched his face.

'Hey, don't forget to breathe,' said Eva, nudging him to release the pause button.

'Fffffffffffff... thanks,' he replied. 'And does he, you know, kill often?'

'I believe so.'

'But why can't he just supply arms and leave it at that?'

'Because in his world the rules are different. Murder achieves far more than simply revenge. It creates fear, which makes people do what he wants them to. It's the bedrock of his very existence.'

Trabant propped himself up on one arm. 'Tell me about him.'

'What would you like to know?'

'Everything.'

'That's quite a lot.'

'I'm sure. But please, start from the beginning.'

'Well, once upon a time, in a far-off land called—'

'Eva, please be serious. I have to know.'

'Okay. He was born and raised in El Chorrillo, a desperately poor and tough neighbourhood in western Panama City. His father was an officer in General Noriega's Panama Defence Force, who preferred to spend his wages on booze and women than to bring it home to the family. For Gunboat's mother, money was a constant worry. At any one time she would have three, perhaps four different jobs, just to make ends meet. And from a very young age, Gunboat used to shine shoes and sell newspapers too, before *and* after school, just to bring extra money home.'

'So when did the arms-selling start?'

'The story goes that one day his father gave him an old pistol to play with, just to keep him quiet, but Gunboat became instantly infatuated. He dismantled it, studied the mechanism, badgered his father to explain the workings, put it back together again, cleaned and polished it, then sold it to one of the bigger kids in the neighbourhood. The money felt wonderful in his hands and, you know, as soon as he went back home he gave every dollar to his mother. Not bad for an eight-year-old boy, eh? He then begged his father for another gun, and another, and before long Gunboat had a waiting list of eager customers – local thugs, gangs and so forth. No more slave to the grind for his mother. No more shoe-shine or paper selling for him. There was infinitely more money to be made selling guns.'

'That's scary.'

Eva nodded in agreement. 'Not long after, his father deserted the family for good, but Gunboat was already the breadwinner and had found new supply lines for his guns, ironically through his father's associates. By the age of seventeen he was selling overseas too.'

'Quite an entrepreneur.'

'Very much so. By the age of twenty he was smuggling huge quantities of weaponry through the ports of Balboa and Colón. You see, Panama is ideally located for gun-running. With the Caribbean Sea to the north, the Pacific Ocean to the south, and the Panama Canal joining the two, it's the perfect transit point.'

'But where were all the weapons going?'

'Anywhere, to anyone that wanted them. Gunboat wasn't selective. By now though, he was making so much money that some other top Panamanian villains thought it time to muscle in. A huge turf war broke out.'

'What happened?' asked Trabant.

'Gunboat took them on.'

'Single-handed?'

'I'm sure he would have done,' replied Eva. 'But by now he had a loyal following, many of whom are still with him today. Enrique Salvador Sánchez; Raúl Núñez Gómez and his brother Ramón, to name but a few.'

'Raúl and Ramón – the two heavies in the yacht club?'

'Yes, the very same,' nodded Eva. 'And his rivals completely underestimated Gunboat's resourcefulness. I mean, he virtually had tanks rolling through the streets of Panama City. The war was over in no time, and those he didn't kill fell to their knees, begging for mercy.'

'So everyone surrendered?'

'All except one, a man named Oscar Conda, who fled and has never been seen since. He is rumoured to still be alive, but no one knows where. Gunboat still considers him a threat.'

'Gunboat threatened? Are you sure?'

'Yes, Bristo. And it's that way of thinking that's kept him one step ahead, for all these years. He never underestimates an enemy. Anyway, Gunboat's victory meant he also inherited all the enterprises of his foes – real estate, hotels, casinos, restaurants, nightclubs. Overnight he went from being premier arms dealer to underworld ruler of Panama too, just like that.'

'So he's a gangster as well?'

'More like global criminal statesman. Throughout Latin America he is known as El Cañonero – the Gunboat. It is a name that will open any door and close any deal. But people whisper it very carefully.'

'The waiter seemed very keen to help him.'

Eva nodded in acknowledgement. 'He is one of Gunboat's fixers on the French Riviera.'

'He couldn't wait to grass me up.'

'Gunboat has informants everywhere. He's a phenomenon; an underworld powerbroker as big and well-connected as they come.'

'Really?' asked Trabant, aghast that one man could wield such influence.

'I'm afraid so. He has a delivery capability unrivalled throughout the world. He is simply the only man to deal with; a one-stop-shop for everything you need to fight a war. Guns, rockets, tanks, planes, helicopters, even warships. Then there's the radar systems, hi-tech electronic surveillance, counter surveillance, technical support, mercenaries, uniforms, medical installations and, of course, billions of rounds of ammunition. The list is—'

'Eva – how come you know so much about Gunboat?'

'Oh, I... er... read an article about him once.'

'Must have been a big... (yawn)... article?'

'Yes. It was a pull-out supplement.'

'But surely the authorities can stop him?'

Eva sat upright. 'That's the really scary part. Gunboat is not to be touched.'

'But why? I don't understand.'

'Because some of the highest-profile governments in the world use him to run covert operations on their behalf.'

'How come?'

'In him they have a man who is discreet, reliable and gets the job done; who will supply whatever they want to whoever they want, leaving the outside world clueless as to what is really going on. In return he receives suitcases stuffed with cash, and guarantees that his other illicit business dealings will be overlooked.'

'That... that's terrible.'

'True, but apparently a price worth paying to achieve a greater good. Of course, Gunboat is fully aware of the bargaining power this gives him, and has made it crystal clear that if any government or intelligence agency dares lift a finger against him, in terms of prosecution or exposé, then he will not hesitate to reveal full details of those clandestine operations to the world. They say he keeps all those secrets in his little black book, and that threat is his way of ensuring everybody works hard at keeping everybody else's mouths firmly shut. Clever, huh? You can imagine how damaging those revelations would be, which is why everyone is so scared of him, and why his dossiers are always filed in the "Best Left Alone" section.'

'I… I see.'

'Even in the underworld his position is invulnerable. He is so crucial to so many people that no one would dare make an attempt on his life, for fear of reprisals from his other clients. Warlords, for example, do not take kindly to spanners being placed in the works of their vital supply chains.'

'Yes, I—'

'What else can I tell you? He is very self-conscious about his weight; er… he harboured a fugitive London car dealer for about a year, in exchange for English lessons; he…'

vi

Eva wasn't sure at what point Trabant fell asleep.

She held him closer, not wanting him to be alone within his torturous nightmares. But he should never have been at the yacht club in the first place, never put within a thousand-mile radius of a man like Gunboat. It was scandalous. Bristo resided at the other end of the spectrum, in a world wrapped in cotton wool; of love and smothering, probably by a doting mother, which, while totally admirable and natural, had left him wholly unprepared for the realities of the parallel universe he'd been

61

thrown into. Someone, somewhere was responsible, and she looked forward to the day when their paths would cross.

Her eyes turned to the window, to the wash and shadows created by the moon. In barely an hour they would be off again, heading for the airport. Yet an uneasiness niggled at her mind, and nothing to do with the significant price now hanging over her head too, or at just how impossibly formidable their opponent truly was. No, it was far more important than that. It was the thought that after they said their farewells, she might never see Bristo Trabant again.

Without realising it, she had started to fall for this unassuming Englishman. Her previous relationship had brought little except hurt and pain, but now, for the first time in years, her heart felt alive, and she knew that the man now lying in her arms wouldn't have a single bad bone in his body.

Her mind replayed the moment when she'd first met him, on the Thursday evening when he'd dined in the restaurant of Le Club Maritime du Soleil. How alone he had seemed, and how she had tried to comfort him as she served his food. She then recalled the events of the next day, when she'd seen him on the beach at Cannes; when a young boy had come screaming from the sea. She'd run to help, but Bristo had been closer; had doused the jellyfish sting with a sachet of vinegar, and begun explaining to the mother, in admittedly broken French, why that was the best remedy.

'Merci, Monsieur, merci,' cried the father, as he ran to fetch the car and take the boy to hospital.

'Lucky I was eating chips,' Bristo had replied. 'I once worked in a public aquarium, so I know all about stings.'

The way he praised the child for being so brave, and the way his eyes flickered, as if he too was sharing the pain. For Eva it revealed so much more about him than she could even begin to contemplate. And now that she'd got to know him better, his qualities had simply been reconfirmed; qualities she found so attractive in a man; qualities she'd never before seen all bundled together within one single body: kindness, compassion, courtesy, manners…

… and the way he moved, and listened, and held her eyes whenever she spoke. He was completely unpretentious, and yes, very good-looking too. Sure, the boxer shorts were unusual, and he'd definitely have to wise up when playing cards, but that aside there was something quite extraordinary about him. For her, attraction had never been about money, or power, or strength. It was about the soul, and he had that in bucketloads. He also had that certain je ne sais quoi that made…

Eva smiled at getting so ahead of herself. There were no guarantees he would have feelings for her, or even be available. Perhaps it was best to just enjoy the moment; enjoy being close to someone again – someone special – if only for a few hours. For even she couldn't predict how many more moments their pursuers would allow.

6

Kiss and Fly

BZZZZZ... BZZZZZ... BZZZZZ...

'Bristo, wake up! It's time to go.'

'Hmmm... just five more minutes.'

'No, we must go now!' replied Eva, wresting the sheets from his clutches.

'But I was in the middle of this fantastic dream.'

'Ooh, was I dressed up as a nurse and about to—'

'No... But we *were* together, with Gunboat, in this expensive restaurant. He was buying us dinner, as an apology for his terrible behaviour.'

'I hope we were running up a huge bill.'

'I think so. You were having champagne and caviar, and I was having my favourite – penne pollo Avante!'

Eva laughed. 'Monsieur Secret Agent, you say all the right things.'

'I try.' Trabant smiled and sat up, rubbed his eyes then planted his feet on the floor. But the connection with terra firma instantly reconfirmed the horrors of last night.

'Stay positive,' said Eva, reading his expression. 'And try these on,' she continued, laying a set of clean clothes at the foot of the bed. 'You need to change your appearance.'

Trabant dressed quickly, and the beige suit, white shirt and soft brown loafers fitted surprisingly well. He walked down the stairs to the lounge and saw Eva standing by the kitchen table checking over her gun. She was wearing a white T-shirt, blue cardigan and shorts. Her hair was tied back again too, now in a yellowy-blue patterned scarf.

'What do you think?' he asked, as if appearing from a clothes shop changing-room.

'Fantastic. You wear it well. But wait...' She stepped forward, noticing all three jacket buttons were done up, and undid the bottom one. 'Top and middle is fine, but never all three. There – irresistible!'

'Thank you.'

'You're welcome. Now, drink this,' she said, handing him a double espresso. 'You need your wits about you from here on. And do you have everything – your passport? Your watch?'

'Yes, but what about my own suit?'

'Leave it here. It is ruined anyway.'

Trabant lowered his head, acknowledging the passing of a dear old friend, then followed her towards the front door.

'Ooh, don't forget this,' she said, reaching towards the arm of the sofa. '*The Beginner's Guide To Being A Secret Agent.* Something to read on the plane.'

ii

Biot slept silently under its pitch-black duvet. Only the eerie swathes of street-lamp yellow remained, still climbing the walls of the narrow alley they had driven into barely hours before.

Eva checked the coast was clear, locked the front door then led them to the little white Alfa. It started first time, filled its lungs with the crisp morning air then set off along the main street, past the restaurant and square, beneath the overhead arch of ivy then hard left back down the corkscrew hill to where the road straightened out.

'Here – this is for you,' said Eva, passing Trabant a curious foil wrap. 'Breakfast – a croissant, which I took the liberty of filling with butter and raspberry jam. I hope you like.'

'Oh, yes. Lovely! Thank you.'

As Trabant tucked in, the Alfa began to stretch its legs, galloping onwards between the intermittent stretches of stone wall, scattered houses and colourful in-fill of summer flowers. To the right lay a valley of terracotta shadows, in no rush to welcome the brand-new day. Trabant's thoughts turned to the countless people still in bed, their worlds safe, their minds untroubled, knowing full well that not so long ago, he too had been one of those people. Mercifully though, for the moment, it seemed they had the world to themselves. Only a heavily laden delivery truck had passed by, heading in the opposite direction, perhaps on its way to market. Trabant thought to ask, but instead held on tight, as Eva pushed on harder.

'And here we turn left,' she said, flicking the Alfa down a fork road and past signs for Villeneuve-Loubet and Cagnes-sur-Mer. 'Wow – what a beautiful sunrise!'

Not as beautiful as you, thought Trabant.

Another few high-speed minutes later, the soft rumble of traffic began to filter through the procession of trees to the right, and then a wide car-dotted stretch of concrete became visible ahead.

'That is the motorway we take, in just a few minutes.'

'That's good,' replied Trabant.

'It is, but…'

'What's wrong?'

'I should drive you to Paris,' she replied, as if it was a thought she could no longer contain. 'It will be a much safer option.'

'But what about my flight? My orders are to head to Vienna.'

Eva turned towards him. 'You could be vulnerable and exposed.'

'… and the rendezvous!' His eyes pleaded for guidance, to

66

help him make the correct decision. 'I daren't miss that. I'm in enough trouble already.'

The terror had returned and Eva paused, annoyed that she had brought it back into focus. 'Will MI6 have the correct procedures in place?'

'Yes, I'm certain they will.'

'And how many operatives will meet you?'

'The whole team, I think.'

'Then you must do what feels most comfortable.'

'D-do you mind?'

'Not at all,' she replied, but against her better judgement. 'I just want you to be safe, Bristo.'

'Thank you. You've helped so much already, and I'm very grateful, really I am. It's just that, well… maybe it's time I started doing what I'm told.'

iii

The outskirts of Nice were barely awake.

Ten minutes from the airport, Eva took a sharp detour and parked the little Alfa on a quiet backstreet.

'Okay – this way!' she said, leading Trabant by the hand a further two blocks until they reached the side entrance of a large hotel. 'Follow me, and act like we're staying here.'

They stepped inside and continued along its winding corridors, out through the lobby and main entrance until finally halting alongside an obsequious concierge on the front steps.

'Un taxi à l'aéroport, s'il vous plaît.'

'Oui, Madame.'

With a click of his fingers, a large red Citroen lurched into action from its resting spot. 'Aéroport départs, s'il vous plaît,' said Eva, following Trabant inside.

'But…' mumbled Trabant.

67

'I'll explain when we're there.'

It was 4.57 a.m. when they pulled into the palm-tree-framed, space-age frontage of Nice Côte d'Azur Airport. A single white coach stood to the right, ejecting holidaymakers intermittently like bubbles from an aquarium air pump. The driver extracted the car-park ticket, waited for the barrier to rise, then drew up just to the left.

'Merci, Monsieur,' said Eva, paying and reaching for the door in one quick movement. And once they'd climbed out and the taxi had moved on, she turned back to Trabant, and spoke in a tone that secured his attention.

'Okay, Bristo, this is what you must do now. Cross the tarmac and mix in with all those holidaymakers, so you don't stand out, and we're not seen together. They're entering the building over there, beneath the sign marked "Départ 4". Once inside, turn to your left and check in. Then turn around and you will see, in the middle of the entrance hall, a giant tropical fish tank. I will meet you the other side of that.'

Trabant did as he was told, then made his way across to the twelve-foot-high cylindrical display, where Eva awaited, hidden behind the pages of *Le Figaro* newspaper.

'Eva, why the taxi? I preferred your Alfa.'

'So did I, but with every pair of eyes looking for it, we needed to change vehicles. And as for the hotel, if Gunboat's men somehow trace us back there from this airport, then all they'll have is a luxury, five-star-rated dead end.'

Trabant smiled. 'You're so clever!'

'It's all about staying alive. Now, you go up that escalator,' she continued, pointing to her right, 'through security then proceed directly to the departure gate. Do not browse the shops. Do not eat in a restaurant. Once on the plane, find your seat and keep your head down. Do not speak to anyone. Become invisible.'

'Invisible. Got it.'

'When you arrive in Vienna, keep your eyes low, walk at your usual pace, turn right out of the arrivals lounge and take an official taxi to the rendezvous – but not the first in line. Go for the third or fourth, just in case. Okay?'

Trabant nodded.

'Good. Now, take this,' she continued, handing him a roll of notes. 'It's two hundred Euros; enough for the taxi at the other end and a healthy slice of apfelstrudel.'

'What's that?'

'Viennese apple pie. It's delicious *and* world famous.'

'Apple pie – my favourite!' smiled Trabant, his face lighting up as if a slice would solve all his problems. 'But I can't take this, it doesn't seem—'

'You need money, and I'm pleased to help. End of problem.'

'Okay, thank you,' he said, reluctantly. 'But I insist on paying you back, if I ever get to see you again, that is.'

Eva smiled. 'Last but most important thing: did you read the sign we passed under in the taxi? It said "Kiss and Fly".'

'Did it?'

'U-huh,' she replied, flashing those wonderful eyes, those dark pools of milk chocolate. 'Which means, Monsieur – as you're doing the flying, I'll do the kissing. Come here…'

Her touch, as before, was electric. 'Now, any further questions?' she asked.

'Hmmm…? Oh, yes – just one. Will I ever see you again?'

Her face softened and she kissed him again, but this time more quickly, to allow him to refocus on the journey ahead. 'Be safe and remember what I said.'

Trabant recalled her instructions, but also began to seriously question the wisdom of leaving the one person who had kept him alive. And she'd sprinkled him with a magic dust; a dust he knew would evaporate the moment she said goodbye.

'This time yesterday I didn't even know you,' he said. 'Now I don't want to say—'

'You have to or you'll miss the flight.'

'Yes, I know.' Trabant looked at her, wanting to say much more than his confidence would allow. 'Thank you for everything.'

'My pleasure.'

'But will I, you know, ever see you again?'

'Get home as quickly as you can, and get out of this business. It is bad for both of us.'

'What do you mean – bad for both of us?'

'Never mind. Just take care and get going. You haven't much time.'

'But…'

'Bristo, darling, you need to get on the plane. Say hello to Vienna for me.'

'Will *you* be okay?' asked Trabant.

'Yes, fine – once I know you're on that plane.'

He reluctantly took his cue. 'Goodbye,' he said softly, and turned towards the escalator.

The cool temperature and bright, sophisticated décor of the departures hall offered zero comfort. He'd been right – with every footstep the magic dust of Eva Avante began to diminish. He instantly felt the need for a top-up, and looked back to see her waiting patiently. She waved. He waved too then turned forward again, almost bumping straight into a middle-aged lady and her two sons.

'Oops… sorry!' he said.

'Pardon aussi,' said the lady.

Trabant looked back to Eva, to acknowledge his clumsiness, to laugh that the accident was partly her fault, but the joke fell on the cold emptiness beside the tall cylindrical tropical fish display. The most beautiful woman in the world had gone.

★   ★   ★

Approximately 6,000 miles away, deep in the rainforests of Sarawak, north-west Borneo, in a clearing just beyond the peat swamps and cobra nests, stood a twenty-acre industrial compound. Strategically placed near the extensive cave system, it consisted of a dozen large wooden huts, a fleet of lorries and living quarters for the hundred-strong workforce. A thirty-foot-high, razor-wired and electrified fence surrounded the complex. Teams of heavily armed guards patrolled the perimeter on foot, and sentry towers looked down from every corner.

A mobile phone rang, which the man at the office desk casually answered during its fourth ring. 'Hola.'

'Oscar Conda?'

'Sí. Who's that?'

'What's the combination?' said the voice, abruptly.

Conda jolted. No problem. He'd recited it endlessly during his eighteen-month wait for this damned call.

'Nine. Five. Sixty-eight. Twenty. Fifty-eight. One. One.'

No reply.

'That's the correct sequence. I know it is,' he insisted. 'Hola? You still there?'

'It is correct,' replied the voice. 'Now, listen carefully…'

Conda pressed the phone to his ear.

'We're on.'

'How come?'

'The catalyst has presented itself. I will visit you within forty-eight hours. Be ready to move.'

'No problem. I will be.'

The line went dead. Conda eased back in his chair, contemplated the enormity of the conversation for a few seconds longer, then reached for his beer and took a swig. Never before had suds tasted so good.

7

In de Mood…

THE OUTLINE OF THE swimming pool was only distinguishable from the air, where its design became unmistakably and chillingly apparent. For it represented the greatest symbol of defiance the world has ever known – the AK-47 assault rifle.

Upon the rippling blue surface a lilo struggled to support the immense bulk of the man sprawled out in a futile attempt at relaxation. Plumes of Cuban cigar smoke took to the air, exhaled in jagged patterns that clearly expressed his mood.

All was not well in the world of Gunboat Charlie Chávez.

ii

Hidden by the dense vegetation upon Ancon Hill, La Fortaleza ('The Fortress') was no average city retreat, as the army of guards and row of empty milk-bottles outside confirmed. It was a brash seven-storey palace of steel and glass, and every bit as intimidating as the man it was built for. Balconies offered the most breathtaking, panoramic views of Panama City, which rolled out in front like a beach-mat across the undulating landscape. Yet more importantly, they provided vantage points through the lush jungle, for snipers to ward off any prying eyes.

To the south-west lay the Bridge of the Americas and the Panama Canal. To the south: the palm-tree-lined Amador

Causeway that stretched into the Pacific like a cradling arm, beckoning to the ever-present queue of container ships waiting for passage through the Canal. To the south-east: the old town of Casco Viejo, a walled peninsula and terracotta scrunch of colonial yesteryear that exuded a vibrancy as edgy and intoxicating as the local rum sold in its many bars. Looking north-east: the view spoke of change, of new money, of modern coastline-hugging skyscrapers at Punta Paitilla, Punta Pacifica and San Francisco. And beyond them lay the ruins of Panama Viejo, where the city's story had begun. The barrio of El Chorrillo, where Gunboat's own story had begun, lay back towards the Canal Zone. It was a neighbourhood plagued with poverty and gang-warfare, but one where those in the know respected the power that he wielded, and the dizzy heights he had reached. For his climb to the top of Ancon Hill was testament to his success, and the AK-47-shaped swimming pool a disquieting explanation of how it had all been paid for.

A glass door that led from the office slid open. Out stepped a tall, wiry man; third-generation weasel, yet casually dressed in white linen trousers and shirt.

'Ah, Enrique... about time!' growled Gunboat, rotating his floating mattress like a tank's gun turret to point directly at his trusted assistant. 'Where the hell you been?'

'Down at de port, Boz, checking de shipments, like I always do Sunday morning.'

'Hmmm...'

Enrique proceeded with caution, knowing the wrong choice of words would act as an incendiary device to the worst temper ever known to Latin America, perhaps even mankind. 'Boz, we need to talk about our orders. Business is getting behind.'

'Oh, I s-o-o-o sorry,' bawled Gunboat, sitting up and almost tipping off his lilo. 'Have you no idea what happen in last twenty-four hour?'

'Yes, Boz. You lose at cards.'

73

'I NO LOSE!' shouted Gunboat. 'HE CHEAT! ENTIENDES? He must have, and now I no can relax until he dead.'

'I understand, Boz. But as you say, twenty-four hours is a long time in de world of war. People are relying on us. Business must go—'

'I too tense.'

'Would de ducks help?'

'Might do...' replied Gunboat, like a child being coaxed out of a sulk. He turned his eyes to the small garden shed alongside the trigger-section of the pool – the type found in most English back gardens. The door was padlocked, and the long side window was covered by a shutter.

Enrique knew his boz well, and also that the ducks inside were perhaps his only chance of securing the time needed to discuss those very pressing business matters.

'ENRIQUE – I WANT THE DUCKS!'

'Great idea, Boz!'

Enrique Salvador Sánchez hurried round the pool. His gold front tooth gleamed in the sunshine, and his neatly cut black hair and clean-shaven jaw confirmed his professionalism and dedication to the position of right-hand man and vital cog in Gunboat's global business machine. The two men went back a long way, to the days when Gunboat had first started out; to the earliest smuggling routes they'd secured up through Mexico and across the border into black-market America. But Enrique was more than just a fixer, he was a friend and confidant, whose cactus-shaped family tree boasted some very impressive spine-shaped connections all of its own, including some of the most infamous bandits to ever rob and plunder. He took great pride in his lofty status within the organisation, and at ensuring everything ran like clockwork. Even so, on this beautiful Panamanian Sunday morning, Gunboat still inspected him with distrust, as he did with everyone when he was angry with the world.

74

Enrique arrived at the shed, lifted a plant pot to retrieve the key, fumbled with the padlock then stepped inside to operate the mechanism.

'Ready when you are, Boz!'

'One moment,' replied Gunboat, paddling his lilo to the pool-side, where he reached across to a small table and picked up a black submachine gun with the words 'Uzi 9mm' stamped on the casing. 'Okay… pull!'

Enrique pressed a button then dived for cover. The window shutter swung down on its hinges, then seconds later a motor whirred and twinkly funfair music started playing, followed by a line of plastic bath toys that nervously made their way across the opening.

Rat-a-tat-a-tat-a-tat-a-tat-a-tat…

'TAKE THAT YOU…!' screamed Gunboat as he opened fire, his terrible aim made worse by the wobbling lilo. The first duck made it across, as did the second, but the third wasn't so lucky. The spray of bullets exploded its yellow plastic body into a million-piece cloud that spiralled down to the water in a kaleidoscope of plastic feathers. Only its orange legs made it to the far side, remaining solidly attached to the conveyor belt.

Ducks numbers four and five now ran the gauntlet with beaks held low, willed across by the earlier survivors. Live ammunition continued to ricochet off everything but the target, until finally, silence prevailed.

'All finished, Boz?' said Enrique, from behind the cover of a palm tree.

Gunboat raised the gun barrel to his nose and sniffed deeply. 'Y-e-a-h… for now.'

Enrique smiled. He knew that to Gunboat, the smell of cordite was as delightful as the scent of jasmine was to his mother. And he also knew that the act of obliteration would temporarily ease his boz's anxiety, like a junkie after a hit, and create the window of calm he must now hasten to exploit.

'Boz, I'll clear up de mess later. Right now we must look at our orders.'

'Orders? Oh, yeah…' replied Gunboat. 'Enrique – to the office!'

Gunboat paddled across to the steps, aligned his feet, grabbed the rails and hauled himself up. His short, squat, hairy body rippled as he moved, yet in no time he was through the open glass doors, and taking his seat behind the huge desk. Enrique was already in position, with a fresh Cuban cigar at the ready to insert between Gunboat's already open fingers.

'So… (puff)… come on then,' hissed Gunboat. 'You gonna ask me about Cannes, or what?'

'Yes, Boz, of course. I just—'

'Cheat, Enrique. The goddam gringo CHEAT!'

'But how?'

'I no know, but he must have. I mean, how else could he have won?'

'Yes, Boz, he must have.'

'I bloomin' hate card cheat. Embarrass me like that in front of all my business associates. And now everyone will think I lose the plot.'

'Dey won't, Boz.'

'THEY WILL!' shouted Gunboat, slamming his fist down on the desk. 'I should have kill him on the spot. I had the gun aimed and everything. All I had do was pull the trigger and… aaarrrggghhh!'

'Boz, calm down. Let's dink about dis. What exactly stop you killing him?'

'Some interfering French hostess sticking her nose in, that what! Suggest I wait. Suggest we lock him in security room and come back later. Only it no was no security room, it was broom cupboard. And when we did come back later he gone, and surprise, surprise, so has she.'

'Any clues where to?'

76

Gunboat drew hard on his cigar, illuminating the end like a fighter-jet's afterburner. 'No. And believe me we turn the place upside down.'

'What about his hotel room? Find anyding dere?'

'No. Turn out he staying over the road. We trash his room but find nothing. Same in the hostess's room. No clue where they run to. The manager did confirm her car was missing. White Alfa Romeo. Raúl circulate the registration plate to our contacts in the region, but again no clue. No a whisper until it captured on CCTV the following morning leaving Nice. And Passport Control telephone to say Trabant had board the 6 a.m. flight to Vienna.'

'With the interfering hostess?' asked Enrique.

'No – alone! But our local amigos see her soon after. They gave chase, shot up her car bad, but just the car, no her, and then she lose them in the roads heading north. No sign since. Anyway, Raúl catch the next flight to Vienna. It only thirty-five minute behind, and Trabant will be tracked from when he land, so no matter where he go, Raúl will be guide in to kill him.'

'Can't a local gringo do de job?'

'No, no, no!' rumbled Gunboat, shaking his head from side to side. 'It has to be one of my top men, to show I in control of the situation and no cracking up.'

Enrique began to lick his lips. 'And how did you instruct Raúl to do de deed, Boz?'

'As painful as possible,' replied Gunboat, his eyes now swelling with malice. 'And public too. You know, a real message to anyone doubting the grip of EL CAÑONERO! Then life get back to normal.'

'Good thinking, Boz.'

'Thing is, Enrique, when I hunt round the yacht club, I find Trabant's jacket on the floor. He slip out of it when try to escape.'

'But it's no your size, Boz, and anyway—'

'I know that!'

'Did you find anything inside it?'

'Sí. That's what I trying to say. Inside one of the pockets I find a room key, no surprise there, but also a book – *The Beginner's Guide To Being Secret Agent*. So maybe he no film critic after all.'

'Yeah, maybe not, Boz.'

'But more important, inside the cover I find this...' Gunboat passed a crumpled piece of paper across the desk. 'It has three telephone number on it, plus some weird writing about... hedgehogs? What the hell is a hedgehog?'

'It's a small, prickly, rodent kind of ding. We have dem too, Boz, but here dey called porcupines.'

Gunboat shrugged his shoulders. 'If you say so. Thing is, the words must be code-words, and at the bottom you see lots of little numbers all grouped together. He definitely work for someone. Get our people at the telephone exchange to check it out. NOW!'

'Sí, Boz.' Enrique dialled rapidly into his mobile phone.

'And find out where the hell Raúl is. He should've killed Trabant by now.'

'Sí, Boz.'

After a brief conversation with the telephone company, Enrique turned to Gunboat. 'Dey gonna call me back in fifteen minutes.'

'THAT TOO LONG!'

'Yes, Boz, I know. But while we waiting, we can look at dese orders?'

Gunboat eyed the tower of papers on the corner of his desk; the weekly lists emailed and faxed in from the battle-ravaged corners of the world. 'Okay, let do it.'

Enrique took the first sheet from the pile. 'Our friends down west want fifteen Challenger Two tanks, dree dousand mortar grenades and another Chinook helicopter.'

'No problem. Next.'

'Er, de Columbians want six more Tornado fighter jets, seventy-five surface-to-air rocket launchers, dree hundred variety boxes of hand grenades, and some of dose lovely cookies dat your granny makes.'

'Cookies?'

'Yeah, Boz. De chocolate-chip ones.'

'No problem,' replied Gunboat. 'I speak to Granny tonight. You phone our man in Florida, get him to do the usual.'

'Sure ding, Boz.'

'Good. What next?'

'Massage oil, a nice bottle of Chilean Merlot, and a hundred red roses.'

'Do what?'

'Er, dis is your shopping list, Boz… from your beloved wife.'

'What on earth I got that for?'

'Señora G has gone into town, Boz. Said she gonna try dat new sexy lingerie store in de mall. Said she planning a romantic evening in, Boz. Apparently tonight is de best night of de year to conceive, so she say *you* got to do de shopping, come back to relax, den get in de mood.'

'In de mood?'

'Yes, you know…' replied Enrique, winking like a naughty schoolboy. 'All romantic, Boz.'

Of course! Tonight – the next instalment in their programme of conception. Gunboat shifted uneasily. He loved his wife dearly, but keeping up with her in the throes of passion would take more energy and resilience than he could muster right now. And then there were the concerns about the efficiency of his equipment. They'd been trying for a baby for months, with no success. Of all people, surely an international arms dealer would be the least likely to fire blanks?

'Anything else on her list?' asked Gunboat.

'Just scented candles, Barry White's *Greatest Love Songs* CD, and strict instructions dat no one is to disturb you tonight.'

Briiing!

Enrique grabbed his phone. 'Sí… u-huh… hold on, I'll ask him.'

'Who is it?' asked Gunboat, desperately. 'Raúl or the telephone people?'

'Neider. It's de man from de Central African Republic, Boz,' said Enrique, cupping the mouthpiece. 'He's wondering what's happened to his side-winder missiles and AK-47s? Our plane was due dere dis morning.'

'Damn! I forgot. Why you no remind me, Enrique?'

'I did, Boz. I telephone you on your jet, on your way back from Cannes. Remember? You told me to stick my ugly Mexican head where de sun don't shine.'

'Did I?'

'Sí, Boz, you did. To be honest, you not been de same since dat English pig beat you at cards.'

'FOR THE LAST TIME – HE NO BEAT ME!' shouted Gunboat, clenching his fists in frustration. 'HE CHEAT! GOT IT?'

'Sí, Boz. But what shall I say to señor African Republic?'

'Tell him he have his shipment tomorrow, without fail. And that I throw in a complimentary battleship to make up for your delay.'

'Nice one, Boz. Good dinking.'

Enrique relayed the message, listened to the reply then cupped the mouthpiece once more. 'Boz, he say de gesture of de battleship is very nice of you, but dere's just one problem.'

'What that?' asked Gunboat, burying his head in his hands.

'Dey ain't got no sea.'

8

In the Presence of Robert Walpole

'HELLO, IT'S THE PLUMBER. The pipe is blown... I repeat...
the pipe is blown. Request instructions as to what to do
now.'

'How badly is the pipe blown?'

'As badly as possible.'

A long pause followed.

'Was the blow caused by failure to follow instructions?'

'Er... y–yes.'

It was perhaps the hundredth time Jones, Chief of Staff, had
listened to the recording. He sat at his desk at MI6 Headquarters,
Vauxhall Cross, London, with his head in his hands, imagining
the countless places he would rather be at 5.47 a.m. on a Sunday
morning – notably back in the bed he'd been so hastily called
in from.

'How on earth did Trabant get himself into such a situation?'
exclaimed Hardcastle, head of the Priority Surveillance Unit,
sitting opposite.

'And how do we now prevent Gunboat blowing up in all
the wrong people's faces?'

Hardcastle shrugged his shoulders.

'There's only one thing for it,' continued Jones, before
taking a deep breath and reaching for his intercom. 'Mary, call
Bravinger's home, please. Tell him we have a Category One
situation, and need him here right away.'

'Yes, sir.'

The intercom soon replied. 'He's coming in, though he said it had better be good.'

'That's the problem – it's very, very bad!'

Within fifteen minutes Jones and Hardcastle were facing the head of MI6 across the same desk that had greeted Trabant just days before.

'This had better be good, gentlemen,' grumbled Bravinger. 'And hurry up, I tee off at nine.'

'Sir, we have terrible news regarding the surveillance op on Gunboat Charlie,' said Jones.

'What's happened?'

'The worst imaginable, sir'

'What? He's given us the slip?'

'Worse than that, sir.'

'For heaven's sake, man – spit it out!'

'Trabant's played Gunboat at cards, sir.'

'NO!'

'I'm afraid there's more, sir,' added Hardcastle. 'He's gone and beaten him too.'

'NO! No, no, no, no, no! Damned fool!'

'Who – me, sir?' asked Jones.

'Oh, shut up. Not you – Trabant!' Bravinger wagged a finger across the desk. 'I told him – whatever you do, don't play him at cards. And what does he do...?'

Bravinger then turned to the head of the Priority Surveillance Unit. 'Hardcastle...'

'Yes, sir.'

'You're fired!'

'W–what?!?'

'This mess is down to you, and Trabant, of course. Get out of my sight.'

'But it was you who—'

'Just go, or I'll have security eject you. Jones...'

'Y-yes, sir,' replied the Chief of Staff, fearing the same fate.

'I'm taking charge of this mess now. You will work by my side – tirelessly – to help clear it up.'

'Sir.'

'Damned IT Department, always cocking things up. Well, there's only one thing for it…'

Bravinger reached forward and pressed the button on his intercom. 'Juliet – get me the Prime Minister!'

ii

'As you know, Prime Minister,' continued Bravinger, carefully balancing his Ten Downing Street teaspoon on the Royal Doulton bone-china saucer, '… for the past few days Gunboat Charlie has been in Cannes, where we've had him under surveillance.'

'Glad to hear it,' replied Prime Minister Cuthbert Hanlon, seated behind his padded desk, in his dressing gown, with slice of hot toast before him; parliamentary jar of marmalade in one hand, Treasury butter-knife in the other. 'But can't all this wait until Monday? It's half past six Sunday morning.'

Hanlon was a tall, polished man of classic appearance. His athletic poise and dashing sweep of silvery-white hair had earned him the nickname Silver Fox, and his reputation for wiliness and tenacity was well established in the gladiatorial arenas of international politics.

Bravinger continued. 'No, I'm afraid it can't wait.'

'Why? What's the problem?'

'Our usual man – Bentley – was sick, so we had to send someone else.'

Hanlon momentarily froze, then looked up from his breakfast. 'What's wrong with him?'

'Chickenpox. And with no other field operatives available,

we had to send a chap from our IT department, named Bristo Trabant.'

Hanlon raised a wary eye.

'Trabant was only supposed to watch Gunboat, that's all.' Bravinger took a deep breath. 'But things went further than they were supposed to.'

'Oh no! Don't say what I think you're going to.'

'I'm afraid it's true, Prime Minster,' winced Bravinger, shifting uneasily in his seat, and glaring at Jones. 'Trabant played Gunboat at cards.'

'Hell no!' cursed Hanlon.

'I told him, Prime Minister. But I'm afraid it gets worse.'

'How can it possibly get any…? Oh, no… don't you dare say that he…'

'He did, sir. Trabant beat him too.'

Prime Minister Hanlon froze, with mouth full of toast and head full of turmoil. Then slowly, after drawing on every ounce of composure gleaned from a long political career, he reached for a napkin, wiped his fingers then pressed the buzzer on his burr walnut intercom. 'Margaret – hold all my calls.'

Bravinger and Jones sat in silence, like naughty schoolboys awaiting the headmaster's verdict. The Silver Fox's eyes were now cloudy and troubled, and robbed of the vigour so adored by the nation he served. 'You *do* realise this is a major international incident.'

'We do, Prime Minister.'

'And what of Trabant? Is he still alive?'

'Miraculously, yes,' continued Bravinger. 'He somehow managed to escape, and telephoned HQ this morning at approximately quarter past two BST. The officer who took the call booked him onto the very next flight out of Nice Côte d'Azur Airport, which happened to be to Vienna. He should be landing in about ten minutes' time. Station V – our Vienna team – will meet him in the city centre, and look after him from there.'

The PM's eyes diverted to an imaginary dot on the ceiling, the same dot he'd used in countless other moments of international crisis. 'You *do* also realise that if Gunboat murders Trabant we'll be compelled to act.'

'I understand, sir. We can't just sit back and do nothing if one of our agents gets killed, no matter *how* stupid he is.'

The Silver Fox threw Bravinger a disapproving look. 'But the pressure from the international community to do nothing would be immense. Everyone is so frightened of Gunboat's dirty secrets that they simply want him left alone, no matter how severe the provocation. If we did act, the heat on us would be unbearable, and that's a situation we can well do without. Which means, gentlemen, that we simply *have* to get to Trabant before Gunboat does. Is that clear?'

'Yes, Prime Minister.'

'And then, somehow, we can try and appease Gunboat's fury.'

'Good thinking.'

'Well, Bravinger – that's why I'm Prime Minister; and that's why you and your whole department will now work around the clock until this mess gets sorted out.'

'Yes, Prime Minister.'

'Cancel all leave. Get every unit mobilised. This could get—'

Buzzzzzz... Buzzzzzz...

Hanlon pressed the intercom. 'Yes, Margaret.'

'Sir, I know you said to hold all your calls, but I have the French Prime Minister for you on line one.'

Hanlon's eyes swelled. 'Okay, put him through.' He swished up the receiver. 'Jacques, how the devil are you? Good... Yes, same old, same old... The odd strike and riot, otherwise all harmonious on the... U-huh... Sure, go on... When?... Today!... Thirty minutes!... Eek... Er, let me just check my diary... Hold on.' Hanlon cupped the phone.

'Everything okay, Prime Minister?' asked Bravinger.

'No! The French are coming! Monsieur Rascous and his team have requested a meeting.'

'Can't you put them off?'

'Not really, seeing as they're just about to land at City Airport. Something to do with a matter of global security. At the last G8 summit I told him: "To France, my doors are always open." But I didn't actually mean 7.30 a.m. on a Sunday morning. Hell!'

Hanlon grimaced once more, then returned to the phone. 'Hello, Jacques. Yes, of course. That's fine. I'll put the kettle on. Just one question before you arrive – is this concerning our friend in Panama? It is… okay, j-just wondered… Yes, see you shortly then… Yes, au revoir.'

Hanlon pressed the intercom. 'Margaret, we have Monsieur Rascous and his team descending on us in less than an hour. Could you kindly ask Mavis to run round with the Hoover, clear the empty wine bottles from the patio, and wake the Foreign Secretary; he's outside asleep in the hammock.'

'I'll see to it, Prime Minister.'

'Good show.' Hanlon turned back. 'Well, gentlemen, it seems bad news travels fast, and that my wife has been sharing diary notes with Madame Rascous, so the French Prime Minister knows that I'm home. It is 7 a.m., which gives me thirty minutes to shave, get dressed and walk the bulldog; and you the same to contact Vienna and make certain they pick up Trabant. Use this phone. I'll see you both back here at 7.25 sharp.'

As Prime Minister Hanlon walked out of his office, Jones turned the desk phone around and dialled. 'Hello, Vienna, Jones here from London HQ… ah, hello, Johann, how are you?… and Little Johann?… Still composing? Bless! Listen, I'm phoning to check you're on standby to pick up our man… Yes, Trabant, that's right – as in the car. All set for 9 a.m. local time, so 8 a.m. here in London. Excellent news. Thanks.'

Jones replaced the phone. 'He said that—'

'Yes, yes, I got the gist,' snapped Bravinger. 'Once Station V have intercepted Trabant we can all relax. Still can't believe you chose to send him in the first place, though.'

'I didn't, sir – you did!'

'Rubbish. It must have been Hardcastle.'

iii

At precisely 7.30 a.m. the famous black front door swung open. Prime Minister Cuthbert Hanlon greeted French Prime Minister Jacques Rascous and his entourage with a shake of hands and kiss of cheeks, before leading them inside, across the black-and-white-marble tiled entrance hall and through to the Cabinet Room.

The room was painted off-white, with large floor-to-ceiling windows along the south-facing wall. Three brass chandeliers hung from the high ceiling, illuminating the huge oval table beneath, around which stood twenty-two carved mahogany chairs, some of which were already occupied. The twenty-third (and the only one with arms) stood in front of the marble fireplace, facing the windows. This was the Prime Minister's chair, with its cushion perfectly moulded (as one would expect after two and a half successful terms in office) to his parliamentary bottom. Above the fireplace hung the only picture in the room: a portrait of Robert Walpole.

'Mesdames et messieurs, ladies and gentlemen, please take your seats,' beamed Hanlon.

'Thank you for seeing us at such short notice,' smiled Jacques Rascous, speaking for himself and entourage, all fresh off the French Government jet. 'It is always nice to see our colleagues from across the Channel, though I wish the occasion was of a more joyous nature.'

Hanlon solemnly dipped his head, waited for the last few arrivals to take their seats, then cleared his throat to set proceedings underway. 'Thank you all for attending this meeting. Bearing in mind the events of the last twenty-four hours, you will agree it is of the highest importance.'

The room nodded in agreement.

'As you are all aware, this meeting is regarding the incident which took place at Le Club Maritime du Soleil in Cannes last night. Our agent, Bristo Trabant, for reasons known only to himself, decided to not only play Gunboat Charlie at cards but to beat him too.'

The room grumbled its displeasure.

'Yes, I know, I know… it's the worst scenario imaginable, but there is a chink of hope, and that is what we need to discuss. But before we do so, I would like to introduce my staff, then hand over to Prime Minister Rascous. Starting to my left: Colonel Bravinger, head of MI6; Jones, MI6 Chief of Staff; Miss Allinson, my long-suffering PA; and finally, the Priority Surveillance Unit's field agent assigned to Southern France *and* Gunboat…' Hanlon paused for effect, 'Bentley.'

Prime Minister Rascous nodded his greetings, and in particular towards Bentley, the man he'd read so much about: the former British Army officer then Special Forces operative, who had transferred to Colonel Bravinger's beloved Priority Surveillance Unit like some prized footballer, and apparently for an undisclosed fee. Bentley's six-foot frame was lean, powerful and handsome; and capped with short black hair, pearl-blue eyes and a jaw-line that glistened with the spit and polish of Sandhurst. Yet there was also a shot-blast toughness about him, and he sipped his carrot juice with indifference, radiating a supreme confidence that no matter the problem troubling both sets of ministers, he alone would be able to resolve it, and of course – as his file stated – be back home again in time for tea.

'Agent Bentley, it is always a pleasure,' said Cuthbert Hanlon. 'And I trust your chickenpox has all but gone?'

'It has, Prime Minister,' he replied.

'Excellent! And just when we need you most. So, Jacques,' continued Hanlon, turning back to Prime Minister Rascous, 'over to you.'

'Merci. Okay, my team: head of DGSE Intelligence Section, Gérard Depouis; Chief of Staff, Xavier L'Acroue; my personal assistant, Genevieve D'Arsang; and finally *our* top agent and head of our taskforce dedicated to the surveillance of Gunboat…' Rascous paused for equal effect, 'Eva Avante.'

iv

The room exchanged pleasantries.

Bravinger leant towards Jones and whispered, 'Just remind me, what does DGSE stand for again?'

'The Direction Générale de la Sécurité Extérieure – France's foreign intelligence agency, sir.'

'Thought so,' replied Bravinger, nodding as if he'd known all along.

Monsieur Rascous, looking every inch le coq sportif, took a sip of water then addressed the room. 'We all know Gunboat of old. He has been tolerated and avoided in equal measures, the reasons for which we are all too aware. I am sorry that your Agent Trabant is in grave danger.'

'Thank you for your concern,' replied Bravinger. 'However, our team in Vienna will collect him in… by my watch, what… approximately twenty minutes' time, so he'll be safe and sound.'

'Have Vienna confirmed they're on standby?' asked Hanlon.

'Yes, Prime Minister,' replied Jones. 'They'll collect Agent Trabant as soon as he arrives at the rendezvous.'

'That is excellent news,' continued Rascous. 'Yet as we all

know, Gunboat will not stop until Agent Trabant is dead. And he will happily blackmail the entire political community if necessary, to get Trabant's head.'

'Jeez, all over a game of cards,' whistled Jones.

'Trivial to us,' replied Hanlon, 'but of paramount importance to Gunboat.'

'Regrettably so,' agreed Rascous. 'Gunboat's fury will be immeasurable. There is no alternative. We simply have to avert this potentially catastrophic situation.'

'We all share your concerns, Prime Minister,' replied Hanlon.

'But it is not only Agent Trabant who is at risk,' continued Rascous, gesturing to his left. 'Our own agent, Miss Avante, is also now on Gunboat's hit-list.'

'How come?' asked Bravinger.

'Because she was the one who rescued Agent Trabant from the yacht club. Helping the condemned man escape carries the same penalty as beating Gunboat at cards. So you see, we are now – as you English say – all in the same boat.'

Hanlon turned to Eva. 'Agent Avante, on behalf of the whole country, may I wholeheartedly thank you for your heroic intervention in saving our man. It is greatly appreciated.'

'My pleasure. Agent Trabant is a fine man.'

'Indeed he is,' replied Hanlon. 'And you have put yourself at great risk, *and* moved like the wind to get here so quickly. It is now 7.43 a.m. How on earth did you do it?'

'After taking Agent Trabant to Nice Côte d'Azur Airport, I phoned ahead to our French Air Force base at Istres, and had them ready a jet. I knew the situation with Gunboat needed immediate attention, as it would quickly escalate. On the way to Istres I was intercepted by men no doubt working for Gunboat, but managed to lose them in the back-doubles around Vence. I then telephoned my team, arranged to meet them and Prime Minister Rascous at London City Airport, then caught the jet. And here we are. But despite gaining an hour with the time difference, I had no chance to change my clothes, so please forgive my casual attire.'

'You look great to me,' replied Hanlon. 'And bravo for such quick thinking and resourcefulness. Well, we owe you a debt of gratitude. Is there anything we can do for you?'

'A strong black coffee would be wonderful,' smiled Eva. 'And also, an introduction to the man responsible for sending Agent Trabant to Cannes in the first place. I wish to give him a piece of my mind.'

Eva followed Hanlon's eyes as they glanced across to Bravinger. So, it was the head of MI6 who was responsible. Colonel or no colonel, she narrowed her eyes and vowed to see to him later.

9

The Towers of the Heathens

BRISTO TRABANT'S FLIGHT TO Vienna had been smooth and uneventful.

While ministers of the British and French governments discussed strategies, he'd remained hidden behind the protective shield of the in-flight magazine, and allowed his thoughts to drift out through the small oval window and beyond the wing tips to the hazy, sun-washed horizon.

The cascading mountains and deep-blue azure of Nice had long since departed, and now, as the rumble of jet engines faded to the back of his mind, he could finally settle with his own thoughts, in his own world, where he felt safest; in a place where even the slamming of overhead lockers and the 'Bing!' of seatbelt warning lights could not reach. And the further the plane crept north-east across the great continent of Europe, the more relaxed he became.

At thirty-five thousand feet the cloud cover became total, like a range of snow-capped mountains floating in the sky before smoothing out into a bleak wilderness, upon which he half-expected to see a mother polar bear leading her two cubs on a search for food, their struggle for survival every bit as perilous as his own. Perhaps they'd also caught scent of the famous Viennese dessert? Perhaps they could all dine together later that night? Trabant allowed himself a smile, and envisaged a pointed wooden sign in the distance, mounted on a solitary cloud, with the words 'Apfelstrudel – 250 KM' painted in tall, mouthwatering, apple-green letters.

And what of Eva? Where would she be now, and for the rest of her life? Tonight, no doubt with husband, friends, children, laughing and eating in some idyllic setting, with a glass in her hand and the world at her feet. His mind drifted but his heart remained firmly back in the departures hall, still locked in her warm, tender embrace. Could there be a place for him in her heart too? Might she also be gazing dreamily out of another window, somewhere else in the world, thinking about him? No, of course not! Their moment had passed, and he'd continued onwards through the doorway of time, to become, at best, just a fleeting memory which she would doubtless soon forget.

'Ladies and gentlemen, we will soon begin our descent into Vienna.'

'Cabin crew, seats for landing.'

The cloud cover thinned then parted to reveal a mosaic of green and brown fields, scatterings of white houses with red-brick roofs, then a river, a motorway, what looked like a huge feed mill and then finally the long stretch of tarmac, upon which the wheels gently kissed. Engines screamed in reverse like banshees, until thankfully the giant lady of the skies gained control of her momentum and slowed to a composed, disinterested amble.

Austrian Airlines Flight OS427 had arrived in the City of Music precisely on time.

ii

A short trundle to the terminal and the journey was complete. Glorious sunshine greeted Trabant, and with no baggage he

93

quickly passed through immigration, the semi-circular arrivals lounge of expectant faces, and out to the taxi rank. Despite the other drivers' protestations, he hailed not the first, but third taxi in line, exactly as Eva had instructed. 'Town centre, please,' he said, closing the door of the white Mercedes.

'Er… you mean Innere Stadt, no?'

'Yes, that's right. As close to St Stephen's Cathedral as you can get me.'

'Okay.' The taxi driver clicked the meter, then eased out into the morning traffic.

'How far is it?'

'About eighteen kilometres.'

'Will we make it by nine o'clock?'

'Ja, no problem. It is only twenty minutes.'

Trabant checked his watch. It was 08.14 – maybe even time for apfelstrudel!

The taxi ploughed onwards, picking up the busy A4 dual-carriageway following signs for 'Wien'. A broad waterway ran parallel on the left, beyond which a parade of grey industrial buildings stood tall, towering with the aura of corporate in-difference. Next, an oil refinery; a power station, then countless apartment blocks with funky roofs and matchbox balconies.

'Is that the Danube River?' asked Trabant.

'Nein, the Danube canal. The river is further east. You here on business, ja?'

'Er, something like that.'

Trabant eased back in the seat to enjoy his new, delicious sense of liberation. He'd made it through the civil aviation network in one piece – thanks to Eva – and now, just perhaps, the horrors of Cannes could finally be considered as no longer applicable.

08.32: The taxi pulled up at the end of a busy street.

'Are we here?' asked Trabant, looking around at the shops and banks on the street named Liliengasse.

94

The driver nodded. 'At Stephansplatz. And there, straight ahead, is St Stephen's Cathedral. Beautiful, ja?'

'Yes, very,' replied Trabant, feasting his eyes on the Gothic masterpiece before him.

'So, are you meeting someone?' asked the driver.

'Hmmm? Oh, yes, at 9 a.m. sharp, beneath the clock, which I'm told is just to the left of the cathedral's main entrance.'

'It is. You cannot miss it. But if you do, just ask Mozart – he will help.'

'I thought he died years ago?'

'Ja, ja… of course. I mean one of the lookalikes selling concert tickets. You'll see.'

'Thank you,' said Trabant, extracting a fifty-Euro note from the bundle Eva had given him. 'And as I'm early, is there a good café you can recommend?'

iii

Outside Café Wiener, rows of silver tables stood within a glass-panelled boundary, and shaded beneath two lines of beige parasols. Trabant took a table in the front right corner, away from the dozen or so tourists, ordered then focused on the large, gold clock set in the sand-coloured cathedral wall opposite.

… and at precisely the same time, the taxi driver completed his phone call, relaying the exact details of which café the target was sitting in; that he had a nine o'clock meeting beneath the clock; and that his beige suit was shadowed by the most curious ears he had ever seen.

08.43: Just as coffee was served at Ten Downing Street, coffee and strudel arrived at Café Wiener. Trabant plunged his fork deep into the compact, sugar-coated layers of pastry-encrusted apple, loaded in a mouthful then braced himself for the legendary explosion of flavours.

'Ooh, yes… delicious!' he muttered to himself. 'Thank you again, Eva.' He paused for a moment, in mid-chew, as if feeling her watching over him like a guardian angel, urging him to remain vigilant despite the closeness of the finishing line. But what could possibly go wrong now?

08.46: With strudel sadly finished, Trabant sipped his coffee and peered across to the far side of the cathedral, to the horse-drawn carriages lined up and the gather of tourists trying to clamber aboard.

08.47: Trabant checked the clock again, wiped a serviette over the brown frothy line encircling his mouth, and prepared to leave.

08.48: The stare burnt like a blowtorch. Trabant turned – and his eyes locked into the gruesome fate that awaited. It was Raúl, Gunboat's heavy, sat at the opposite corner of the café, his pockmarked skin even more sinister in the cold light of day. But Cannes was a thousand miles away. How could he…?

08.49: The walls of Vienna closed in like an industrial crusher. But the café was filling. Thank heavens for public places. Surely too many witnesses to kill him here? Yes, he was safe… if he remained in his seat… for as long as it took… forever if necessary, or until one of them died of old age, whichever came the sooner. Ah, but no! He couldn't wait… the RENDEZVOUS!

08.51: Trabant stole a look behind him. Inside the café there must be a toilet, perhaps with a small window he could clamber through. All toilets had those, right? But how to get there unnoticed? 'Ooh, pardon, Madame.'

'This is Austria, sir – not France,' replied the waitress. 'You want more coffee?'

'No, I need your help. You see, I'm about to be murdered!'

'Really? How terrible for you,' she replied sarcastically. 'What's wrong? Not enough to pay the bill?'

'I'm serious. The man sitting on the far side of the café is going to kill me.'

The waitress looked across. 'What man?'

'The big, ugly one with—'

'There is no one there, sir.'

Trabant spun round, disbelieving the now empty space. 'But where did he go?'

'I do not know,' replied the waitress. 'But it's still eight Euros to pay, or do I need to call my manager?'

08.56: 'Here, keep the change.'

'Thank you,' she said. 'Enjoy your—'

'Wait! Do you have toilets inside? You know, with a small window, the kind I can climb out of?'

'Toilet… ja. Small window… nein.'

'Nine! Oh, thank heavens. I really only need one, but—'

'No, you misunderstand me, sir. We-have-no-toilets-with-windows. Understand?'

'Oh…' Trabant slapped down another ten-Euro note on the table. 'Any other ideas?'

'I have now!' she smiled. 'If I was about to be murdered, I'd use our fire-exit. Run inside, veer to the right and you'll see it.'

08.57: Trabant slalomed the tables, ran inside to the fire-exit and pushed down hard on the silver bar. The doors flew open, launching him out into a narrow, shadow-littered alley – the kind that always give murderers the unfair advantage. He sprinted to the end, turned right onto a main street then right again, praying his inbuilt compass would somehow return him to the cathedral. A tram clattered into view, forcing him to divert left around its tail, onto the far side of the street, past the gift shops, until mercifully back into Stephansplatz, to face the clock from the other side.

08.59: Made it. Now come on, contact – where are you?

The golden hands moved to precisely 9 a.m.

B-o-n-g!

Trabant ignored the bell chime to scan every face, left-to-right then—

B-o-n-g!

… back again, as if watching a tennis—

B-o-n-g!

… match! Double fault, foot-fault, but this was all his own—

B-o-n-g!

… fault. Jeez – help! Look inconspicuous… just blend in. What, like at the yacht club? Look how—

B-o-n-g!

… that turned out! But this would be different. The contact would have a—

B-o-n-g!

… photo to work from. Being found should be easy, a for—

B-o-n-g!

… mality. Yes, and especially with ears such as his. Come on, where are—

B-o-n-g!

… hell, that's loud! Why not rendezvous at half past the hour, when there's only one… oh, silence. Maybe that was—

B-O-N-G!

09.03: Nothing.

09.07: Still nothing. Something wasn't right.

09.09: He caught the eye of a broad-shouldered woman heading straight for him, dressed in blue jeans and black fleece jacket, complete with ruddy complexion and mousy-brown hair that bounced in flagging curls. Did she look like an agent from Station V? Did anyone?

Calm down… look inconspicuous. Inconspicuous…

She pounded the last few metres like a rugby prop-forward, until stopping directly in front of him. 'Good morning. Are you taking the guided walking tour?'

98

'Huh?'

'The walking tour,' she repeated, with eyebrows lowered in slight confusion. 'I noticed you immediately. You look very conspicuous standing here, so I figured it must be you.'

'Er... aren't you supposed to ask about hedgehogs?' replied Trabant, thinking of the MI6 phrase-codes Bravinger had issued him.

'No. We did the nature trail yesterday, and now we're here to learn about the historical wonders of Vienna. I'm Natalie Fisher, Head Mistress of Chancery Royal School for Girls.'

'Pleased to meet you. But I...'

'Oh, didn't head office tell you? Well, we booked ages ago, and there's thirty of us, Mr...?'

'Trabant.'

'Oh, that's a funny name. As in the—'

'Car? Yes, but I—'

'Look, here come the girls, getting off the coach.' She turned to yell at the gaggle of school kids clattering down the bus steps. 'COME ON, GIRLS!' She turned back to Trabant. 'We're spending the day in Vienna before heading to the Alps. Schönbrunn this afternoon; the Opera House tonight. How exciting! And the girls have been *so* looking forward to your walking tour, so don't let us down now.'

The terrifying prospect of conducting a walking tour suddenly grew in appeal – as Raúl reappeared.

'Please, Mr Trabant,' urged Natalie Fisher. 'Can we get started?'

'Yes, definitely! Right away,' he replied, urging the wide-eyed huddle of teenager expectation closer. 'That's it, gather all around, so you can hear what I, er... say.'

Ominously, Raúl stepped closer too.

Trabant took a deep breath, and desperately tried to recall the terminology used by the London guides on their walking tours. 'Now, I'm just waiting for, er... one more person to arrive, and then we can begin. I'm sorry for the delay, but it really is a matter of life and—'

'He no coming.' Raúl's words frosted the whole group.

'H–how do you mean?' asked Trabant.

'I see to it. Permanent.'

A bluster of fear circulated.

'I don't like that man,' whispered one of the girls to her friend, nodding towards Raúl. 'Bet he's just escaped from the local loony-bin.'

'I know. You get some real weirdos on these tourist trips.'

'And look at his eyebrows,' added another girl. 'They meet in the middle. You know what they say about people whose—'

'Quiet, girls!' barked Natalie Fisher. 'So, Mr Trabant, if there's no one else to wait for, perhaps you can now begin?'

'Sí, you really *must* begin,' chuckled Raúl.

'Must I?'

'Yes!' snapped Natalie Fisher.

'O–okay. Well, er… good morning, everyone. My name is Bristo Trabant.'

'G–o–o–d m–o–r–n–i–n–g, M–i–s–t–e–r T–r–a–b–a–n–t,' replied the girls (and Raúl) in unison.

'I am your guide for the next few hours; in fact for as long as it takes, and I will… er, show you some memorable sites of Vienna. And where better to start than right here, at St Stephen's Cathedral. Please take as long as you like to marvel at the breathtaking architecture, most notably the twin Roman towers – known as the Towers of the Heathens – and the awesome Giant's Door.'

'Wow! Magnificent!' gasped the group.

'What's a heathen?' asked one of the girls at the front.

'Well, Naomi,' replied Natalie Fisher. 'One definition would be a person lacking morals or principles. The word dates back centuries, to when people roamed the open countryside, or heaths, and were regarded as savages.'

Trabant eyed Raúl, the modern-day equivalent, then continued his recital of the in-flight magazine's blurb, risking copyright infringement for the sake of self-preservation. 'The first cathedral was built on this site in 1160, of which, sadly, there are few remains.'

'Boo!'

'However, major reconstruction continued until 1511—'

'Hurray!'

'... and repair work and loving restoration continues—' A movement caught Trabant's eye, as Raúl's right hand slid inside his jacket pocket, exactly as Gunboat's had in Le Club Maritime du Soleil. 'But enough about that, let's *quickly* move on, er... this way.'

Trabant hurried to his left, across the main entrance and round the corner, with the girls bounding along in hot pursuit.

'Mr Trabant, are you okay?' asked Natalie Fisher. 'You look pale.'

'Yes, fine,' he answered, hastily reassembling his human shield. 'Just a little queasy.'

'Good, then perhaps you can tell us the significance of this miniature replica?'

'Which one?'

'This one – the only one!' She glared, pointing down to a jet-black, plinth-mounted, model cathedral.

'Oh, *that* one... is special; a gift donated by the... er, friends of Vienna for all—'

Raúl reappeared. Trabant faltered and lost his thread, as his head spun... like a wheel... a wheel inside the cage... the cage of a... 'Mouse!' he blurted. 'I mean... mice. It's a shelter for, er... local mice. In winter.'

'That's ridiculous!' exclaimed Natalie Fisher.

'Not at all,' replied Trabant, with no option but to continue. 'It gets extremely cold here. And Viennese rodents are very religious too.'

The first breeze of discontent claimed the air. Trabant moved quickly, leading the group around the back of the cathedral to the far side, where even more horse-drawn carriages waited for tourists.

'Okay, here we are, to take a look at er… more examples of beautiful Viennese window design.'

'What's that?' asked one of the girls, pointing to an adjacent building.

'Hmmm? Oh, that's the Dom Museum.'

'Who's he?'

'Good question,' replied Trabant. 'Anyone like to take a guess?'

'It's the museum of the cathedral itself,' stated Natalie Fisher, through gritted teeth.

Discontent now blustered. Trabant decided to tack. 'Vienna is also famous for apfelstrudel…' blank faces stared back, '… and its cafés, which are great places to renew old acquaintances, welcome or… oh, you have a question?'

'Yes,' replied another girl. 'Did Johann Strauss live nearby?'

'Which one – the first?'

'No, the second.'

'Yes, I believe it was somewhere just over… there!' gestured Trabant, vaguely in a south-westerly direction.

'What about Mozart?' asked another girl. 'Did he live there too?'

'Probably…'

'At the same time?'

'Er… possibly.'

'Wow! Did you hear that, Miss Fisher?' said the girl. 'Strauss and Mozart were flatmates. How cool is that!'

'I'm sorry to shatter your enthusiasm, Emily, but Mr Trabant is quite incorrect. Mozart died in 1791, and Johann Strauss the second wasn't even born until 1825.'

Trabant stood exposed, the batsman bowled clean, his stumps of fabrication despatched to the frosty atmosphere.

Natalie Fisher wasn't finished. 'In light of Mr Trabant's confusion over elementary historical dates, perhaps he'd be kind enough to tell us what the names Mahler, Schubert, Brahms, Schoenberg and Haydn mean to him?'

'Er... members of the Austrian national football team?'

'Pah! And I suppose the street named Philharmonikerstrasse, upon which our hotel is situated, was named after a man called Phil, who owned a harmonica, and used to busk there for his dinner money?'

'Perhaps.'

Raúl looked up to the adjacent street sign, astounded that one name could contain so many letters.

'Miss Fisher,' whispered another girl. 'This tour is crap!'

'I agree. Look here, Mr Trabant,' Natalie Fisher continued, turning back. 'We're not happy with ...'

But Bristo Trabant had gone. Raúl looked back too, with instant disbelief, and barged through the group, furious at his oversight, and quickly began to scan the vicinity for the irregular, jagged movements of his quarry.

'There he is – over there!' shouted one of the girls.

'Oh yes, so he is,' replied Natalie Fisher. 'I say there, Mr Trabant...'

A clattering sandwich-board confirmed Trabant's position. Raúl zeroed in – running faster and faster – with fists clenched and eyes ablaze. And as Trabant picked himself up off the ground, their eyes met in another telepathic exchange of precisely the fate that awaited.

The starting pistol of life and death had fired once more.

Hell Hath No Fury Like a…

BRITISH PRIME MINISTER CUTHBERT Hanlon stole another glance at his watch. It was 08.19 and still no news.

'Bravinger – contact Station V. Ask them what the hell's going on?'

'Yes, Prime Minister. Personally!' The head of MI6 swivelled in his chair. 'Jones, get on to that straight away.'

'Yes, sir.'

As Jones dialled his mobile, Bravinger turned to Jacques Rascous. 'While we're waiting, I'd like to apologise for Trabant. You see, he was all we had available. If it's any consolation, we're all hopping mad with him. He's completely incompetent and daft as a brush to boot.'

'Amateur,' sneered Bentley.

Eva had heard enough. 'Gentlemen, Agent Trabant is not trained in espionage, counter-intelligence, or any related fields. You both know he should never have been sent to watch Gunboat.'

'I hear your sentiments, Agent Avante,' replied Bravinger, 'but I'm telling you, there *was* no alternative.'

'There is always an—'

'What!?!' exclaimed Jones, stopping Eva in mid-flow. 'But how? Yes, I'm with the Prime Minister right now… okay, keep me posted… out.'

Jones ended the call, ashen-faced.

'What's happened?' asked Bravinger.

'Bad news, I'm afraid. Trabant's flight arrived on time, but Station V haven't got him.'

'WHAT!' exclaimed Eva.

'The local operative sent to meet him at the rendezvous never made it. Radio contact ceased at roughly ten minutes to nine. He's only just been found, in the back of a frankfurter delivery van heading south for Eisenstadt.'

'How is he?' asked Eva.

'Left for dead, though thankfully still alive. But Agent Trabant – has vanished!'

The first scent of genuine concern wafted through the room.

'Ladies and gentlemen, let us not panic,' said Hanlon, with deliberate calmness. 'Let us put our heads together and think.'

'I fear we may be too late,' said Jones.

'Maybe not,' replied Hanlon. 'If Trabant's as dizzy as Colonel Bravinger says, then maybe he gave up on the rendezvous and went to see the sights?'

'With respect, Prime Minister, I think not,' said Eva. 'He was very scared when I left him at Nice airport. He would've made the rendezvous, and certainly phoned MI6 HQ if no one from your Station V showed. Without doubt, something is very wrong. And forgive my directness, but I fear you have an informer in your Vienna office.'

Hanlon nodded in pained agreement.

Gérard Depouis, Head of DGSE Intelligence Section, spoke up for the first time. 'We must assume the worst – that Agent Trabant has been captured by Gunboat.'

'I agree,' said Eva. 'In which case, Prime Minister Hanlon, with your permission I would like to suggest a plan.'

'Please. Be my guest.'

Eva chose her words carefully, knowing the apportioning of blame – MI6's chain of command, Station V and herself for not driving Bristo directly to Paris – must wait. Right now, all that mattered was Bristo's life, and the lightning-fast action required to stand any chance at all of saving it.

'Ladies and gentlemen, I will speak quickly because time is short. For the past eighteen months I have led a surveillance operation on Gunboat. I have learnt of his strengths and weaknesses. It is correct to assume that Agent Trabant has fallen into his clutches, and if Gunboat hasn't already killed him, then the only way to stop him doing so is to create a *live* value for Agent Trabant.'

'How do you mean?' asked Hanlon.

'Give Gunboat a reason to keep him alive.'

'But he wants him dead. More than anything,' scoffed Bravinger.

'Precisely,' added Hanlon. 'How on earth are we going to do that?'

Eva continued. 'Let us consider what we already know. Gunboat hates losing at cards, because of what people might think. In truth, no one cares, but Gunboat doesn't know that. And that is what we need to focus on.'

'Go on,' said Hanlon.

'He doesn't care at all about *our* opinions, but with the underworld it is different. If we can force some of his known associates and clients to directly question both his invincibility and his continued ability to supply arms, then his worst fears will appear to have become reality. He'll go crazy with worry. We then force those associates to insist that Gunboat prove his ability to continue as before, and the only way he can do that – is by holding a rematch.'

'A REMATCH!' gasped the room.

'That's crazy!' exclaimed Bravinger.

'No, Colonel Bravinger, that's genius!' beamed Hanlon. 'Gunboat cannot possibly refuse.'

Eva nodded in agreement. 'We instruct the associates to set the date for this coming Saturday, which will buy us six days to find Agent Trabant. We then treble our surveillance on Gunboat, which will hopefully lead us straight to him.'

'And if it doesn't?' asked Bravinger.

'Then we wait until the rematch, wherever that might be, and snatch Agent Trabant back, by force if necessary.'

The room shifted nervously.

'Easy, everyone,' said Hanlon. 'Her Majesty's Royal Marines will handle that, if it comes to it. Bravinger, see me afterwards to prime that angle.' Hanlon then turned back towards Eva. 'Forgive my interruption, Agent Avante. Please continue.'

'Once Agent Trabant is back in my... I mean, *our* safe hands, we can decide what to do about Gunboat.'

Bravinger frowned. 'The question, of course, is whether Trabant *is* still alive?'

'Agreed. And the only way to know that is to propose the rematch. If Gunboat agrees to it, then we know Agent Trabant is still alive. We must act right now – this very second – because at this very moment Agent Trabant could be facing a bullet.' Eva picked up some papers from the table in front of her. 'I have taken the liberty of compiling a list. It details the ten highest-profile contacts Gunboat has spoken to in the last week. And with the room's permission I request that both myself and Monsieur Jones immediately adjourn and phone these ten names, and insist they each phone Gunboat within the next five minutes to demand the rematch.'

'Next five minutes?' scoffed Bravinger. 'These things take time.'

'No, they do not,' replied Eva, dismissively.

Bravinger leant forward. 'And how do you propose we get these *names* to cooperate? Ask them politely? They are far more afraid of Gunboat than they will ever be of us.'

'I appreciate that, sir,' replied Eva, not caring about the bite in her voice. 'And perhaps not all will cooperate. But I am certain some will, if we threaten to blitz certain areas of their criminal enterprises that have, shall we say, traditionally been overlooked. Once they appreciate the extreme heat they will come under, and the financial implications that will follow, I have no doubt they will play ball. Unless, of course, Colonel Bravinger, you have some personal objections the room should know about?'

'No, not at all. It's just that—'

'Good,' continued Eva, deliberately cutting him short. 'These contacts will also be instructed that under no circumstances are they to breathe a word of our request. It is absolutely imperative Gunboat does not know what is really happening.'

'And I presume these criminals must also be instructed to inform us the moment Gunboat agrees?' asked Hanlon.

'Correct. And to also pass on the precise location of the rematch. Gunboat will need to tell them in advance so they can make their travel arrangements. Prime Minister, we must do this immediately or Agent Trabant will die. It is as simple as that.'

'Are we all agreed?' asked Cuthbert Hanlon, addressing the room. 'Good! Agent Avante and Jones – please use the adjoining room.'

Jones quickly followed Eva through the open doors. Twenty minutes later they returned.

'All okay?' asked Hanlon.

'Every contact has been instructed. They were given no choice. The outcome is now in the will of the gods.'

'You know, this *could* just work,' mused Hanlon.

Eva sat back down. 'Next, Monsieur Jones and I will phone even more of Gunboat's contacts and get them to demand the same. The more people who state their displeasure, the better our chances.'

Hanlon nodded. 'I know a few people in Manila who can be counted on for their discretion. I'll make some enquiries.'

'Thank you, Prime Minister.'

Hanlon offered a smile of hope. 'Bravinger, Jones – liaise with Agent Avante's team to contact all remaining associates of Gunboat immediately.'

'Yes, sir.'

'Ooh, and one more thing before we close this meeting,' added Hanlon. 'This operation needs a codename, to ensure tip-top secrecy at all times. Any suggestions?'

'Yes, I have the perfect name to remind us all of Trabant,' beamed Bravinger, his eyes twinkling at Eva. 'How about "Operation Dipstick"?'

'Perfect,' laughed Bentley.

'That suggestion, Colonel Bravinger, is wholly disrespectful.'

'To who – dipsticks?'

Eva glared back.

'Operation Dipstick it is,' continued Hanlon. 'Apologies, Agent Avante, but we haven't time to choose an alternative. So, mesdames et messieurs, ladies and gentlemen, if that's everything, let's get cracking, and may the gods of mercy shower us with good fortune. We're certainly going to need it.'

ii

While Eva's master plan was put into effect, Bristo Trabant continued running for his life through the narrow, tourist-filled alleys of Vienna. But Raúl was gaining, with every pounding footstep.

'MOVE – PLEASE!' shouted Trabant, as he approached another alley. The men jumped aside, as if a runaway car was heading straight for them, shrugged their shoulders then regrouped, only to step directly into the path of Raúl, who despatched them like pins in a bowling alley. Alley number two offered similar terrain, but with even more tourists and ever-decreasing gaps. Trabant ran faster still, willing his body on, praying for— 'Aaaaah!'

An elderly lady stepped out from nowhere. He dived to his left, avoiding contact but only to career headfirst into the tables and chairs of the adjacent café. People screamed and drinks sprayed everywhere.

'S-sorry,' exclaimed Trabant, but Raúl was now on the scene, arriving like an emergency service, yet with far darker motives... and at a speed too great for the seeping pool of froth. His feet lost traction, and as the assassin flailed, Trabant rose, like the second coming, scrambling away from the crash scene of furniture and back out into the sunshine.

'TRABANT!'

Once more the heavy was upon him. Trabant toppled a postcard stand to trip the beast, then veered right for the parasols and hedgerows of the upcoming beer house, then left beneath an archway, clueless as to where the cobbled street led, just that if offered sounds of life and roaring traffic. Yes, lots of traffic, and a view of both the canal and St Stephen's cathedral!?! Hell, he'd come full circle!

Ding ding ding!

A tram sounded its disgust as Trabant ran in front and onto a pedestrian island. He looked back. Raúl had momentarily disappeared behind the convoy of red-and-white carriages. And now, to the left, five lanes of traffic revved their engines like the starting grid of the Austrian Grand Prix. The lights changed to green, but Trabant went for it, across the din of blaring horns to the bridge that led over the murky-green, graffiti-bordered canal, then down some steps and along the towpath. But Raúl was unshakeable, getting ever closer; his hands at the ready to swipe and kill.

Ahead – a group of schoolchildren would certainly block his way. Trabant diverted up the next flight of stairs, back up to street level, veered across yet more traffic and made a final dash towards the maze of streets to the left. But the city was getting quieter, with fewer people about.

Trabant changed direction, but slipped, and Raúl was upon him in seconds, lifting then frogmarching him onwards, past a children's play area to the dimly lit rear entrance of an apartment block. Two steps led up to a tall, frosted-glass door. To the left stood a column of letter-boxes and door buzzers. To the right, a funeral parade of cold, grey dustbins.

'Please, I…'

Raúl's fist smashed into Trabant's back, sending him tumbling to the ground. And another blow was imminent, but this time from the gun now aimed firmly at the top of his head.

'PLEASE!'

'No beautiful hostess to save you this time.'

'But I—'

Brrrr… Brrrr… Brrrr…

'Who the hell…?' The gun remained pointed, while Raúl's other hand retrieved his mobile phone. 'Sí? Oh, hola, Mama, cómo está? Sí, sí… Gracias… Working hard… Yeah, yeah, I eating properly. Listen Mama, I call you back in five minute, okay? Just got to fire someone. Yeah, love you too. Adiós.'

'H-how is your m-mother?' gasped Trabant, desperate to buy some time.

'Shut up.'

'Please, I—'

Brrrr… Brrrr… Brrrr…

'Jeez! What now?' Raúl's gun didn't move as he angrily answered his phone again. 'Mama, please, I very… Oh! Hello, boss… no, no yet; just about to… sí, of course… whatever you say, boss… Adiós.'

Raúl's face was etched with disappointment. 'That was my boss.'

'Y-yes, I gathered. How is he?'

'He no happy! But it your lucky day.'

'You could've fooled me.'

'Oh, it your very lucky day. Wanna know why?'

'P-please.'

Raúl grabbed Trabant by his collar and lifted him to his feet. 'It seems señor Gunboat wants you brought back alive.'

iii

In London and Paris, telecommunications networks fizzled throughout the remainder of the day and into the evening. MI6 and DGSE teams worked relentlessly, mobilising agents around the world to call on those most likely to cooperate. Hoodlums were woken from their sleep; corrupt judges interrupted at the eighteenth tee; middlemen visited at the most inconvenient times, and all given the ultimatum. Some refused, but some could not.

'Well, that's the last call,' yawned Jones, dropping his battered MI6 phone into its cradle. It was 23.42 – a full eighteen hours since he'd first replayed the tape and heard Trabant's soul-chilling message. He slumped back in his chair, rubbed his eyes and tried to reassure himself that he'd done all he possibly could.

'Now listen here, Jones,' grumbled Bravinger, stepping into the office. 'It's not on, you know.'

'What's that, sir?'

'Letting the French steal the show. You should've had the last word. Don't let it happen again.'

'Sorry, sir,' replied Jones, too weary to protest. 'It's been a long day. Shame about your golf match.'

'Shame about a lot of things.'

Ring… Ring…

Jones wearily lifted the phone. 'Yes… u-huh… WHAT!?! Yes, t-thank you. Straight away!' He turned to Bravinger, re-energised. 'He's made the phone call, sir.'

112

'Who?'

'Gunboat Charlie! He's started telling people he *will* organise a rematch, and that it'll be held this coming Saturday. He's fallen for it – hook, line and sinker. Bristo is still alive! And once we have details of the location of the rematch, we can get him back. That gives us, what – a full five days to find out. It's worked. It's damned well worked. Congratulations, sir.'

Bravinger leant back in his chair to absorb the adulation. 'Well, Jones, when you've been in the service as long as I have, you get a feeling for these things. Now go on, reveal all. Who phoned us first?'

'Frankie Fugazi, the Florentine forger. He told Gunboat that concern over his card-game defeat was making him smudge. Not good with the holiday period coming up.'

Bravinger nodded in agreement. 'Artists of whatever genre, legal or otherwise, never want their arms twisted too far.'

'Apparently Gunboat hurled obscenities down the phone. But when the Columbians and the Sicilian Mafia called too, well… he had no alternative *but* to agree. Honestly, sir, you should've heard Agent Avante on the phone. I've never heard anyone so persuasive. And I've never known planning and contingency like it.'

'I think you've had too much coffee, Jones.'

'But it's true, sir. Don't you agree?'

'Yes, well, I have to admit, she is extremely capable. But she mustn't push Gunboat too far. We don't want the whole operation to self-combust before we achieve our goal.'

'How do you mean, sir?'

'I mean we're all playing with fire. If Gunboat finds out he's been tricked, the fallout will be catastrophic.' Bravinger removed his bifocals and looked Jones straight in the eye. 'In fact, Jones, it will be far worse than either you, I, Agent Avante or Prime Minister Hanlon could possibly imagine.'

'Will it really, sir?'

'Yes, Jones, it will. There's a saying that echoes throughout every single continent on this earth that endorses what I'm saying. Surprised you haven't heard it.'

'I haven't, sir. Please tell—'

Bravinger emptied his face of any humour. 'Hell hath no fury like a Gunboat scorned.'

Señor Gringo Loco

THE LEARJET RACED ACROSS the sky, piercing every cloud that dared stand in its way. Only a quick stop in Dakar for fuel and chicken yassa had eased the tension. But at last the jet crossed the final stretch of the North Atlantic to begin its homeward descent. Beneath, the volcanic island arc of the Lesser Antilles smiled back; the gateway to the Caribbean running north to south like a skeleton's backbone; its vertebrae highlighted in the turquoise water by rings of golden sand.

'Hola, señores,' mumbled the pilot through the intercom. 'We land in ten minutes.'

The wings tipped slightly as the jet altered its course for the south-west corner of the Caribbean and the isthmus of Panama. And soon the sea gave way to a landscape of dense rainforest, scattered housing, and a mountain range as rugged as it was vast. Then finally, the jet eased out of the sky to touch down at Aeropuerto Marcos A Gelabert, Panama City's domestic hub.

'Bienvenidos, señores,' said the pilot. 'Home sweet home.'

ii

Aeropuerto Marcos A Gelabert was located immediately north-west of Ancon Hill, and bordered by the Canal and Balboa Port complex, where herds of giraffe-like cranes picked at the spread of transport containers as if collecting fallen fruit from the ground. The airport was small, minimalist and defined by a wire-mesh fence that offered little deterrent, even to the orchids and creepers that poked through wherever possible.

The Learjet taxied off the runway and came to a standstill between the two rows of hangars. The door quickly opened and two men – one huge, the other skinny with big ears – climbed down the steps and hurried across the tarmac to the waiting helicopter, which immediately returned them to the skies, barely reaching altitude before descending back through the canopy of trees covering Ancon Hill and onto the huge G-shaped landing pad. A welcoming committee of fifteen hefty men awaited, each aiming an AK-47 at the prisoner's head.

One of the guards ducked beneath the rotor downwash, opened the door and beckoned the prisoner out. Trabant remained still, frozen with terror, until Raúl effortlessly shoved him out and down onto the burning tarmac, where he remained, lying motionless beneath the shards of piercing sunlight.

'That gringo is loco,' smiled a guard.

'Sí, and crash-landed too!' added another, to a chorus of raucous laughter. But the laughter soon stopped…

'Get up!' snarled a voice.

Trabant warily opened his eyes. Before him stood a pair of squat, hairy, flip-flop-wearing feet, with toes thick and stubby like shotgun cartridges. He scanned further up, beyond the white surf shorts and garish Hawaiian shirt, to meet the blaze in Gunboat's eyes.

'Señor, I say – GET UP!'

Two guards hauled the prisoner to his feet.

'P-please, I…'

Gunboat stepped closer, eyeballing Trabant like a boxer before the opening bell. 'I no like you,' he growled, in a tone far more venomous than any heard at Le Club Maritime du Soleil.

'Honestly, I n-never meant for this...'

Gunboat turned to his guards. 'Bring the gringo inside. I want talk to him.'

'Sí, Boz.'

The AK-47 dug hard into Trabant's back, forcing him inside the huge building complex, through an arrivals lounge then down two flights of stairs, along a corridor and finally out into a vast open-plan office, the outer walls of which were glass, and fitted with sliding doors that led out onto a huge balcony offering views of the ocean. At the far end sat a large desk, with papers strewn all over; a bank of telephones poised on the left, and a half-finished box of chocolate éclairs to the right. Gunboat took his seat in the black leather chair behind.

'Now you see my power, my plane, my airport *and* my hill. So perhaps now you understand calibre of the man you mess with?'

'Yes, I think I—'

'You crossed me, señor. That a bad mistake.'

As if on cue, a dog raised its head from the basket in the corner and snarled.

'Ssssh, Bazooka. You get a piece of him soon. Sit.'

'Who – me or the dog?' asked Trabant.

'BOTH!'

The dog recoiled; Trabant too, onto the edge of the nearest chair.

'You like Bazooka, señor Trabant?'

'Yes, he's... adorable. What breed is—'

'Golden bull mastiff, so say the lady at the kennels. But I prefer golden revolver.'

'Oh, really? We had a golden retr—'

'He rip your head off, señor. And so will I. Every inch of me want to kill you, right now, with these…' Gunboat opened his massive paws to highlight their capability.

'Y-yes, I can imagine.'

'Can you?' replied Gunboat, through gritted teeth. 'Can you *really* imagine how angry I am? There I was, in my favourite yacht club, enjoying nice evening until you come along, señor Loco, with your blatant cheat and señorita Apple Juice to ruin everything – AND I MEAN EVERYTHING!'

'But I…'

'I SAY – EVERYTHING!' The fist smashed down with tremendous power, sending an expeditionary force of paperweights into the air. 'Who the hell you think… you are?' continued Gunboat, distracted by the clattering return of desk junk. 'And now look what you do to my ornaments.' He slumped back in his chair as Raúl started rearranging the paraphernalia.

'So tell me,' continued Gunboat, 'who you work for?'

'L-like I said – the *Pimlico & District Chronicle*.'

'YOU LIE TO ME!'

'Honestly, I—'

'And what about that book – *The Beginner's Guide To Being Secret Agent?*'

'I b-bought it at the airport.'

'Liar! And the piece of paper inside it, with telephone numbers on?'

'Oh, t-that's to contact my, er… editor.'

Gunboat offered a chilling smile. 'We see when I ring him, eh?'

'There's really no need.'

'YOU MUST BE SPY! WHO YOU WORK FOR – MI6?'

'N-no! I'm a journalist. Film correspond—'

'PA!' shouted Gunboat. 'I know you lie, *and* cheat at cards! But the worst thing: I can no even kill you. Not yet. Oh, no,

118

I have to wait… keep you alive longer. You know why?'

'Beats me.'

'Because your cheat in that card game make my business associates nervous. Some now want guarantees I still able to supply their precious military requirements. And the only way I can convince them of that – is to beat you in a rematch.'

'A rematch!'

'Sí, a stupid, loco REMATCH! Which is why you here and no smeared across the street in Vienna. I can no kill you until I have lay everyone's fears to rest, and right in front of their eyes.'

'But I don't understand.'

'You and me both! But let me tell you something,' he continued, pointing his finger like a missile launcher. 'After I beat you on Saturday, and all my guests watch you endure the most violent death possible, then whole planet will once again understand that the word of El Cañonero is no to be questioned.'

'Who?'

'EL CAÑONERO! ME – GUNBOAT CHARLIE CHÁVEZ!'

'Oh yes, of course…' replied Trabant, now recalling Eva's explanation.

Gunboat leant forward on his knuckles. 'In Panama we have word for people like you: Loco – crazy! You crazy to cross me, señor, and you pay with your life, as will those who demand this rematch. They too will wish they no ever been born. So, until Saturday you stay here as my prisoner, under key and lock. You no escape again, for sure. And that remind me, what *did* happen to that interfering French hostess?'

'I honestly have no idea.'

'When you last see her?'

'As she c-closed the door of the broom cupboard, in Le Club Maritime du Soleil.'

'You lie again, señor. You stand right next to her while she batter my two men in the car park outside.'

'R–really? I don't recall...'

'Well, they recall, once they wake up in hospital. Anyhow, some of my other men catch up with her on outskirts of town. Put plenty bullet holes in her car, but somehow she still get away – again!'

Trabant closed his eyes, relieved at Eva's escape, yet horrified at the repercussions she had already begun to face.

'So, come on then, señor Loco. How d'ya do it?'

'D–do what?'

'Win at cards. You cheat, right?'

'Er…'

'I knew it! You bloomin' cheat. That the only way you *could* beat me.'

'Honestly, I…'

The knife-slit eyes reformed. 'Have you any idea how much trouble you cause?'

'I can only begin to—'

'And you still want to lie to me, eh?'

'No, not at all.'

Gunboat emitted a plume of cigar smoke. 'Señor Loco, there two types of liars in this world: those who do it for love, and those who do it for… you know, to be malicious.'

'But I—'

'My grandfather lie to me. As a kid he sit me on his knee and tell story of how he single-handedly dug the Panama Canal, with just bucket and spoon. He was my hero, and because of that I believe him. Some years later I realise the truth, and sure I was disappoint, but it no matter because I love him, and I know he only try to fill my head with family pride. But you, señor Trabant, your motives are dirty, stinking, vindictive—'

Ring ring…

Gunboat swooped a paw at the telephone. 'WHAT?'

'Boz, señor Imran has arrived at Pedro Miguélez.'

'Oh, okay. Prepare the helicopter. Tell him I be there in

120

twenty minute.' Gunboat slammed down the receiver, stood to leave but then paused. 'Señor Loco, I think you come too.'

'W-where?'

'To one of my storage compounds. It now time you *see* precisely the business of the man you mess with.'

iii

The helicopter began its descent onto an airstrip, cut out of the dense surrounding forest like a championship golf course. Trabant checked his watch. They'd only been flying ten minutes.

'Welcome to Pedro Miguélez Airport, or that's what I call it this week,' smiled Gunboat, half-turning his head. 'Used to be American Air Force base, like Marco A Gelabert, but this one is forgotten about. We use it for storage.'

The helicopter gently nestled down. The two men in the air-traffic-control tower waved like long-lost friends then returned to their beers and newspapers. Raúl's wagging gun ordered Trabant out into the searing heat, and onwards across the tarmac, following Gunboat towards the adjacent hangar, where he jabbed a podgy finger at the red button marked 'UP'. With instant obedience, orange lights flashed and an army of motors shook the gigantic metal door into action.

'Prepare to be amaze.' With that, Gunboat stepped inside, flicked a switch and waited as row after row of fluorescent tubes lit up the cavernous space.

Trabant inhaled sharply. The hangar stretched back as far as he could see, and each side was lined with aircraft. But not just everyday planes, these were military jets – perhaps as many as thirty – as if a whole national air force had convened for the onset of war.

'This is my dispatch area. Every plane here is sold.' Gunboat

121

led them down the centre aisle. 'That one is a U-2 high-altitude reconnaissance aircraft,' he continued, pointing towards a long, thin black craft being hastily polished. 'A US Air Force model, nicknamed the "Dragon Lady". And this one is a MiG-29, design of course in Soviet Union.'

'A MiG – wow!' gasped Trabant, feigning interest. 'She's very, er… sleek.'

'Aerodynamics very similar to the Sukhoi Su-29. You know, the Russian aerobatics aircraft.'

'Yes, of course…' lied Trabant.

A studious man with round spectacles and ink-strewn clipboard shuffled up from the left, seeking a signature. Without breaking stride, Gunboat snatched the pad and pen, scribbled haphazardly then sent the man on his way. 'The tanks, artillery and larger aircraft are kept elsewhere,' he continued. 'The ships and submarines are constantly on the move. But here I also keep rockets, guns and ammunition. Wanna see some?'

'Y-yes, okay.'

'This one is my favourite,' he continued, extracting a gleaming black assault rifle from a nearby wooden crate. 'Such beauty I no ever seen before. Just had to have her, and all her brothers and sisters.'

'How many have you sold?' asked Trabant.

'Señor, I lose count. Millions? After the Cold War end and the Soviet Union finally crumble, there were many, many new countries with mountains of weapons to sell. Lots of these assault rifles, plus tanks, missiles and rockets, and so on. These countries need hard cash. I fly my planes in, buy the lot, fly out, and sell on to anyone who pay me the dollars.'

'Anyone?'

'Yep. I buy lots of weapons from elsewhere too, but this one – this assault rifle – is always muy popular. She the first choice of rebels and freedom fighters all round the world.'

'How come?'

122

''Cos she a very reliable lady. She no jam if submerge in water, sand or mud. Ask any guerrilla and they choose her over the American M-16 any day. And she cheap too, only twenty-five to thirty of your pounds sterling – tops. But sometimes I give her away for free, as sweetener for bigger deal.'

'What's her name?'

'AK-47. The darling of terrorists, insurgents, militias etc all over the world. You wanna hold her?'

'No, thank you,' replied Trabant, squirming away like a child rejecting a disgusting medicine. But he then instantly recognised the opportunity Eva would've seized, literally with both hands, in an attempt to escape.

'Okay, suit yourself. Perhaps you prefer to hold one of these?'

This time Trabant readily agreed.

'It called the Vinto 227 Sling-Shooter. Far more suitable for a gringo like you.'

'U-huh,' replied Trabant, holding the silver, light-weight plastic pistol in his hands. 'How many rounds does it fire per minute?'

'Squirts, you mean? About four, then you refill at the tap. It a water pistol, señor Loco, part of a job lot from Taiwan.'

As Gunboat and Raúl burst out laughing, Trabant lowered his head in embarrassment, then returned the pistol to its crate.

Bong… bing… bong.

'Gunboat, please proceed to de second-hand sales area,' said the tannoy.

'Crazy gringo – come this way!' ordered Gunboat.

Trabant nodded and slowly withdrew his hands from the crate… but at the last moment, he carefully slipped the water pistol up the inside of his jacket sleeve.

'Boz,' asked Raúl. 'Is Imran buying that new jet?'

'I hope so,' replied Gunboat, his eyes full of dollar signs.

Trabant followed on close behind, his own eyes loaded with

123

guilt, yet also with the euphoria of seemingly getting away with his deception. He'd never stolen anything before in his life, but when you're a dead man, you need all the help you can get.

iv

'She a beauty, huh, señor Imran?' beamed Gunboat, as he finally reached the second-hand sales area in the far right-hand corner, where half a dozen more fighter jets stood patiently beneath a stream of bunting, and with a selection of price boards, spec sheets and money-off stickers pasted inside their windscreens.

'Indeed she is, señor Gunboat,' replied Imran, a tall man dressed in a black suit, white shirt, and holding a briefcase. 'And thank you for seeing me. I also received your invitation to the rematch, and of course will be there to cheer you on.'

'Muchas gracias,' replied Gunboat, shaking his hand. 'I knew I could count on your support. And perhaps you like to meet the gringo who cause all this trouble. Señor Imran – meet Bristo Trabant.'

Señor Imran threw a scornful glance. 'So, it was you!'

'Really, I never—'

'If this beautiful floor did not belong to my dear amigo Gunboat, I would spit at your feet – right now.'

'But I…'

'Silence. You have said too much already,' hissed Imran. 'I just wish for your death to be unbearably painful.'

'Oh, it will be,' beamed Gunboat. 'Excruciatingly so, and very spectacular too. I think we all enjoy it. Except, of course, señor Gringo Loco here. But meantime… down to business.'

'Yes,' replied Imran, turning back towards the plane, and the man now polishing the endless contours of her bodywork. 'Tell me more about this tantalising weapon of destruction.'

124

'Well, she a 2005 model F-16 Falcon fighter jet. One careful owner, full service history, leather seats, air con, CD player, and a special limited-edition anniversary model, so she have tinted windows, wide wheels and golden cup-holder. You like her, huh?'

'Very much. She ever been shot down?'

'Only the once. We repaint the nearside wing and fill in a few bullet holes, part from that she good as new. Even thought to keep her myself, but if you interest I could be persuade to let her go.'

'Goodie. What's the price?'

'Price!?!' replied Gunboat, feigning surprise at the very mention of the word. 'Please, señor Imran. When discussing such fine example of military air supremacy, price is merely an incon... er... an incon—'

'Inconsequential?' offered Trabant.

'Gracias. An inconsequential detail.'

'Please forgive me,' replied Imran. 'I'm getting ahead of myself. Let me rephrase. How much compensation would it take to wrestle this beautiful lady of annihilation from your protective, loving bosom?'

'Ten million dollar. Cash.'

'Nine and a half,' countered Imran.

'Eleven.'

'Ten?'

'Sold!' Gunboat shook the hand of the proud new owner. 'You make excellent decision.'

'I think so too.'

Gunboat turned towards Trabant and smiled. 'There you go. And as my old friend from London Old Kent Road would say – another satisfy punter.'

12

A Glass of Chilled Rosé
on a Hot Summer's Evening

PARIS LAY HUDDLED UNDER a grey, patchwork-quilt sky. Ominous clouds twisted and conspired, then launched a torrent of rain that sent passers-by dashing for cover. Traffic splashed its way through puddles, windscreen wipers worked double-time, and the roads became more like ice rinks, hazardous beneath their shining innocence.

Eva Avante's mind drifted across the rooftops and chimney stacks, and refused to allow the scene outside her fifth-floor office window to dampen her spirits. Inspiration would have to come from elsewhere, at the time when it was most needed. Because from now on there could be no let-up, no pause to catch breath. Every single moment would be critical.

ii

The return flight from London (and awaiting agency car) had delivered Eva back to DGSE headquarters at 141 Boulevard Mortier in the XXe arrondissement of Paris (approximately one kilometre outside the city centre) just before 5 p.m. The sliding steel gate finally allowed passage and in they drove, through the eighteen-foot-high, razor-wired, stone-wall perimeter and on between the lawns and horse chestnut trees to the white, faceless buildings that formed the heart of France's external intelligence agency. Centre stage, a lone steel-lattice tower reached for the clouds, upon which clusters of satellite dishes huddled like disgruntled birds dreaming of better weather. Yet their resolve was unceasing, as was the flood of communication they fed back down to the army of operatives, decoders, interceptors and taskforce leaders stationed in the countless offices beneath, who worked tirelessly in the search for, and exploitation of, intelligence relevant to the security of France.

Inside the tallest white building, the department known as Administration took the first two floors, Strategy the third and fourth, and Intelligence the top; the rationale being that Intelligence required the best vantage point of all. Intelligence was itself divided into two sub-sections: Technical and Action. Action was responsible for planning and performing clandestine surveillance operations against potential and existing threats.

Eva's rise within the DGSE had been remarkable. To become taskforce leader at the age of thirty was unheard of, yet it had been earned through a combination of natural panache and sheer hard work, as had her whole military career. At nineteen, when she'd joined the Armée de Terre as a raw recruit, her flair for close-quarter espionage immediately became apparent. Tours of duty in Afghanistan and East Africa moulded her into a highly efficient combat soldier, yet also as a deeply caring humanitarian coordinator, working with the innocent civilians so often caught in the crossfire. Her passion for this role was immense, and despite winning the French Army's prestigious Miss Battlefield beauty contest six years running, her focus continued undeterred. She became known as 'La Belle Éponge' (The Beautiful Sponge) for her good looks and astonishing retention of detail.

At twenty-five, she joined French Special Forces detachments to master covert surveillance techniques, and to work on some of the numerous behind-enemy-lines missions deployed by the Marine Nationale; so many, in fact, that she gained automatic qualification for the French Navy's equally prestigious Miss Flight Deck beauty contest, which she subsequently won for her next three years of service.

It was not long before she was noticed by the highest echelons of national security. And so, when the DGSE came calling, the opportunities were simply too appealing to resist. Eva transferred, and for the next two years cut her teeth working within the Action Department on counter-terrorism initiatives. The intelligence, which she collated at substantial personal risk, shaped policy and hugely influenced France's negotiating strategy with other nations. This was a role of paramount importance, which directly affected the safety of the people she now observed down on the gloomy Parisian pavements. Yet it was a closely related issue, and one of epidemic proportions, that finally provided the platform to fly.

The flow of arms into conflict zones around the world, many in which France had a direct interest, had reached unprecedented proportions. Instability ruled supreme, and every time a new conflict flared up, one man's name was whispered as having made it all possible: Gunboat Charlie Chávez.

Regarded as the best in her field, Eva was empowered to lead a new, dedicated taskforce to build a case against Gunboat so watertight, so damning, that should an arrest ever be made, the evidence compiled would finally shut down his global enterprise and send him to prison for years. The operation, however, was seen by many as a poisoned chalice. For no matter how methodically and precisely the intelligence was accumulated, no action was ever likely to be taken, on account of the dark secrets Gunboat held, and his promise to reveal them and implicate some of the most powerful people in the world, should an arrest ever be made.

Nonetheless, for the next two years Action worked tirelessly at building a picture of Gunboat's world. Files were stacked up to the ceilings, and endless photographs of known contacts were pinned to the control-room walls. Names, dates and times were continually entered into one huge central database, which cross-checked the cross-checks until finally a pattern of movements emerged, and a chilling roll-call of associates from every walk of life began to take shape.

iii

Rain continued to pitter-patter on the window.

Eva's mind wandered to the events of the past few days; to the seemingly routine surveillance operation at Le Club Maritime du Soleil that had suddenly been turned on its head. In one moment, she had blown two years of anonymity out of the water, and added her own name to the very top of Gunboat's death list. And surely with his connections, any CCTV images would soon lead to the discovery of her true identity. Yet she'd had to step in. She couldn't stand back and let an innocent man die, even if that meant risking her operation, let alone herself. And what's more, she knew she'd do exactly the same again. Yes, rescuing Bristo Trabant had been exactly the right thing to do. She just hadn't envisaged falling for him in the process.

Knock, knock.

'Entrez.'

'Madame, I have your travel documents and itinerary,' said Yvette Claron, Eva's PA, poking her attractive, twenty-seven-year-old, Marseille-raised head around the office door.

'Ah, thank you. Please, come in.'

Yvette walked into the office and placed a folder on the desk. 'Your plane leaves at seven o'clock tomorrow morning. Our local agent is Alvaro Francisco Leonardo Samporo López Heguiela – thankfully known just as Big Al, you'll be relieved to know, who will meet you at Costa Rica's Juan Santamaría Airport. From there he will drive you across the border, and on to our safe house in Panama City.'

'Excellent. Is it a high-rise flat?'

'Yes, just as you asked for, Madame. It's a fifteenth-floor apartment with views of both Gunboat's Fortress and the Panama City Aquarium. Our local scouts have done well.'

'So have you,' smiled Eva. 'And what are the latest intelligence reports from around the world?'

Yvette sat on the soft velvet chair. Round glasses encircled her hazel eyes, and her face glowed with fondness for her boss.

'Across the United States the CIA are staking out all Gunboat's known haunts,' she said, 'in the search for Agent Trabant. Er, pardon, Madame... may I ask – Agent Trabant's surname... is that Trabant as in the—'

'Car? Yes. It's a sort of nickname. I don't know the full story, but once he is safe I shall find out.'

Yvette smiled. 'And safe he will become, Madame. So, to continue: in Europe, Interpol are scouring the entire continent from north to south, east to west. And it is the same throughout Asia, including Indonesia and the Philippines, where all the national forces are working together. Africa, however, holds little hope, stating it would be easier to find a needle in a Serengeti haystack; and the South Americans, sadly, are equally pessimistic.'

'Gunboat's influence there is almost total. The person you spoke to is probably already on his payroll. Now, tell me about Panama.'

'As you requested,' replied Yvette, 'we have taken on the bulk of the surveillance ourselves. So Gunboat's portfolio of hotels, restaurants, bars, strip clubs, jewellers, pawn shops... gee, the list seems endless... are all being watched.'

'Wow, that's a lot of places.'

'Yes, and a lot of surveillance. All holidays have been cancelled. Overtime is compulsory. I just hope—'

Eva detected the apprehension in her friend's voice. 'Yvette, what is on your mind?'

'Madame, the team is worried about you. Would it not be wise to stay hidden until this trouble is over?'

Eva smiled. 'Thank you for your concern, but it's what I'm trained for. And the vast knowledge our team has collected will be crucial. We may only get one chance to save Agent Trabant. Talking of which, is there any news as to the location of the rematch?'

'No, Madame, though we are working around the clock.'

Eva glanced over her PA's shoulder, through the glass partition into the operations room, where rows of agents sat at computer screens, with heads down and fingers tapping furiously at keyboards.

'Madame, is it true the British will undertake military action if required?'

'Yes. A British Royal Navy aircraft carrier is en route to Panama as we speak.'

'So the rematch will be held there?'

'Most likely. My hunch is that Gunboat will want to make a real display of power, and there's no place like home to do that. Hopefully I'm right, and we'll hear early enough to get into position.'

'Good luck, Madame. And do take care.'

'Oh, there *is* one more thing,' said Eva, catching Yvette before she stood to leave.

'Yes, of course, Madame. How can I help?'

'I need to ask your opinion, between you and I; strictly off the record, about a bear called Rupert. You know, the comic-strip character.'

'Ah, Monsieur Rupert!' she replied, with fond recollection. 'I read all his books as a child. What would you like to know?'

'It's more concerning his fans, rather than him specifically.'

'Please, ask away.'

'Okay. Well, if a man – a grown man – was to wear Rupert Bear boxer shorts, would you think that to be odd, or cute, or perhaps a little quirky?'

'Oh, no, Madame – very cute! It shows a softer, playful, less serious side that is all too rare in the modern-day male.'

'My thoughts precisely.'

'I would love to find a man like that,' continued Yvette, 'but alas, they prove as elusive as… the Siberian tiger, the mountain gorilla, or… er… any other animal that faces extinction. You find a man like that, Madame, you should hold on to him tightly, with both hands.'

'I intend to.'

Yvette's eyes swelled. 'Madame, you have met such a man?'

'Maybe. I'll keep you posted.'

'Then I shall cross my fingers for you.'

'Thank you, Yvette, to you and the whole team for your efforts. It is greatly appreciated.'

'My pleasure. Everything will work out fine, Madame. You'll see.'

Yvette smiled once more, then left the office.

iv

Eva sat back and drifted into deep contemplation. The logistics of the operation did not particularly bother her, but the thought of never seeing Bristo again did. Without detection, this unassuming Englishman had tiptoed through her defences, bypassed the alarm bells and picked the lock to her heart – the impregnable fortress she'd painstakingly created to ensure no one would ever hurt her again. Not after last time.

At the age of twenty-seven she had married Jean-Marc Gistard, a French army officer. Their relationship enjoyed a great beginning, yet after only eighteen months had come to a tragic end. His initial smothering evolved into a suffocating possessiveness, and his heavy drinking fuelled a dark, jealous monster that became consumed with insecurity and envy. Her shining career became the catalyst for his rage, and her constant trips abroad unsettled him to a point where even the slightest mention of another man's name could mean only one thing. The arguments became worse until, one day, they left Eva with a bruised eye and a cut lip, lying amongst the scattered debris of their broken relationship.

The line had been crossed. No longer did she want to gather up the pieces and put them back together again. It was over, and she would tell him so when he returned later that evening, drunk and full of remorse, as he always did. Fate, however, denied her the opportunity. Within two hours the telephone had rung. The voice from police headquarters explained in detail. There had been a fight. Witnesses said Gistard had been like a wild man, looking for trouble wherever he could. A small group obliged, and a knife was pulled, by whom the police were uncertain. Two men had been arrested, and one had died. Gistard.

Within an hour Eva had identified the body. Within two she had arranged the funeral. Within a week he had been cremated, together with the dark truths she vowed never to recount, so as to preserve his gleaming image in the inconsolable eyes of his adoring mother. Yet her own pain was also deep, and for more than the loss of the man she had once truly loved. He had exposed a weakness in her armoury, a vulnerability to pain from a source she had, to that point, always considered safe – a loved one. Never had she imagined things getting so out of hand. Never in a million years had she thought he would raise a hand to her. But he had, and she knew she could never allow that to happen again. Her family she trusted without question, but to let another outsider in would be a risk; and the only way to eliminate that risk was to never let anyone come close again.

Her friends considered this a monumental overreaction, but she didn't care. It was her life, and her choice. She needed to be secure and so, as on any other professional assignment, she took control, closed down her emotions and tied off that part of her life. The impregnable fortress had been constructed, and the cracks welded over. No one would get close again. Ever.

As the weeks became months, Eva grew ever more convinced she didn't actually need anyone in her life. She had never wanted anyone to provide for her, protect her – only for someone to love her. But now even that seemed surplus to requirements, and she resigned herself to the fact that perhaps, in spite of all her childhood dreams of raising a family and living happily ever after, it wasn't meant to be.

And so work became the prime constituent of her life. The cheeky, bubbly exterior remained, but her closest friends could see it was manufactured, and nothing more than a glossy overcoat to hide the sad embers of a fire that once burnt so brightly inside. They also knew that to relight that fire would take an approach so radical, from a man so unconventional and unique that even Eva – the lady with perhaps more surveillance resources at her disposal than anyone else in Europe – wouldn't see it coming. But could a miracle really happen? Her friends lived in hope, but they doubted such a man actually existed.

Eva flicked through her travel documents. Yvette's planning, as always, was exemplary. The only frustration was having to wait until morning for the next flight.

So what *was* Bristo's secret? There was no golden patter, no mercurial technique that rendered her defenceless to his endearing charms. No, it was far more effective than that – he had simply been himself, which was, more to the point, quite unlike any man she had ever met before. In her world of inflated egos and supercharged testosterone, his shyness was a breath of fresh air; his innocence a dream – refreshing like a glass of chilled rosé on a hot summer's evening. And the very

134

fact he didn't consider himself to be special, made him – in her eyes – very special indeed. And if others queried the attraction, well… she couldn't care less. She was the beholder, and her eye was delightfully focused.

More memories came flooding back; to her cover at Le Club Maritime du Soleil, which included working as a waitress on the 6 – 10 p.m. shift. She recalled when she'd first seen him, sitting alone in the restaurant on the Thursday night, tucked away in the far corner, lost amid the dazzle of jewellery and laughter coming from every other table. To her, he had far more than any other person in that restaurant that night. He was simply, well… wow! – and to a point where she'd begun to double-check herself in the mirror, to ensure she looked her best. He'd only just arrived (she'd checked); was travelling alone (she'd checked that also) and was on assignment as a film critic (which she'd dismissed as false within thirty seconds of conversation).

Eva smiled again, and remembered how he'd struggled to understand the French-only menu; how she'd explained that coq au vin was not actually the method by which the chicken arrived; and how on the very next evening he'd ordered the exact same, but this time with total assurance. They'd shared the joke, and after he'd finished eating she'd deliberately taken an age to clear his plate, to keep him talking, to enjoy his company, in the hope he wouldn't have to leave too soon. But of course eventually he'd had to leave, to retire to his hotel. And it wasn't until the next day that she'd seen him again, on the beach, when he'd helped the boy who'd been stung by the jellyfish.

Yes, the memories were lovely, but they were now tinged with guilt of having left him at the airport instead of driving him straight to Paris. Eva shook her head in self-disgust. The very real possibility of never seeing him again was now her own fault. Yes, she'd headed back to the airport to try and change his mind, but the black Mercedes had aborted that attempt. And then somewhere between his plane landing and his rendezvous, he'd been intercepted. Again she cursed her error of judgement, and Bravinger's decision to send Bristo to Cannes in the first place; *and* his description of him being 'daft as a brush'. How dare he?

Picasso would never have described a brush in such derogatory terms. Oh, no. A brush was vital, a tool of expression and every bit as important as paint and canvas. Where would Picasso have been without a brush? Or Rembrandt, or Van Gogh? Nowhere, that's where. Just a selection of frustrated artists wilting in the shadow of unfulfilled potential.

Eva chewed her bottom lip. Bristo's potential was also huge, of that she had no doubt. He just needed someone to believe in him; to point him in the right direction. But before all that, he needed someone to rescue him, which she would do, and all on her own if necessary. She would deal with Bravinger later. Right now she had to—

Brrring... Brrring...

Eva swished up the telephone receiver.

'Oui.'

'Pardon, Madame, I have Monsieur Bentley from MI6 on line four.'

Eva hesitated. She disliked Bentley, and for more than his arrogance and overbearing self-importance. A trusted sixth sense put her on guard, but against precisely what she couldn't be sure. 'Okay, put him through. Bonjour, Monsieur Bentley.'

'Bonjour, Eva, how are you? Been thinking about me?'

'No.'

'Okay, whatever. So tell me, are all the women in the French Secret Service as pretty as you?'

'What can I do for you, Bentley?' she replied, abruptly.

'Just wondered on progress?'

'Our surveillance operation is underway. How are things at your end?'

'My end? Oh, pert – as you will have noticed.'

'I meant your operation, not the state of your bottom.'

'Sure?'

'Yes!'

'Fair enough. Look, I hear you're going out to Panama to watch Gunboat?'

'Yes. My flight leaves in the morning. And you?'

'I'll be there in a day or so, to wrap the whole thing up, as usual.'

'Why so long?' snapped Eva. 'Don't you understand the urgency?'

'I appreciate this is a big deal for you guys. But for me it's just another day in the office.'

'Must be great being so fantastic,' replied Eva, sarcastically.

'Glad you noticed.'

Eva's hackles rose further.

'Stick with me, Agent Avante,' continued Bentley, 'I'm always on the winning team. But look at Trabant. British Intelligence? There's a contradiction if ever I heard one.'

'I think he is a great man.'

'Hmmm… Anyway, enough about Trabant – what about us? I think it's time we got to know each other better. How about dinner tonight?'

'I think you should be working as hard as everyone else in locating Agent Trabant, don't you?'

'Listen, if you ask me, he's cocked everything up. He knew the rules. If Gunboat kills him, so what? It's no big deal.'

'I can't believe you just said that.'

'Oh, come on! He's hardly a loss to government resources, is he?'

'He shouldn't have been out there in the first place.' Eva scowled.

'Trabant is clearly a waste of space. Whereas me, I'm just on the express lane to a better life, honey.'

'I am not your honey.'

'Not yet. See you in Panama.'

The line went dead.

Eva replaced the receiver in disgust. Bentley's arrogance was astounding, and the conversation had gone just as expected – plenty of self-congratulatory waffle, but zero substance to help the cause.

She gathered up her travel documents, flicked off the light and left her office. Bentley was of no importance to her. There was another man far more deserving of her attention.

13

The Man in the Light-Blue Suit

A RHYTHMIC SHRILL PIPED up from deep in Borneo's Sarawak rainforest, and joined in with the countless other rhythmic whoops and tweets to complete that afternoon's impromptu jungle ensemble. But Oscar Conda wasn't interested. He'd never had the slightest interest in things of natural beauty, and it could have been the trees making all the noise, for all he cared. He was, however, convinced that the monkeys were laughing at him. Well, he hated them back, with a passion; and the birds, and the snakes. Though most of all, he hated Gunboat Charlie Chávez.

Conda cast his eyes around his thatched, wooden office and contemplated his jealousy; jealousy and a deep-rooted envy of the legend that was Gunboat Charlie; of Gunboat's lofty position as the *número uno* of international crime, and the abundant trappings and virtual celebrity status that came with it. Everyone was in awe of Gunboat. He was a great ally but a fearful enemy. A man as ruthless and brutal as they came, who commanded both respect and loyalty in equal measures – something Conda could only dream of.

An overhead fan chopped at the humidity, and the sun shone through the window, bathing his office in a glorious post-rainstorm glow. With hands gently resting upon his globe-like belly, Conda peered back out the window across the earthy, puddle-littered ground to the storage huts that nestled tight against the towering barbed-wire perimeter fence of his Borneo compound. Men wearing military fatigues criss-crossed before his eyes, a pick-up truck braced itself for another heavy load, and amongst the dense vegetation that pressed in from all sides, if he listened very carefully, the whispers of optimism could be heard growing louder. Perhaps better days really were just round the corner. Perhaps the phone call he'd received less than forty-eight hours ago really could change his fortune.

Convinced another beer might also help, he retrieved one from the corner refrigerator, flicked the top, then returned to his chair and hoisted his feet back up on the desk in a single well-practised manoeuvre. As he swigged, his eyes settled on a picture nailed to the opposite wall, of him posing with friends in Panama City; a group of gangsters whose future success and prosperity had once seemed certain, until their fateful underestimation of Gunboat. And now only he – Oscar Ramírez Conda – remained alive. Alive but alone, cut off and still licking his wounds from the hurtful beating in the Panama City turf war. That was ten years ago, yet his desire for revenge burned as brightly as ever. And he still wanted everything Gunboat had, and all for himself. That went without question. But precisely how he could achieve that *and* remain alive was simply beyond him. Surely only a tactical masterstroke could deliver what he truly desired.

Briiiiing!

The telephone interrupted another delicious icy swig of beer. 'Hola,' he grumbled.

'He's here!'

Conda stood immediately, wiped the froth from his unkempt moustache and looked out expectantly through the window. To the left the guards were opening the main gate. The whole compound paused with anticipation until slowly, from between the eerie shards of light that sliced through the rainforest canopy, stepped a man dressed in a light-blue single-breasted linen suit and white open-neck shirt. And he brought no bag

140

or bodyguards, just a purposeful stride and a glow of devilish intent that strongly recommended caution.

Conda's tactical masterstroke had arrived.

With the athletic grace of a panther, the man in the light-blue suit passed through the security perimeter cordon and strode onwards to the main office. While feigning indifference to the guards' attention, he calculated numbers and distances and decided he could more than handle any threat they might pose, so he effortlessly skipped up the three steps and entered the thatched wooden office.

'You took your time,' grumbled Conda, slowly turning to shake his guest's hand.

'Nice to see you too,' replied the man in the light-blue suit. 'I said within forty-eight hours. Stop complaining and give me a beer.'

Conda retrieved a precious cold bottle of suds, flicked the top and handed it over.

'Thank you.'

Both men swigged, and took the moment to eye each other suspiciously.

'So you made it past the headhunters then?' smiled Conda.

'I saw the signs,' replied the man, savouring another taste of the ice-cool liquid. 'Thought that died out years ago.'

'Who knows for sure? And while there's uncertainty, no one will come within fifty kilometres of this place. The only visitors are those who are invited, people like you with important news to tell. So let's go somewhere very private to hear it. Follow me.'

ii

The vast, rugged outline of Mount Kinabalu peered down with suspicion, as Conda led the man back across the compound to

141

the far side, occasionally acknowledging one of his workers with a half-hearted nod. Distant squawks from the rainforest still punctuated the silence, while sweat claimed everything else.

Past four wooden storage huts, another security gate opened before them, beyond which a narrow pathway led to the mouth of an enormous cave.

'Follow me,' continued Conda, clumsily straddling a few boulders.

'Where you taking me?'

'Inside. It's the best place to talk. Borneo has probably the largest cave system in the world. No one could ever find us in here.'

The man in the light-blue suit followed him into the dank black hole, slowed his pace as he negotiated the rock-bed floor, and watched out for the erratic contours of the jagged walls.

'Why on earth *are* we here?' he asked.

'Like I said,' replied Conda. 'To talk.'

'Eugh… yuk! I've just trodden in something.'

'Guano.'

'Same to you!'

'No, guano – bat droppings. Piles of it,' beamed Conda. 'I sell it as a fertiliser. It's an industry worth over a billion dollars a year, but I'm tired of dealing in bat poo. Profitable yes, but glamorous, no. I want to get back into the arms trade.'

'Did you say bats?'

'Yes, up there.'

They both looked up and saw a million pairs of eyes staring back down at them, squabbling and jostling for position, as if ready to swoop at any moment. 'This is where I come to talk business,' continued Conda. 'Most people hate deep dark caves, but many more hate bats. Put the two together and you have the perfect environment for deterring eavesdroppers.'

The man in the light-blue suit scrunched his face. 'How on earth can bat droppings be worth billions?'

'Guano consists of many things. Ammonia, also uric, oxalic and carbonic acids, some earth salts, nitrates and, of course, impurities. It is also very rich in phosphorus, vast volumes of which are needed to produce fertiliser. It's an essential plant macronutrient.'

'Really?'

'Yes. It's better than horse manure.'

'Well, thank you for the biology lesson,' replied the man in the light-blue suit, dismissively. 'Now, can we get down to more pressing matters, such as why I've travelled all the way to this god-forsaken hole?'

'Go for it.'

'And you're certain your beloved bats can keep a secret?'

Conda gazed affectionately at the rippling black ceiling. 'I think so. Of the three hundred or so species, none have ever been known to understand English, let alone operate surveillance equipment. I think we're safe. Now, what have you to tell me?'

The man in the light-blue suit stepped closer. 'The time has almost come for us to make our move.'

'I've been waiting eighteen months to hear that. What took you so long?'

'We had to wait for a catalyst, for the right opportunity. Now that opportunity has arrived. Gunboat is about to commit murder. Blatant cold-blooded murder. Once he has done so, I can ensure he goes to prison for a very long time.'

'Pah! Gunboat commits murder like you and I have sausages for breakfast – regularly and well done. What's so different this time?'

'Because the victim is to be a British MI6 agent.'

'Really?' Conda's eyes widened with interest. 'How come?'

'The fool only went and beat Gunboat at cards.'

'Still don't see how that helps us.'

'Because, Einstein,' groaned the man in the light-blue suit, 'the moment Gunboat kills him, I will inform MI6. They will listen to me, and I'll get them all the proof they could ever need. Then, indirectly of course, I'll leak the entire story to the world media, to ensure MI6 act against Gunboat, rather than sweeping the whole thing under the carpet like they usually do.'

'You think that will work?'

'When the story breaks there will be public outrage. I can see the headlines now: "MI6 and the Arms Dealer – Money, Murder and Corruption at Vauxhall Cross." MI6 will crumble, and the government will fall. But, as politicians always do, they'll scrabble around in a futile attempt at redemption, and that will mean arresting Gunboat, which will create the huge void into which you – with my invaluable assistance – will seamlessly and effortlessly step.'

'But what about his little black book of secrets?' asked Conda nervously. 'Will the British Government seriously risk those secrets being aired?'

'They'll have no choice. The case will be ugly and messy, and the fallout colossal. But, by then, Gunboat will be decomposing in some dirty, stinking cell until sentence is passed, and the key is thrown away forever.'

'But what if he gets off?'

'He won't. Take it from me.'

'But this is El Cañonero! He makes the rules.'

'Not this time. I'm pulling the strings, and you will become the dominant force in one of the world's largest industries. You can forget vampire poo forever.'

'Not all bats are vampires. In fact only three species feed on—'

'I'm really not interested, okay?' replied the man in the light-blue suit. 'Just understand that with my help it can all be yours.'

'So what's going to happen? Taking on Gunboat's soldiers, even with him in prison, is suicide.'

'Never had much stomach for the fight, have you, Conda.'

'Some wars aren't worth restarting.'

Their voices echoed eerily in the cave.

'That's the beauty. There is no need for a war. We sit back and let Gunboat self-destruct, then simply move in and take over the reins. That way our hands appear clean.'

'Very cunning, Mr—'

'Uh-uh. No names, remember, in case we're overheard. That's the discipline.' The man in the light-blue suit wagged his finger at Conda. 'I don't trust anyone, even your precious bats. Now tell me, is your infrastructure in place to take over Gunboat's operation, as we discussed?'

'Yeah, pretty much.'

'How many planes do you have?'

'Six. Is that enough?'

'No! Gunboat has at least fifty. Get more.'

'From where?'

'Anywhere. Just use your imagination. A lot of Gunboat's equipment will be inheritable, but I can't say how much will be seized by the authorities once he is behind bars.'

'Okay, more planes,' repeated Conda, etching a mental note. 'And how about pilots?'

'Might be handy, eh?' replied the man sarcastically. 'Get as many as you can. Some of Gunboat's may jump ship, especially when the prospect of no wages dawns, but most will remain loyal.'

'When do we make our move?'

'The moment Gunboat is arrested. That act alone will send shock-waves through his client database. Most of his customers just want their arms delivered on time. If we can promise to fill the gap and offer the same level of service, then we're well on our way.'

'Sounds simple enough.'

'It will be if you prepare properly. When the time comes, just make sure you deliver what they want, where they want, and on time. Got it?'

'Yes,' replied Conda. 'And you'll source the weapons?'

The man nodded. 'I'll tell you where to go and whom to see to get whatever is required. But you must stay on top of every detail. Gunboat is extremely customer-focused, and will be a hard act to follow.'

'Okay, I'll make sure.'

'Get everything ready and wait for my contact. Do not... I repeat... do not do *anything* until I contact you. Understood?'

'Yes... pretty much.'

'Oscar, get with it. This is a multi-billion-dollar global industry. For this to work, it has to be a seamless transfer. You'll be dealing with governments, revolutionaries, freedom fighters. The list is endless. I will ensure all his contacts buy from you. I will give you all the government secrets and tip-offs you could dream of. I will arrange everything at my end, but the rest – my short, balding, pot-bellied friend – is up to you.'

'Okay, okay!'

'And smarten up too, for chrissakes. Your appearance is a mess.'

'What's wrong?' asked Conda, looking at the remnants of last night's TV dinner still clinging to his singlet.

'You need to look the part. And now the price,' continued the man in the light-blue suit. 'It'll cost you ten million dollars a year, paid directly into this Swiss bank account.' He transferred a sheet of paper from his inside jacket pocket into Conda's grubby mitt.

'How much?!?' shrieked Conda, as he studied the written information.

'Don't make me laugh. I'm handing you this industry on a plate. Ten million is a snip compared with the profits you'll make.'

'Still seems a large slice for you, especially with the risk I have to take,' said Conda.

'Listen, if I gave it to you for free, you'd still ask for change.'

'A risk is a risk.'

'No risk – no reward. Let's be honest, Oscar, the only reason I'm offering it to you is because I want a better cut than I already have. Gunboat Charlie has stood still for years, not paying me a proper percentage for the deals I've brought him. I want what I deserve. So I'm not doing this for the love of it, or because you're a nice bloke – which, incidentally, everyone tells me you're not. It's all about the money, Oscar. This is business.'

'What guarantees do I have? I don't want a war.'

'I bet you don't!' The man smiled. 'Gunboat really kicked your hide last time, didn't he? Well, if you do exactly as I say, he will have no idea that it was you and I who plotted his downfall. Of course, if you're losing your bottle, then I'm sure there will be plenty of other interested parties who—'

'No. No. I'm in, I'm in. As long as there's no chance of him finding out.'

'There won't be, as long as you follow my instructions precisely.'

Conda nodded as his desire to put one over on Gunboat became totally overwhelming.

'Okay,' continued the man in the light-blue suit. 'Gunboat will kill Bristo Trabant on—'

'That's a funny name. What, as in the—'

'Car? Yes. Now, don't interrupt. Gunboat will kill him on Saturday. Today is Tuesday. So that means we need to be ready to move three days from now. Understand?'

'Yes.'

The man in the light-blue suit leant forward and looked Conda hard in the eye. 'Now, you must remember these three rules.'

'Go on.'

'Number one: you never, ever contact me. I always contact you. Agreed?'

Conda nodded.

'Secondly, you mention our conversations to no one. Agreed?'

'Agreed.'

'And finally, you pay me my money on time, every time, with no exceptions, or believe me I'll drop you harder than I'm going to drop Gunboat.' The man in the light-blue suit clicked his fingers for effect. 'Got it?'

'You have a deal,' replied Oscar.

'Do exactly as I say and you can kiss your guano goodbye.'

'Really?'

'Yes – figuratively speaking, of course. Now, get moving. You have a lot to do. I'll call you the moment Gunboat is arrested.'

With that the two men walked silently back towards the glistening daylight. Within five minutes Conda was back in his office and the man in the light-blue suit had vanished into the shadows beneath the rainforest canopy.

Conda sat back to dream of the riches that would soon be his, ironically without firing a single bullet. He flicked the top off another bottle of beer and raised it to the air, to propose a toast.

'To Bristo Trabant – whoever the hell you are.'

14

'Please, Call Me Mrs G'

'IT'S THE PANAMA CITY Aquarium, sir!'

'What is?'

'The location of the rematch,' exclaimed Jones, a golden beacon of optimism shining through the doorway into Bravinger's office.

'Well, I'll be damned. Owned by none other than Gunboat himself. Thought he'd pick some backstreet hellhole of a place, not somewhere virtually visible from the moon.'

'And it's only a short helicopter ride from his home too, sir.'

'Has no fear, that man,' replied Bravinger, removing his glasses to facilitate even deeper contemplation. 'Who'd we find out from?

'Ibrahim "Jolly Roger" Cohanya – the Somalian Pirate. The threat of us sinking his mothership ensured his cooperation.'

'Excellent. And let's hope we've heard the news before the—'

Bzzzzzzzzzzzz...

'Yes, Juliet.'

'Sir, I have the French Prime Minister for you.'

'A-ha! Great news! Now we can rub it in for once.' Bravinger lifted the receiver. 'Prime Minister Rascous, bonjour! We have great news. We've found out where the... Oh, you already know?' Bravinger wrinkled his brow. 'Yes, we were surprised too... U-huh, yes... Bentley is on his way out there now. And Agent Avante? On her way too... Oh, okay, yes, yes of course,

149

as soon as we hear of Trabant's whereabouts we'll let you know. Bye for now.'

Bravinger slammed the receiver back into its cradle. 'Damn French! Always one step ahead. Well, at least we'll have the last laugh when Bentley saves the day. Apparently he's teaming up with Agent Avante.'

'Lucky Bentley.'

'Pardon?'

'Nothing, sir.'

'Keep your mind on your work, Jones,' barked Bravinger as he pressed the intercom. 'Juliet, get me the Prime Minister again, will you?'

'Which one, sir – ours or the French?'

'Our one, of course.' Bravinger rolled his eyes, then flopped back in his seat. 'Things are moving fast, Jones. Faster than I thought.'

Bzzzzzzzzzzzz…

'Jeez! Yes, Juliet.'

'Prime Minister Hanlon for you.'

'Ah, right, thank you. Prime Minister, sorry to disturb you, but we now know where the rematch is to be held… Oh, right… Yes, s-straight away.'

This time the receiver was carefully replaced.

'What's wrong now, sir?' asked Jones.

'We've been summoned to Number Ten again. Apparently Admiral Sims-Hopewell – the top man in the Royal Navy – is already there, as is Jack Venison, the Foreign Secretary. Hell, if only I'd known, I'd have worn my Winchester tweed. I said to my wife, there's a lot going on at the moment, Daphne. I really should wear the Winchester tweed. But oh, no, she knew better, and now…'

'Ah, Bravinger, Jones, come in,' said Prime Minister Hanlon fifteen minutes later, welcoming the two men into the private meeting room at Number Ten Downing Street. 'Gentlemen, you know the Admiral, and Jack Venison.'

'Yes,' replied Bravinger, as he draped his coat over the arms of the butler.

The room nodded its hello.

'Right, take a seat and let's get cracking,' continued Hanlon. 'Now we know the location of the rematch, we can confirm that Her Majesty's Royal Navy will, in whatever capacity, have to get involved. Agreed?'

'Yes, Prime Minster,' replied the room.

'So, Admiral Sims-Hopewell, please take us on from here.'

'My pleasure.'

The Admiral took a final sip of tea then returned his cup to its saucer with helicopter accuracy, hovering then lowering the bone-china drinks-vessel directly into the central circular recess. His tall, beanpole body was draped in a navy-blue suit that rippled every time he moved, like the ensign flown from every one of Her Majesty's ships, and his weathered complexion was framed by a bluster of grey hair.

'Well, gentlemen,' he said, 'thankfully our *Invincible*-class aircraft carrier HMS *Indomitable* is currently on manoeuvres off Baja California, together with supply ship RFA *Gallant* and destroyer HMS *Defiant*. They have been informed of the situation and are hightailing it south as we speak. HMS *Nautilus* – our fleet's newest submarine – is racing up from the Scotia Sea to join them. HMS *Warrior* is on her way too. She was halfway to Hawaii. Both will complete the taskforce. All five should arrive off the Pacific coast of Panama late Friday night.'

'Excellent,' said Hanlon.

'But, Prime Minister,' asked Bravinger. 'Do we really need all that muscle?'

'Yes, Colonel Bravinger, we do. This is Gunboat Charlie we're talking about.'

'Plus,' added the Admiral, '*Indomitable* cannot launch the LCVP landing craft we'll need to get the Royal Marines ashore. HMS *Warrior* is an LPD.'

'Er... what's that?'

'A Landing Platform Dock. Meaning she has the capability to flood her well deck to approximately ten feet, thus floating the landing craft. The stern gate is then opened and out they go. And all done at open sea. It's a sight to behold.'

'Yes, I can imagine.'

'I'm presuming, Prime Minister,' continued the Admiral, 'that all diplomatic channels will have been covered by the time the taskforce arrives, to ensure smooth passage into Panamanian waters?'

Hanlon turned to Foreign Secretary Jack Venison. 'Is that the case?'

'Yes. Panamanian President señor Roberto Caballero is overseas on a state visit to China, which is a gift from the gods of political mercy. In his absence we contacted Caballero's deputy, a man named Pasco Fostas, and told him the British Government wished to arrange a maritime surprise for señor Caballero's return, and sneak in Her Majesty's favourite warship, plus friends, to welcome him home on Sunday. Fostas thought it an excellent idea, signed every bit of paper we presented, *and* vowed to keep schtum.'

'You think he will do so?' asked Hanlon, warily.

'Yes. But to be sure, at ten o'clock local time this morning an SAS unit bundled him into the back of a furniture removals van, and are on their way to a remote safe house as we speak. For the time being they'll blame it on kidnappers from across the Colombian border, or something like that.'

The room shifted very uneasily.

Hanlon raised his hand. 'The point is, anything goes to stop Gunboat killing Trabant. Yes, I know – the murky water just gets murkier, but we can bargain and compensate once the situation is in hand. Our priority is to get Trabant safe, and I have every confidence the Royal Marines will do exactly that, after which the whole taskforce can slip away, citing a mechanical defect or similar for their hasty departure; the specifics of which I will leave to you, Admiral.'

'No problem.'

'And Gunboat will just take this lying down?' asked Bravinger.

'No. But we're hoping the presence of *Indomitable*, plus a few little sweeteners from moi, will make him re-evaluate things. So, I repeat, we get hold of Trabant with minimum fuss, get the hell out of there, and then we can bargain. Agreed?'

The room nodded unanimously.

'Good. Now, if that's all – let's get cracking.'

iii

Eva's fears for Trabant's safety were well founded. One more piece of seafood soufflé and he was sure to explode.

'Go on, have another slice,' said señora Chávez, sat in the sumptuous lounge of La Fortaleza. 'You need feeding up.'

'Honestly, I...' Trabant looked across to the cream leather sofa, from where Gunboat's exquisitely groomed and lavishly dressed wife stared back. She was a woman of large bones and broad features, with an aura that bubbled every bit as menacingly as her husband's. Yet it was framed in a flowery softness that made the whole effect even more unsettling.

'Don't get me wrong, señora Chávez, it's delicious, but I'm full.'

'Please, call me Mrs G – I know it's the English way,' she

replied, inserting another pickled onion into her powerful, scrunching mouth. 'My first name is Antoinette, as in the Queen of France. My father was a fan. My great-great-grandfather was from Lyons in France and came here to work on the first attempt at the Canal. But it failed, so we don't talk about that.'

'Ah, okay.'

'Anyway,' she continued, 'I thought you must be starving after my husband locked you up in that tiny broom cupboard. I don't know what's the matter with him lately. Normally our guests stay in the luxurious splendour of Annex Fourteen.'

Trabant tried to imagine its opulence. It couldn't be plusher than this lounge, which was straight out of a million-dollar catalogue. The ceiling boasted a chandelier worthy of any French monarch, and magnolia walls displayed grenade-shaped spotlights and a collection of abstract paintings set in garish gold-leaf frames. Vast white rugs lay upon the parquet flooring, and to the rear, beyond the sliding glass doors, lay the stunning views of the Pacific Ocean.

'I must admit,' continued Mrs G, leaning closer, 'I do have an ulterior motive for bringing you up here.'

'Really?'

'Don't look so worried! I'm simply desperate to learn more about England. My husband says that with business so good he'll need to buy a big residence over there. And when he mentioned that you – an English gringo from England – would be staying, I just had to pick your brains, especially when he added that after Saturday you will never, ever be seen again.'

Trabant closed his eyes.

'What a strange thing to say,' continued Mrs G, thoughtfully. 'He works too hard these days, and seems very anxious and grumpy. Can't imagine why.'

'Hasn't he, er... said anything to you?'

'No. He never tells me anything about his business. All I know is that since he returned from Cannes he's been totally

154

preoccupied. But enough of that. Tell me, whereabouts in England do you live?'

'London.'

'Oh, marvellous! So you know the Queen then?'

'Not personally, but my house isn't far from Buckingham Palace.'

'How far?'

'Fifteen minutes' walk.'

'What's the neighbourhood called?'

'Pimlico. My Aunt Rose says it's one of London's best-kept secrets.'

'Sounds perfect. I think we'll buy it. Now tell me, is she a wonderful neighbour?'

'Who – my aunt?'

'No – the Queen.'

'Oh yes, the best.'

'But don't her garden parties ever get a bit, you know... rowdy?'

'Never.'

'No, of course they wouldn't,' replied Mrs G, chastising herself for even thinking such a thing. 'She's so kind and considerate. By the way, I hope *we* didn't make too much noise last night?'

'Didn't hear a thing.'

Mrs G leant closer still. 'Can you keep a secret?'

'Not really.'

'Well you must, because if I don't confide in someone I'm sure to explode. You see, we're trying for a baby!'

'Oh, wow! Congratulations!'

'Muchas gracias, señor,' replied Mrs G, unable to contain her smile. 'The hot springs of passion bubbled over last night. Oh, Charles is such a tiger, and I just know that this time *is* the time, if you get what I mean? We've wanted a little Gunboat for ages.'

'I'm very happy for you.'

155

'Thank you. Now, get this: Gunboat is throwing a party on Saturday at the aquarium.'

'Aquarium?'

'Sí. The Panama City Aquarium. You've not been yet? Oh, you really must before you leave. It's wonderful. The penguins are my favourite.'

Trabant shuddered in realisation, that the aquarium must be the venue for the rematch.

'Anyway, lots of his business associates will be coming,' continued Mrs G. 'Thing is, he doesn't know I know, but I overhead him making the arrangements. He's been very secretive, so I think it *must* be a surprise party. You know, to make the big announcement. It's *so* exciting. I hope you'll be able to come too?'

'Oh, yes,' replied Trabant, with reluctant certainty. 'I'm sure I'll be there…' His words tapered as a distant vibration became louder… and louder… sending eerie ripples across the brine in the jar of pickled onions. 'I–is that a washing machine?'

'No, that's my husband,' replied Mrs G, checking her hair. 'Returning from a hard day's gun-running. Bless.'

Trabant shifted uneasily in his seat. The mechanical whir of rotor blades crescendoed then softened as the helicopter settled on the rooftop landing pad. Mrs G stood expectantly, but Trabant inched further back into his chair, as the sound of footsteps came ever closer.

'Honey, I h-o-m-e!'

'Hello, sugar,' said Mrs G. 'How was your day?'

'Very productive,' replied Gunboat, waddling forward to kiss his beloved, an expression of total devotion upon his face, until he caught the outline of Trabant in the corner of his eye. 'What the hell *he* doing up here?'

'Señor Trabant has been telling me about London. And guess what? He knows the Queen.'

'Well, I don't exactly…'

'He suppose to be lock in broom cupboard,' snarled Gunboat.

156

'Yeah, de broom cupboard,' repeated Enrique, as he too entered the room.

'But he's our guest, and it's been such a lovely day.'

Trabant studied Mrs G's expression, now certain she hadn't a clue as to why he was actually there.

'So tell me,' she continued, 'where have you been today?'

'Mexico City. Saw a very large man about a very large dog.' Bazooka raised a jealous ear. 'We discuss things over nice plate of fajitas.'

'Well, I hope you haven't spoilt your appetite?' tutted Mrs G. 'Chef's been slaving away all day.'

'Sweetie, you know I always hungry. Is there any seafood soufflé left?'

'Yes, señor Trabant has left you two slices.'

'Oh, muchas gracias, señor Loco. How generous! Make yourself at home, huh?'

'Honestly, I…'

Gunboat narrowed his eyes. 'You finish those apology letter yet?'

'N-not quite.'

Mrs G could contain her enthusiasm no longer. 'Señor Trabant has made London sound *so* wonderful. We *must* go there. I'd love to meet the Queen, and maybe we could get a corgi as a friend for Bazooka?'

'We see,' growled Gunboat. 'Guard – take señor Trabant down to broom cupboard. Let him get on with writing. Enrique – come with me to my office.'

'Sí, Boz.'

iv

The guard shoved the prisoner inside, then slammed the door behind. Trabant listened as the footsteps began to fade, then

157

turned to face his cell. The gunmetal bars on the solitary window were already slicing the moonwash into rectangles of silver on the opposite wall. In an hour or two it would be midnight, and then Wednesday – another day closer to the rematch.

He sat down on the bed and buried his head in his hands. The impossibility of the situation was overwhelming. The only option was to pray for a miracle and, in the meantime, do whatever Gunboat said. So he turned to the bedside table, picked up paper and pen and continued writing.

Only two hundred and eighty-seven to go…

Dear Guest of the Rematch,

My name is Bristo Trabant and I am writing to apologise for my conduct when playing Gunboat at cards in Le Club Maritime du Soleil.

The outcome gave the impression that Gunboat was losing the plot, and therefore no longer invincible or fit to do business with. However, I would like to point out that I only won because I cheated, and therefore Gunboat's invincibility and dependability in business remains intact.

I wish to express sorrow and regret for my actions. It was the only way I could stand a chance of winning against such a skilful opponent. I am clearly an inferior card player, and was completely wrong to do what I did.

Gunboat is as strong, ruthless and murderous as ever, and I categorically and unequivocally apologise for any tarnish to his good name.

Again, I am very, very sorry for all the trouble I have caused, and after my inevitable defeat in the rematch, I sincerely hope you will enjoy the full horrors of my gruesome death.

Yours apologetically,

Bristo Trabant

'So, what exactly *is* wrong with me entertaining our guest?' growled Mrs G, as the waiting staff cleared the plates away after dinner.

'I no want him in your way, sweetie,' replied Gunboat. 'That all.'

'Honestly, Charles, you can be so secretive sometimes. You didn't even tell me he was coming. I need to be informed. Chef needs to be informed. He doesn't have a crystal ball, you know. And speaking of cooking, don't forget we have the Chief of Police and his wife coming to dinner next Thursday. Make sure you're here.'

'Yes, sweetie.'

'And I suppose it's also up to me to show señor Trabant around, while you're off doing your deals, huh?'

'No! He stay here!'

'Does he? And what will he tell his friends when he gets back to England? "Oh – Panamanians are *so* inhospitable. They kept me locked up all day. Didn't even see the Canal." Is that what you want him to say? Because we know that's not true, don't we? Us Panamanians are muy hospitable.'

Gunboat bubbled with frustration. 'But sweetness, he no here to see the Canal.'

'Then why *is* he here?'

'I can no say.'

'You never do say, do you?'

'No.'

'Well, in that case I'll be the judge of where señor Trabant spends his time.'

'NO!'

Suddenly a glint shone in Mrs G's eye. 'Oh, unless of course he is here for something that might be happening on Saturday?'

'Maybe.'

'Well, in that case, I might let you have your way.' With that she bent forward and planted a huge kiss on Gunboat's cheek. 'Why didn't you say so earlier, my little tiger.'

'Er…'

'It's okay, not another word. I understand.' She winked. 'I'm off to bed now, to catch up on the soaps. I'll leave you and Enrique to discuss whatever it is you boys have to discuss at ten thirty at night.'

'Okay, dear, I no be long,' replied Gunboat, watching until the shadow of his beloved finally disappeared through the doorway.

vi

The dark Pacific Ocean tossed and turned, in an attempt to get comfortable for the night. Back in his office, sleep was not on the agenda for Gunboat Charlie Chávez.

'Okay, we go over the running order once more.'

'But, Boz, we done it twenty times already.'

'I no care, Enrique. From the top!'

'Okay. All de guests will arrive at Aeropuerto Marcos A Gelabert on Saturday morning, by 9 a.m. From dere, we move dem quickly to de aquarium by helicopter shuttle service.'

'And from there?'

'At 10.45 a.m. we move everyone into de main auditorium, to take deir seats and build de atmosphere for de rematch. Upon each seat will be one of de English pig's apology letters, and undernead: a selection of rotten indigenous fruit and vegetables for de guests to drow.'

'Drow!?! You mean – throw?'

'Sí – drow! Den, at eleven o'clock sharp, it's show time. You

160

win de rematch, make your speech, and den it's over to your special plan for de English pig.'

'Yeah, you gonna like that,' beamed Gunboat.

'I'm sure I will, Boz! After which, it a fond farewell and all de guests leave, via helicopter shuttle back to de airport; safe in de knowledge dat your reputation is fully restored, and normal service is resumed.'

'Good. And have you… (puff)… made it clear to the public that the… (puff)… aquarium will be close on Saturday for a private event?'

'Sí, Boz. All taken care of.'

'And have you organised the food?'

Enrique nodded. 'Dere will be carimañolas upon arrival, and bucketloads of sancocho.'

'Mmmm… good!' replied Gunboat, drifting for a moment amid thoughts of Panama's beloved national dish. 'Everyone will love our spicy chicken-and-vegetable stew, especially our French and Italian guests, who think the only decent food comes from their neck of the wood.'

'Sí, Boz.'

'Ooh, and nibbles! No dare forget the nibbles. Every good international party has nibbles.'

'Er… what *is* a nibble, Boz?'

Gunboat narrowed his eyes. 'You no know nothing, Enrique? They crispy things that go in bowls, for the guests to munch while talking. Had them at arms fair in Zurich. Boy, they went down well. I want to cover all the angles.'

'Dis event must be costing you a fortune, Boz.'

'No worry. I claim it back as corporate entertaining. Now, about the catering staff – they been checked out?'

'Sí, Boz. Every single one has a criminal record, so dey one of us.'

'Excellent. Can no be too careful these days. And security?'

'Trebled, Boz, and all briefed on the building layout.'

'Bravo! Well, I think that covers everything.'

Enrique tentatively raised his hand. 'I do have one more question, if I may?'

'Sure. Go on.'

'Why *are* you holding de rematch at de aquarium, Boz?'

'Well…' replied Gunboat, leaning back in his large, soft chair. 'After I win the rematch it is feeding time, and you know what food the sharks like best?'

'No, Boz, what's dat?'

'English pig. Ha ha ha!'

15

Avenida B and Calle Nueve Este

THE MIDDAY SUN BLAZED down on Casco Viejo and projected the immense and eerie shadow of the man across the pastel-coloured colonial townhouses of Panama City's old town. Death accompanied his every footstep, and the cool strands of breeze faded to nothing, as if even they held their breath until the man had passed by.

Despite his best efforts, the elderly newspaper vendor had little choice but to turn and face this colossal living monolith, as it scanned the racks then pointed a brutish finger at *La Crítica*, one of Panama's daily tabloids. The vendor shivered, and suddenly cherished his wife and children more than ever before. He extracted the newspaper, smoothed its cover, then carefully placed it on the rickety table.

As the colossus sifted through a handful of coins, the vendor studied his face. The eyes were dead as a cadaver's, and the broken nose boasted tunnel-like nostrils – exhaust pipes, no doubt, for the by-products of the evil manufactured within. Narrow lips encircled the wide mouth, and the set of white, serrated teeth were clearly longing to bite and tear. Razor-stubble joined the crop of black hair like the frontier of an ancient civilization, and the tanned skin was rough and leathery, contouring the muscular body like a suit of corrugated iron. He wore an unbuttoned dark-blue shirt, and a white vest that stretched around his broad circumference. Combat trousers and polished boots completed the profile.

Army? Couldn't be. No single authority could control such a man. Nor escapee. This man would run from no one.

A selection of coins landed in the vendor's hand, and at last the huge man continued on his way. The elderly paper seller slumped back on his stool, and released the breath he'd been holding too long for someone of his advanced years; watched the man finally disappear out of sight, then quickly began to close down his stall. One brush with death was enough for any day.

ii

Vatu Greolle was a force of nature, a solitary hunter most active at night. Cold, efficient, and unhindered by the baggage of passion or love, he was built for violence and born to kill. At seven feet tall and seventeen stone, his body was a battle-hardened superstructure. Death energised his spirit, and there was never a flicker of remorse for the way he made his living. Emotion too had been eroded by conflict, about the same time his soul had defected to hell, where it was welcomed with open arms.

Nine years in the French Foreign Legion had transformed him from bare-knuckle club fighter into highly polished killing machine. Tours of Afghanistan, the Central African Republic and the Gulf further enhanced his reputation, but a growing reluctance to cease fire and obey orders had meant regular summons before the disciplinary committee. The penalties were severe, but Greolle wasn't listening. By year ten the regiment had finally lost its appeal. So he quit to go freelance, to auction his services, and there could be no higher bidder than Gunboat Charlie Chávez.

Within days he was put to work, to kill and cull with devastating and previously unseen ferocity. He was given a new

164

identity, and a name personally chosen by Gunboat – inspired by one of the ocean's most feared predators, in recognition of the qualities they shared. Both lived a nomadic existence, conducted their business with chilling stealth, and made their kills in the most brutal and destructive fashion. The oceanic predator's scientific name sounded almost human too. It was the ideal choice.

Galeocerdo Cuvier: the Tiger Shark.

iii

The concrete peninsula winced beneath the impossible heat. People took to the shade to catch their breath and chat, while overhead, the flowers upon the balconies gasped for water like travellers lost in the Sahara desert.

A bright yellow Panama City taxi eased along a narrow, cobbled street as it headed towards the Pacific headland. Cuvier waited for it to pass, then crossed into La Plaza de la Independencia – an open, red-brick square sprinkled with tall, pink cherry blossom trees and neatly enclosed corner gardens. He took a seat on the nearest bench and scanned the surroundings – an old Legion habit. Busts of historical figures looked in from every side, a dark stone roll-call of those who had fought for each chapter in his adopted nation's colourful history. The white central bandstand stood tall, overlooked by the magnificent Catedral de Nuestra Señora de la Asunción.

Cuvier double-checked at right angles, then peered down yet more cobbled streets that disappeared into the distance, into the past. Some offered views of the adjacent ocean, others the shoulder-to-shoulder contrast of picturesque restoration and ramshackle neglect. In the far corner of the square, a hunched-up old woman busied herself with coloured beads and a chesty, resonant cough. And to the right – another street vendor, dressed in white shirt and brimmed hat, toiled over his portable drinks trolley, shaving ice from a huge block into a cup for a couple of tourists, before squirting the pile with cherry-coloured liquid and holding open his hand for remuneration. All seemed normal, just another lazy day in sun-blessed Casco. Yet Cuvier remained vigilant. He waited another five minutes until totally satisfied, then finally opened his copy of *La Crítica*, turned to the Lonely Hearts column and scanned each advert in turn.

MEN SEEKING WOMEN

> *39 YO Colombian would like to*
> *meet lady for fun and possibly more.*

Cuvier shook his head.

> *45 YO Cannibal would like to meet*
> *groups for home cooking and fine wine.*

Again, no.

> *34 YO Pacific Islander required for*
> *solution to extra-marital affair. Urgent*
> *response required. Call Box 52663.*

Cuvier reread the pre-agreed text that signalled his call to arms, then checked his surroundings once more. The old woman remained, now busy feeding the birds, and the tourists were having their photo taken with the ice-scraping street vendor. With the newspaper still open, Cuvier stood up then walked back across the street to the nearest phone box and dialled.

'Gracias por llamar a 52663. Deje su mensaje después del tono – please leave your message after the tone. B-e-e-p.'

Cuvier checked his watch then spoke. 'Two o'clock this afternoon. Corner of Avenida B and Calle Nueve Este.'

At two o'clock sharp a flower delivery van pulled up. The driver climbed out, retrieved a bouquet of tropical flowers from the back, handed it to Cuvier, then jumped back inside and quickly disappeared into the afternoon traffic.

In less than ten minutes, Cuvier had closed the door of his rented apartment and torn open the coloured wrapping paper, to extract the envelope hidden within the red and yellow stems of heliconia. Inside he found a wedge of cash and a photograph of a man. He studied the man's features meticulously. Early to mid-thirties, English, he guessed, and with a manufactured smile that begged to be extinguished. He then read the words written on the back, that detailed the how, when and where. The man was indeed English; the kill must be made after the rematch, and in a very public way, for the world to see.

Cuvier stifled his disappointment at not being able to break the man with his own hands, and turned his mind to the sniper's rifle he'd used on countless previous occasions. He was a crack shot. He never missed.

Next, he pulled a match from his top pocket and drew it swiftly across his left cheek. The stubble ignited the flame, the flame lit the photograph, and the man's image twisted and curled as it dropped to the floor, just as the man himself would do in a few days' time.

Cuvier's eyes were impassive as he stubbed out the remains with his foot. He then knelt, pulled up a floorboard, inserted his hand and retrieved a bullet and hacksaw. He sat back on the bed, focused his narrowed eyes and slowly, meticulously began to engrave the Englishman's name onto the side of the bullet. With each cut, the filings sprinkled to the floor like the sands of time ebbing away for the victim. After a few minutes Cuvier blew away the debris and raised the bullet to the light to inspect his handiwork. It was perfect.

Silently and efficiently he returned the bullet, hacksaw and cash to the hideaway, replaced the floorboard, dusted away the mess, reassembled the bouquet, then walked out of his apartment. Back on the street, he handed the flowers to the first lady he saw, ignored her thanks, then disappeared into the cobbled maze of Casco Viejo.

The Tiger Shark was on the move.

16

Calypso Abajo

THE LITTLE AEROPLANE CONTINUED south-west across the Bay of Panama. Trailing behind, a thirty-foot-long banner rippled in the air like a long, white eel, projecting the slogan 'Welcome to Panama, Have a Great Day!'

Eva sat alongside the pilot and looked inland, across the sprawling metropolis of Panama City to the rolling expanse of rainforest, which eventually gathered height and became the mountains of the Continental Divide that separated Panama's Caribbean and Pacific sides.

As the plane turned inland, Eva surveyed the never-ending stream of cars and lorries making their way in from the distant neighbourhoods of Pueblo Nuevo and San Miguelito, towards the workplaces in the financial district of El Cangrejo, or perhaps the Canal Zone. Some of the roads had ground to a standstill, probably amid the usual chorus of a thousand car horns.

The coastline now presented the headland of Punta Pacifica; its back prickly with yet more skyscrapers. And on the outermost tip sat a large, square, glass-covered building, coloured blue by the reflecting sky, and capped with a silver dome and the garish bright-red letters that spelt out 'Panama City Aquarium'.

Eva let out a cynical chuckle. The aquarium was Gunboat's facade of respectability that allowed him to pose in local newspapers and industry journals. If only they knew how it had really been paid for. Well, that exposé would have to wait its turn. Right now she was just thankful the location of the rematch had been ascertained, and that all efforts could be focused on finding Bristo. But where would Gunboat be keeping him? Down town? Out of town? Or perhaps not even in Panama at all.

She exhaled deeply, in an attempt to purge her body of the weight of the task, because the possibilities were endless, but time wasn't. It was running out – fast.

ii

The container ships were lined up as normal along the horizon. Eva waited until the plane was almost over the Canal entrance, then signalled to the pilot to veer east, as if picking up the flight path for Aeropuerto Marcos A Gelabert, which conveniently passed directly over the summit of Ancon Hill.

The plane levelled and eased lower, seemingly now beneath the tip of the pole from which the huge national flag rippled with pride. For a moment, Eva became transfixed by its design; pleasingly symmetrical and sectioned into four quarters: the top left rectangle white with a blue star, the bottom right white with a red star, and then the opposite quarters – plain red at the top right and plain blue on the bottom left.

'Madame, shall I fly any lower?'

'Yes, please. As close as you can get.'

From a distance, every inch of the 654-foot-high hill seemed to be covered in dense vegetation, but as they flew closer gaps began to appear, and Eva started to recognise features from her team's comprehensive intelligence documents: the outlines of a large building; the G-shaped helicopter pad, and then the huge AK-47-shaped swimming pool, complete with bullet-riddled garden shed and docking bay for an armada of lilos.

The pilot kept the white Cessna steady. Eva shifted in her

seat and peered hard through the window as they passed over the monstrous palace of glass. Already a dozen armed men were on the perimeter walls, glaring back, their guns held high with unmistakable intent. By the time the Cessna had banked hard right again and passed back over, that number had swelled to over twenty. Civil aviation guidelines didn't warn against negotiating this section of terrain, but common sense certainly did.

'Quick, let's get out of here!' urged Eva. The pilot nodded nervously, then hit the throttle. The propeller screwed into the air with all its might, whirring and biting with feverish energy to lift the aeroplane towards the safety of the blue horizon. As the world spun upside down, Eva craned her neck for one last look, to absorb every detail and dimension of La Fortaleza – just in case.

Masquerading as a tourist-board aeroplane had bought them a few extra seconds, just enough to get in and out intact. But now beads of sweat danced upon Eva's forehead – a stark reminder of the very real danger that Gunboat represented.

'Heading back to base?' asked the pilot, hopefully.

'Oh, yes. That's enough excitement for one morning.'

iii

An hour later, Eva stood in the hastily assembled DGSE surveillance headquarters, a large top-floor apartment in one of the most westerly towerblocks downtown, chosen for its dual views of La Fortaleza and the Panama City Aquarium.

Two bedrooms accommodated the team of five officers, each of whom cat-napped in strict rotation to ensure round-the-clock observation. The living and dining rooms were furnished with a metallic cornucopia of surveillance equipment and little else. Large wall-mounted TV screens gave permanent views of the key locations Gunboat might visit. Three desks were bunched together centrally, upon which banks of computer screens displayed yet more information – flight times, local times around the world, air-traffic-control updates. And in between, in the nooks and crannies, lay the obligatory stack of empty pizza boxes and half-finished cups of coffee; the kitchen itself a testament to the French Secret Service's lost art of washing-up. Through the north-facing balcony doors stood a high-powered telescope; its huge eye trained on La Fortaleza, peering through the layers of plant-life, and scanning for the face of the man who also appeared in the photographs gaffer-taped to the surrounding walls.

'Any sign of Bristo yet?' asked Eva, walking up to the cluster of desks, sipping from a bottle of chilled water.

'No, Madame,' replied her friend and colleague Thierry, busily tapping away at his laptop. 'Not even a hint of a clue – anywhere! Gunboat left Aeropuerto Marcos A Gelabert very early this morning with his sidekick Enrique, and his Learjet has been tracked into Bolivian airspace, but they haven't returned yet. All's quiet.'

'Well, we nearly got shot out of the sky this morning, and Gunboat's fortress is more heavily armed than usual, which I guess is to be expected. But likewise, no sign of Bristo at all. Where on earth can he be?'

'No idea,' replied Thierry. 'At least we still have four days to locate him.'

'Make that three – today, tomorrow and Friday. Leaving it to the day of the rematch is too close for comfort. We simply *have* to find Bristo beforehand.'

Eva's choice of words made Thierry look up. He'd noticed her addressing the target by his first name, even more so as the hours counted down. He knew her well. They'd worked together since she'd joined the DGSE and he considered her a close friend. If she did have personal motives then he would work even harder to assist her.

172

'What is it?' asked Eva, questioning his smile.

'Nothing, Madame,' he replied, turning back to his keyboard to begin tapping even faster.

Eva walked over to the balcony, to another colleague, who'd been glued to the telescope for the past three hours. 'Want a break, Claude?'

'Oh, yes please, Madame.'

Claude stood, yawned, and began to rub away the circular indentation from around his eye.

'Anything happening at the aquarium?' she asked.

'Just the general… (yawn)… public going in and out.'

'And La Fortaleza?'

'Ten minutes ago a guard topped up the drinks tray for the hummingbirds, but that's all.'

Eva sat in the chair and quickly adjusted the viewfinder to her eye. The overhanging branches and termite nests soon came into focus, as did La Fortaleza. It was enormous – balcony after balcony, window after window, seemingly never-ending, and at certain angles the refracted sunlight formed prisms of light that sparkled like jewels. A remarkable feat of engineering, and quite how Gunboat had managed to build it up there in the first place she could barely—

'Oh, look!' she exclaimed. 'Sitting on that branch – a sloth. How cute. Wish we could get an agent that close.' Eva continued scanning then focused on the open glass doors that led out from what looked like a lounge area.

'Can you see anything else, Madame?' asked Claude.

'Yes… yes, I can. Señora Chávez has just come into sight… she's talking to someone, but I cannot see who. And now… she's eating what looks like a… pickled onion?'

'Yes, Madame, that is correct,' replied Claude, beaming at his own efficiency. 'According to our intelligence database, she is most partial to the variety from—'

'Wait!' cut in Eva. 'I can see more movement… something

173

pushing behind the curtain… here it comes… wait… wait… ah, yes – the doggy.'

'Yes, Madame, according to our intelligence database, the dog's name is—'

'Bazooka?'

'Oui, Madame, that is correct. Though his full kennel name is Earl Bazooka De Monte—'

'It's okay, Claude, you can take your break now. I'll be fine, honestly.'

Claude hovered. 'Madame, may I ask something?'

'Yes, of course.'

'Who will man this afternoon's reconnaissance flight? It's just that Françoise always goes, which I don't think is fair. Is it okay if I go?'

'Of course,' smiled Eva, looking up from the telescope. 'Go with Thierry. I'll keep watch here. Just stay clear of La Fortaleza. They'll be waiting for us to return.'

iv

With Claude and Thierry gone, Eva refocused the telescope and painstakingly inspected each individual window. La Fortaleza now looked still, as if not a living soul were present – very different from a moment ago. The huge eye zoomed in on the top floor, then dropped down until it settled on another balcony and a bustle of… hovering, darting hummingbirds – as Claude had mentioned – encircling a red feeding platform suspended from a hook. They were so beautiful, so captivating, so busy… but unable to signal just where to look. Eva moved her eye onwards, to where the doors were open and net curtains flapped in the morning breeze. There must be more people inside, someone who—

There he was! Clear as day! And just for the briefest of

moments, in the open doorway, before shuffling out of sight.

'IT'S BRISTO! I CAN SEE HIM!'

But the room did not reply. Of course! The team had gone to look elsewhere, just when she needed them most.

She turned in a flash towards the adjacent table, where her radio was ready and waiting, but beside it lay Thierry's… and Claude's… and Françoise's. Damn! The argument about manning the next surveillance flight had got the better of them. Eva shook her head in frustration. They'd doubtless be back as soon as they realised, but how long would that be? Half an hour? Perhaps even longer if they stopped off at the empanada snack shop on Via Argentina.

Okay, stay calm. Think clearly…

She refocused on La Fortaleza. Had Bristo only just arrived, or been there all the time? Gunboat must have slipped him in immediately after he'd been captured in Vienna, in the few hours before the surveillance unit was set up. But now, with Gunboat and Enrique out of town, this was the best chance she could hope for.

But how to…?

Bingo! An idea…

Eva ran inside to the computer, typed in her request and waited with bated breath until the monstrous search engine finally displayed all known telephone numbers for La Fortaleza.

Next, how to get past the most trigger-happy private security service in Central America? Even a direct assault by a DGSE Action Unit would be a tall order. No, there had to be another way to get Bristo… to get him out… yes, that was it! She had to get *them* out… lure señora Chávez out of the building, with Trabant in tow… somehow…

Think… think…

Well, Gunboat was notorious for not telling his wife about the nitty-gritty of his business dealings, or so the marriage counsellors said. So it was highly likely she wouldn't know why Bristo was really there, or about the necessity to keep him inside La Fortaleza at all times. So what would tempt her out?

Eva began to pace the room. What did she really like? Pickled onions, Ferrero Rocher chocolates, er… anything expensive. No, it needed to be something living, vibrant, irresistible, like… calypso music! Yes, señora Chávez was a devotee.

Eva chewed her bottom lip in deeper contemplation. It was one hell of a long shot, but worth the gamble. Again she tapped frantically at the keyboard, and this time brought up on screen a list of señora Chávez's favourite social haunts.

'A-ha!' Calypso Abajo – one of Panama City's finest clubs, situated in the West Indian neighbourhood of Rio Abajo. And in that moment of realisation, Eva loved her team more than ever before; for the dull, bland process of data input that drove them all crazy had suddenly laid its golden egg. Local intelligence had noted señora Chávez visiting Calypso Abajo at least five times in the past month, and it was open twenty-four hours a day, seven days a week.

Eva picked up the telephone and dialled; her heart beating like a drum. The line rang once then answered.

'Sí?'

'Señora Chávez, por favor.'

'Espera.'

Eva waited as instructed… and waited. Were they tracing her call? They'd have to break the encryption device first, and even then, they'd—

'Hola.'

'Ah, is that señora Chávez?'

'Yes, it is she. Who is that?'

'I'm calling from Calypso Abajo, in Río Abajo.'

'Oh, hello. What a nice surprise. I was only with you last week. Is everything okay?'

'Yes, fine. In fact, it's because of your highly valued custom that I'm calling… to make you aware of a very special offer, only available *today*, for VIP customers like yourself.'

'Oh, I *do* love special offers. Tell me more.'

'Well, if you are able to come to our club this afternoon, and bring with you an Englishman whose initials are *B* and *T*, then you will receive a free lunch, a case of champagne *and*, er… lifetime membership of our establishment.'

'Oh, I say, that *is* interesting,' replied Mrs G, gripping the receiver tight, in excited anticipation. 'But I don't know any Englishmen with those initials. *B* and *T*, you say – as in Bocas del Toro?'

'Yes, that's right.'

'No… I'm quite sure I don't know any. That *is* a shame.'

'Please can you check.'

'I'm really quite sure, you know,' replied Mrs G.

'Don't you have *any* Englishmen staying with you at the moment?'

'Well, just the one.'

'Please, you really must check his initials.'

'Okay, okay. Hang on…'

Eva could hear the muffled conversation as the phone was cupped, then Mrs G's mutterings of disbelief at her incredible good fortune. 'Hello, you won't believe this, but it just so happens I *do* have an Englishman staying here with those initials.'

'Really? Well, that truly *is* a remarkable coincidence.'

'Sure is. And guess what? He's only here until Saturday, after which my husband says I'll never see him again, so it's lucky you phoned when you did. Well, I accept your kind invitation. What time do you want us there?'

'IMMEDIATELY!'

'Oh! Not sure I can do that. How about one o'clock?'

Eva checked her watch – 11.20 a.m. 'That will be perfect,'

she replied, with deliberate composure. 'And please bring the Englishman's mobile phone and passport, for identification.'

'Well, okay, if you insist.'

'I do! And one final thing, señora. We are extremely short of space, so I must request you do not bring hundreds of your bodyguards.'

'Oh, okay, if you think it's for the best. I'll just bring Raúl.'

'That is fine,' agreed Eva, knowing señora Chávez never travelled completely alone.

'Well, if that's all, I look forward to seeing you at one o'clock – and make sure you save us the best table now.'

'Yes, of course, señora. Only the very, very best.'

V

Calypso Abajo stood just off Calle Don Santos. It was a wide building, and painted orange, blue and yellow, in keeping with all the other colourful single-storey houses and apartment blocks that gave the neighbourhood its flavour. Music really did play twenty-four seven, and everyone in the neighbourhood set their watches to the beat of the calypso wafting through the air. Numerous other bars in the area played calypso too, but none as exuberantly as the Abajo.

The black Mercedes limousine pulled up out front. Raúl climbed out, opened the rear door for señora Chávez, then followed both her and Trabant inside.

The Abajo froze. People looked at each other with an oh-jeez-do-you-know-who-that-is expression on their faces.

'Tres rum pintados,' ordered Raúl.

The barman leapt into action, and the waitress ushered a group of drinkers away to clear three bar stools, then produced a match to light señora Chávez' cigar.

'Muchas… (puff)… gracias,' she replied, then quickly took

a sip of rum, after which, once she'd nodded her approval, the club's hum of conversation dared tiptoe back to its previous level.

The Abajo seemed to hold the same promise as Panama City itself – that a full-blown carnival could break out at any moment. Trabant scanned the room. It was even bigger than the exterior suggested, and to the right, the long bar was lined with an apron of wicker beach mats. Every table was occupied by men in bright shirts and women in skimpy dresses. And at the far end stood a stage, full of musical instruments.

'You like my favourite haunt, señor Trabant?'

'Y–yes, it's very… atmospheric.'

'When people came from the West Indies to Panama to work on the Canal,' continued Mrs G, 'they brought calypso with them. This whole neighbourhood – Río Abajo – was built to give them somewhere to live. Many older generations have come back to—'

'I sorry to interrupt, señora,' cut in Raúl, as he returned to Mrs G's side, 'but the management no have recollection of a special offer of free lunch, champagne and lifetime membership upon the presentation of Englishman with the initials *B* and *T*.'

'WHAT? But the lady phoned me this morning. Tell them to think again, or else.'

Raúl nodded, then disappeared back across the room, returning moments later with the indentation of the manager's teeth set deep into his knuckles.

'Well?' barked Mrs G.

'The manager has seen error of his way, and apologise for his loco incompetence.'

'I should think so too,' replied Mrs G, watching a group being ejected from their front-of-house table. 'Now, come on, señor Trabant – let's take our seats, relax, and enjoy the rhythms of the isthmus of Panama.'

17

The Eyes of Cerro Ancón

THE HOUSE LIGHTS OF Calypso Abajo dimmed. A tall West Indian man wearing a brightly coloured shirt, shorts and flip-flops walked onstage to join the other five West Indian men wearing brightly coloured shirts, shorts and flip-flops. And once in position, they started playing the selection of instruments spread out across the stage.

The room cheered.

'Having a good time, señor Trabant?' Mrs G smiled.

'Oh, y-yes. Thank you.'

'My pleasure. I don't know what's wrong with my husband – keeping you cooped up in that broom cupboard like some delinquent rooster, when he should be showing you the sights. Us Panamanians are very hospitable, you know.'

'I never imagined I'd be—'

'Oh, look! It's Franco and Estanza Rodríguez! Haven't seen them in months. Won't be a mo…'

Trabant watched her cross the room, then turned his mind back to the music, which really was wonderful, and infectious, but just too damned loud to let him formulate an escape plan.

'Drink, sir?'

'No, thanks.'

'Are you sure, sir?'

'Yes, very. Thank you,' repeated Trabant, agitated at the interruption.

'Then how about a slice of apfelstrudel?'

'Ooh, yes. Now that would be... EVA!' he exclaimed. 'But... how did you...?'

'Sssssh!' she replied softly, placing an index finger over her mouth, while pretending to collect glasses from the table. 'I've been watching La Fortaleza, in case you were there.'

'Really?' he replied, his mind racing, and noticing her more casual work attire of T-shirt, skirt and trainers. 'But what about your job at Le Club Maritime du Soleil?'

Eva's look of confusion was brief, until she remembered that he still didn't know her true identity. 'Bristo, there is much to explain, but not right now. First we must escape, and I have a plan.'

'I'm all ears.'

'Yes, my darling,' she replied, admiring the sides of his head. 'Indeed you are.'

ii

The red toilet sign was a faint glimmer in the far right-hand corner, mounted above a set of swing doors. Trabant double-checked that Raúl was still distracted by the menu, then slowly stood and made a bee-line, advancing through the maze of packed tables as calmly as he possibly could.

'And where are you off to?' asked Mrs G, heading him off at the pass.

'I need the... have to go to the... in fact it's really quite urgent...'

'Hmmm... you do look a little flushed. Go on, before you have an accident. Lunch will soon be served.'

Think confidence... just keep walking...

Trabant continued towards the red neon sign, then on through the swing doors and straight ahead – now running – through another set of doors that led into a kitchen; into a

181

cacophonic mayhem of chefs shouting, of metronomic chopping, of sweat-stained tiles and bubbling saucepans.

Keep walking… act as if you belong…

Trabant ducked beneath the crossfire of expletives and made for the far end, pushed through the fire exit and out into the bright afternoon sunshine, where Eva waited, to take his hand and lead him across the street and down the adjacent avenue.

The afternoon heat was already formidable. They ran towards a stretch of sidewalk shaded by a row of colonial-style townhouses, and kept moving, quickly as possible, eyeing the constant stream of vehicles that glided past. But none of them were taxis.

'Quick – this way!' said Eva, diverting them back through the maze of neighbourhood until they reached the next large intersection. Finally, a beaten-up yellow taxi turned the corner ahead and ambled its way closer. Eva flagged it down.

'Amador Causeway, por favor,' she said, climbing inside after Trabant.

'Sí,' replied the hoarse voice.

'Gracias. You speak English, señor?'

'A little.'

Eva studied the driver's eyes in the rear-view mirror. They seemed relaxed and carefree, but the instinct to distrust had always served her well. She positioned her hand on her gun, but the driver's only movement was to lean forward, turn up the radio and fill the car with calypso.

The taxi pulled off. It was old and tired, just like its owner. A set of red beads hung from the rear-view mirror and, on the dashboard, miniature flags of Panama and FC Barcelona stood side by side. Its scent was musty, testament to the thousand previous customers who'd also clung on for dear life, as the little chariot did battle with the darting, horn-blaring traffic.

Eva checked back down the road for signs of pursuit. But

Trabant could only smile, unable to contain his joy. 'Oh, Eva. It's so good to see you again. I thought—'

'Yes, I know. Me too,' she replied, quickly raising her index finger to stem his flow. 'We have lots to talk about, but later… understand?' She flicked her eyes towards the driver.

'Oh, yes. I see…'

Eva smiled, gently squeezed his hand then continued her vigil. The taxi was now trundling along Via España, the opposite way Mrs G's limousine had come earlier, then it picked up Avenida de los Mártires, heading west. To the left, beyond the grass and palm tree-lined promenade, lay the Pacific Ocean. To the right were shops, bars and a swathe of residential blocks. Overhead, the large green road signs pointed towards Balboa Container Port, Amador Causeway and the Canal.

'Can the driver go any faster?' whispered Trabant.

'We're nearly there,' replied Eva, still on high alert.

After the next few interchanges the taxi turned left and swooped round onto Calle Amador, a narrow causeway that stretched far out into the bay.

'Only a few minutes now,' said Eva, calmly.

Trabant tried to smile, but the tension was unbearable. And Ancon Hill – or Cerro Ancón, as Lili the live-in cleaner called it – was still ominous, as if it had eyes… the eyes of Gunboat himself, about to—

'Atención! Attention!' crackled the taxi's radio. 'This is head office. On the look-out for an English man and French woman. He's got really big ears, she's drop-dead gorgeous. Just escaped from Calypso Abajo. Maximum priority. Request comes from the big man himself. Anyone seen them? Over.'

The driver's eyes immediately flicked to the rear-view mirror, barely a second before Eva's gun pushed hard into the back of his head. 'Keep driving, señor. Don't try anything, or you'll be needing windscreen wipers on the inside. Entiendes?'

'Sí,' hissed the driver. 'Entiendo.'

They continued along the causeway for another few tension-laced minutes, past numerous shops, restaurants and little coves filled with yachts and pleasure craft. After passing a sign for Isla Flamenco, the taxi followed the road left and into a huge car park fringed with manicured lawns and pink cherry blossom trees. Beyond stood a large, two-storey building with magnolia walls, white sash-windows and a long balcony, its ground floor awash with restaurants that overlooked a sumptuous marina.

'Pull over there,' said Eva sternly, directing the driver to the very far side of the car park. The driver eased to the curb, but his eyes – alive, hawk-like – returned to the mirror, ready for something Eva could not predict.

'Turn off the engine. And, if you want to live, put your hands on the wheel,' she instructed, pushing the gun harder to reinforce her commands. 'Good. Now, just to ensure…'

Eva drove the butt of her gun hard into the driver's jaw, bouncing his head against the side window, where it remained. She then rolled up her skirt, extracted a long black cable-tie from inside her stocking, leant forward and looped it round the driver's hands and steering wheel, and zipped it up tight.

'Okay, Bristo, let's get moving,' she said, flinging open the taxi's door. 'The whole of Panama will be looking for us now.'

In a moment they were running hand in hand towards the marina. As they rounded the corner, they could see a line of huge gangways leading down to enormous rectangular concrete jetties, where half a dozen ships and ferries waited impatiently. People seemed to be everywhere, waving and kissing goodbye to loved ones, taking photographs, or just ogling the breathtaking cityscape across the bay. Officious-looking crew guided elderly-looking tourists down the last few steps, and deckhands toiled and slackened the broad, snake-like ropes.

'Okay, to the ticket office – over there.'

'Can we rest, just for a moment?'

'No, Bristo. If we stop, we're dead! We must get away as quickly as possible.' Eva led them over to the booth. 'Okay, we need a ferry to take us north,' she said, studying the destinations on offer. 'And we haven't got long until most depart – perhaps seven minutes max.'

'What are those?' asked Trabant, staring at the powder-blue sky.

'Hmmm? Oh, vultures,' replied Eva, following his eyes. 'But don't worry, they won't be getting a piece of us.'

As Eva looked back down, a movement to the right caught her eye. She peered closer, and her instincts went into overdrive. A car had parked up, positioned awkwardly, and with doors left wide open, and occupants no longer inside.

'Eva, are you okay? What's wrong?' asked Trabant, confused at her distraction.

She continued to look away and scan the crowd, searching for the faces that didn't fit; then she saw the three men advancing quickly, with guns barely concealed. She looked back to Trabant, and in that instant knew she couldn't tell him. To explain would take an age; to contain his panic would be too great a hindrance to what she now had to do.

'Bristo, take this,' she said, handing him a wad of dollar bills. 'I need you to buy the tickets.'

'Okay,' he replied, looking increasingly confused. 'But something's wrong, isn't it? I can tell.'

'Yes. I, er... need the loo. What a time, huh?' she laughed, rolling her eyes.

'But you can go on board.'

'This can't wait, so please listen very carefully.' Eva spoke, with controlled calmness. 'We have to head north. At least two of the ferries are going in that direction. Buy tickets for either under a false married name, get yourself on board, leave my ticket with the official on the gangway, then make your way to the bow.'

'Which end is that?'

'The pointed one.'

'Ah, okay.'

'Stand there so I can see which ferry you are on. I will join you on board. And thank you,' she said, kissing him hard on the mouth.

Trabant contemplated Eva's kiss, which she'd delivered with far greater passion than a trip to the toilet really warranted. 'You will come back, won't you?' he called out, as she disappeared into the crowd.

'Yes, I promise. Just make sure we head north.'

'No problem,' he replied, before turning to the lady in the booth.

iii

The men were approaching fast, barely fifty metres away, fanning out and barging their way through the crowd. The area seemed impossibly full, and even more tourists were exiting the furthest gangway, creating a whirlpool of cameras, sunhats and garish tracksuits.

Eva rechecked her watch. Seven minutes had just become five, leaving just over a minute to disable each man, then a final minute to get herself on board. Thank heavens this time she had proper footwear. She then patted her thigh to check her gun was ready and waiting. It was, but bullets had to be the last resort – gunfire caused panic, panic meant pandemonium, pandemonium meant security shutdown, and that meant no ferries would be heading north, south or anywhere.

Deep breaths crystallised her plan.

She took one more look at the sea of people, then dipped beneath the surface and made her way across the melee until directly between Trabant and man number one.

Twenty-five metres…

Fifteen metres…

The crowd was thick – ideal cover. Ten metres…

Five metres…

Now! Attacking from depth, she swept the man's legs and dropped him to the floor. A few tourists tutted at the inconvenience, by which time Eva had punched the man hard to the jaw and solar plexus, to comprehensively end his afternoon's work. She then dragged him by the shoulders, propped him up against a bin, retrieved his hat and tilted it down over his face. 'Sleep tight,' she whispered, then advanced towards man number two.

Just over four minutes left.

A quick glance back to the ticket office revealed Bristo had gone. She scanned across to see him heading towards the gangways, then looked further still to pick up man number two, who had seen exactly the same. Man number two ran faster, Eva faster still – as fast as she could – to head him off with barely ten metres to spare.

Whack!

She judged the angle of impact to perfection – forty-five degrees – her elbow delivered to his jaw with such force and disguise the man didn't even see its shadow. And in the few footsteps before he fell, Eva guided him onto a nearby bench; threw his gun into the ocean, then arranged his head and limbs as if he too had decided to take an afternoon nap.

'I saw what you did,' stated a frowning American tourist. 'You hit him with your arm.'

'Yes, you're quite correct,' replied Eva. 'But so would you if he'd been sleeping with your sister.'

Eva's conviction was total, and the lady's face began to scowl. 'Damn right,' she replied. 'Well, in that case, let me do this.' She stepped forward and kicked the brute hard on the ankle. 'There! Take that, you swine!'

'Thank you, my friend,' smiled Eva. 'And please, let this be our little secret.'

'Mum's the word,' smiled the lady, tapping the side of her nose. 'Us women need to stick together.'

Brrrrrrrrrrrrrr… Brrrrrrrrrrrrrrrr…

Numerous ships and ferries sounded their departure, oblivious to the drama unfolding. Gigantic ropes were slowly loosened, and gangways readied for removal.

Eva rechecked her watch: two minutes forty-five to go.

She turned and ran back into the crowd, looking for man number three. There he was, but now with men four and five. Where the hell had they come from? Their eyes were wild and unsure, their guns unhidden and obvious, their feet gaining pace through the crowd towards the gangways. She had to stop them, divert them, but how?

Brrrrrrrrrrrrrr… Brrrrrrrrrrrrrrrr…

Eva zigzagged through the crowd – blindside – gaining as much speed as possible to…

Wham!

…body-check man number three into numbers four and five. They stumbled, but not for long, and in time to see Eva running inside the main building. They licked their lips and took the bait.

Man number three barely made it through the door before being tripped then kicked hard on the jaw, to end sprawled out like a starfish. The surprise on the face of man number four cost him dear – his forward motion transmuted via a judo throw into a three-sixty-degree panoramic view of the shopping mall that ended back down on the unforgiving ceramic floor. His groans were short-lived, ended by a ferocious open-handed blow.

Onlookers froze in disbelief. Eva turned in a flash towards man number five, her prowess giving him a serious crisis of confidence, but instead of running, he aimed his gun and began to fire wildly.

Onlookers dived for cover, and Eva threw herself into the nearest shop, a gift boutique, thankfully empty except for the startled assistant, who now ran screaming towards the rear. More bullets chased Eva inside, exploding the glass door and window into a shower of a billion pieces. But then... silence.

Eva crouched low behind a display cabinet, drew her gun, and rechecked her watch. One minute ten to go... couldn't be! She cursed herself for not disabling man number five, and for provoking him into the worst possible scenario – a gunfight in a public place.

Fragments of glass began to crunch beneath man number five's slowly advancing feet, but Eva waited, coiled like a spring, surveying the layout, counting down his distance. The shop was narrow and deep. To the left were postcards, fridge magnets and T-shirts; to the right: books, flags and CDs; and behind, on the back wall, a row of almost human-sized soft toys.

Suddenly a door creaked open. Eva turned in a flash to see the shop assistant disappear into the back office, and slam the door behind. Thank heavens.

Eva inched her head round the end of the cabinet to see man number five getting closer, scanning his gun like a metal detector. From the way he moved he wasn't a pro, none of them were, just hired guns who'd never seen active service like she had. It was time to bring this to an end.

She leapt to her feet then ran across the back of the shop to draw the man's fire. His bullets followed, but with horrendous inaccuracy, and Mickey Mouse took three in the guts. Plumes of his stuffing took to the air like nuclear mushroom clouds, billowing everywhere, and within three seconds the rear of the shop resembled a severely shaken Christmas paperweight. Eva instantly hit the deck, beating the curtain of white as it descended, and crawled forward on her stomach to take aim. She'd done alpine training with the French Special Forces, and figured much would also be applicable to stuffing blizzards. Yes it was, and she could hear the enemy advancing – slowly and erratically.

The stuffing continued to fall, and much thicker than she could have imagined. Gee, Mickey must have been tightly packed, or perhaps Donald and Pluto had been shot as well.

Eva rechecked her watch. Forty-five seconds to go.

Come on… come on…

The man's outline slowly reappeared. The time for half-measures had passed. She aimed at his ankle, then scanned upwards to where his thigh would be – and fired.

The man fell amid screams of agony. But his gun remained in his hand, and as Eva rolled away to the left behind a display cabinet, he opened fire at her passing shadow.

Bang. Bang. Click…

He fumbled for a clip, but Eva had already re-emerged through the blizzard, with her gun pointed directly at the man's head. 'Dead man's click, that's what they call it.'

'Huh?' whimpered the man, clutching his blood-soaked leg.

'When you're out of bullets. You used most of yours on poor Mickey back there. How could you?'

The man cursed in Spanish, until Eva stepped forward to claim his silence.

Whack!

The man's wound was significant, but not life-threatening, – just as she'd intended. She grabbed a scarf from the adjacent shelf, tied it firmly above the injury to stem the blood flow, then ran back to the locked office door and knocked.

'Señorita, you still in there?'

No answer.

'You speak English?'

'S-sí…'

'Okay. The bad men have gone. But wait another two minutes before coming out, then call an ambulance. Entiendes?'

'Sí, sí.'

Eva returned her gun to its garter then ran back outside, where thankfully the world seemed oblivious to the fight. She continued on towards the gangways, wiping her face clear of stuffing as she zigzagged the crowd.

Twenty-seven seconds.

Bristo, where are you!?!

Her eyes scanned each ferry, most now with ropes off and gangways all but removed. Which one? WHICH ONE!?!

There! Pacing up and down nervously – Bristo!

Eva cut through the last line of onlookers and accelerated down gangway number two.

'You have my ticket,' she said to the man.

'Ah, yes. Señora Loco, I presume?'

'Er, yes… that's right.'

The man looked at her disapprovingly, tore the ticket in half and waved her on board.

'Muchas gracias,' she smiled, unable to contain her sense of achievement. 'And look – three seconds to go,' she uttered to herself. 'No problem.'

iv

'What kept you?' exclaimed Trabant. 'You nearly missed the boat.'

'Don't ask,' she replied. 'Just follow señora Loco inside – quickly!'

'But, Eva, you're covered in fluff. What on earth happened?'

Eva looked at him and smiled. 'I ran into Mickey Mouse. He sends his regards.'

Trabant's look of suspicion faded as Eva led them past the other passengers, to a small alcove as secluded and out of sight as they could find. And in no time they felt the gentle vibrations through the floor, and the ferry easing away from the jetty.

'I hate fluff,' said Eva, brushing the last remnants from her arms.

'Yes, me too,' replied Trabant, just as an elderly American couple ambled past.

'Well, Jethro,' said the American lady. 'I'm sure sad to be leaving Panama City.'

Trabant smiled at her words. He couldn't wait to get out of the place.

'Me too, Charlese,' replied her husband. 'But heading south is sure gonna be fun too.'

Trabant froze. Heading south? No, they couldn't be! He sat bolt upright and looked out of the windows. The ferry had cleared the breakwater and was gaining speed.

'Bristo, are you okay?' asked Eva. 'You don't look very happy to be rescued.'

'Oh, I am… very happy, honestly. It's just that…'

'What? What is it?'

Trabant looked at Eva with horror in his eyes.

'I think we're on the wrong ship.'

18

Cornelia Cortez

'THIS ISN'T EVEN A ferry, Bristo. It's more like an ocean liner.'

'I thought the tickets were expensive.'

Eva stepped up to the railings to get her bearings. The ship was certainly ocean going, but not full-sized, with perhaps only five upper decks. 'We're heading south for sure. First stop probably Ecuador.'

'Is that good?'

'Right now, anywhere out of Panama is good.'

Bristo Trabant lowered his head. 'I'm sorry about getting on the wrong ship. They all looked the same to me.'

'It's okay. It's an easy mistake. We just needed to head north, that's all, where I have contacts; people who can get us home fast. In South America it's a whole different ball game.'

Trabant attempted redemption. 'Would it help matters if I bought you an ice-cream?'

ii

Shoulder to shoulder they devoured their vanilla cones, sitting on a bench at the rear of the upper deck, allowing their eyes to wander freely amongst the white lines of froth that trailed behind the ship.

'So, I'm señora Loco now, eh?' joked Eva.

'Yes, sorry about that. It was all I could think of. Those last few minutes before we set sail were ever so stressful. They just don't queue in Panama like they do in England; the lady in the ticket booth only spoke Spanish, and then I spilt my raspberry fruit-crush all over the floor.'

Eva smiled. 'I'll get you another one.'

'It's okay. This ice-cream is much nicer. Talking of which… here's your change.' Trabant produced a pile of notes and coins from his trouser pocket. 'I'm sorry, I haven't got your other money yet.'

'What money's that?'

'The Euros you lent me at Nice airport. I *will* pay you back, honestly, just as soon as I can.'

'Don't worry about it.'

'No, I insist.' He paused, quickly licked a run of vanilla before it reached his hand, then continued. 'So, do you work freelance?'

'How do you mean?'

'As a hostess? First Cannes, now Panama. Guess you go where the money is, huh?'

Eva lowered her cone, unable to conceal her huge, warm smile.

'What?'

'Bristo, I have something to tell you. I'm not really a hostess. I'm a secret agent, just like you.'

Trabant's jaw dropped. 'No way!'

'It's true. I work for the DGSE – the French Secret Service. I head a taskforce dedicated to the surveillance of Gunboat, which is why I was at Le Club Maritime du Soleil.'

'Well, you had me fooled. I thought you were an excellent hostess.'

'Thank you. Maybe I missed my vocation in life?'

'Maybe. But a real hostess might not have saved my life.'

Eva leant closer. 'But I'm sure she'd have fancied you just the same.'

Trabant blushed. 'So, er… why didn't you tell me sooner, about you being a secret agent?'

'Isn't that the first rule of undercover work?'

'What?'

'Not telling anyone you're undercover.' She winked.

'Yes, I suppose so,' he replied, thoughtfully. 'And your cover – is it totally blown?'

'Yep. Pretty much.'

'And Gunboat will now want to kill you too?'

'U-huh.'

Trabant lowered his head once more. 'Eva, I'm so sorry to have got you mixed up in all this.'

'Hey, it was my choice, remember?'

'But if I hadn't—'

'Bristo, it's not your fault – it's Gunboat's! He's the creator of this dark, violent world; the one who fuels countless wars around the world. And he *will* get his comeuppance.'

'I'll vote for that.'

'Thought you might. Anyway, the house we stayed at after escaping the yacht club, it's a DGSE safe house, which is why spare clothes were there, and the line was safe for you to call London.'

Trabant's eyes remained curious. '"Get out of this business – it is bad for both of us." Why did you say that?'

'It was my subconscious, reaching out to you in sympathy. This business can be bad for anyone's soul.'

'Wow,' replied Trabant. 'Do all ice-cream flavours make you this philosophical?'

'Yes, except strawberry. But you'll have to cook me your famous steak and kidney pie first to see the effect that has.'

Trabant blushed again.

'Anyway,' continued Eva, 'things have moved fast since Cannes. Our governments have indirectly forced Gunboat into holding a rematch.'

Trabant's eyes swelled. 'But I don't want to play a rematch. I just want to go home.'

'You won't have to. It was just a means to buy time, to find you. I chose to search Panama City, saw you in La Fortaleza, et voilà – here you are.'

'Wow! How very smart. Thank you again.' Trabant pondered the enormity of the developments a moment longer, then turned back to Eva. 'So what happens now?'

'Well, I get you to safety, then let our governments try and appease Gunboat. The thing is, I haven't yet confirmed that I've rescued you, so everyone will still be searching.'

'I have my mobile phone on me,' replied Trabant, patting his jacket.

'Brilliant. Then let's finish our ice-creams, work out precisely where we're heading, then inform our people before Gunboat's net closes in.'

iii

They walked back along the deck, downstairs and through the busy restaurant, and out into the customer reception area, where Eva stopped at a wall-mounted deck plan.

'*Cornelia Cortez* – such a pretty name,' she said, reading the ship's blurb. 'Registered in Ecuador. Ninety metres long, two thousand three hundred tonnes, crew of sixty, and complete with three bars, two restaurants, and a hot-tub and sauna.'

'Ooh… can we?'

'Sure, if we have time.'

The adjacent wall offered a map showing destination arrows from all the ports she used. 'We'll either be heading straight out to the Galapagos Islands, or down to Ecuador, then on to Peru,' said Eva, tracing her finger along the lines of dots leaving Panama City.

'Perhaps we could ask this man if—'

Eva turned to look. 'No!' she said quickly.

'But…'

As the man passed by, her suspicions were confirmed. Despite the white shirt and epaulettes, his hooked nose and parrot-friendly shoulders indicated an ominous family connection to Blackbeard the pirate, or similar.

'Bristo, we must remain invisible!'

iv

The ship ploughed onwards through the blue wilderness.

Eva led the way back across the deck towards the stern. At one of the smaller bars they purchased club sandwiches and two bottles of water, then found the most out-of-the-way table they could to concentrate on remaining invisible.

'Eva, there's a cabin number on our tickets.'

'Really?'

'Yes, number eighty-eight.'

She turned in a flash to double-check. 'You're right! Let's get moving.'

With food trays in hand, they walked back out to the gangway and followed the signs. 'Should be just along here,' said Eva. 'Eight-six… eighty-seven… here it is!'

They hurried inside and closed the door behind. It was small and basic, with minimal furniture and bland decor, but an ideal hideaway. There were keys left waiting in the inside door lock, and a compact double bed was pushed up in the far corner, at the foot of which was a door to a closet-sized bathroom, which had towels, a bathrobe and a bar of soap.

'About time we had some luck,' said Trabant.

'I agree.' With that, Eva quickly locked the cabin door, pulled a chair across and wedged it beneath the handle. 'Okay, so we keep the door locked at all times, the chair wedged like this, and we don't answer the phone.'

'And if there's a knock at the door?' asked Trabant.

'Then we—'

Knock. Knock.

Eva's eyes swelled in disbelief. 'Er… momento!' she called out.

She beckoned Trabant towards the bathroom, and began to whisper. 'Lean into the toilet, pretend to be seasick. I will do the talking.' She then quickly tore off her trainers and stockings, pulled on the bathrobe, wrapped the bath towel round her head, rubbed the soap under the tap and smeared the froth all over her face, then sprinted back, pushed the chair aside and opened the door ajar. 'Er… pardon.'

'Oh! Er… triste, sorry er… señora Loco?'

'Señora Locomovich. I, er… Slovakia.'

The ship's officer looked at her apologetically, having clearly interrupted her in the bathroom. 'Er… billetes… tickets, por favor.'

'Vstupenky?' replied Eva, with a confused look on her face. 'Er… these?' she added quickly, handing over their tickets then watching intently as the officer tore off a section and politely handed them back. 'So, is all okay?'

The officer nodded. 'Sí, all okay. Muchas gracias. Er, excusar… excuse me, we are look for two people. Er… English man… big ears, and er, French woman… gorgeous, with long black hair. You see?'

'Er, I… Slovakia,' she replied. 'Señor Locomovich… he also Slovakia. He in toilet. He… bbbluuuuuuurgh… sick of sea. You listen…' Eva opened the door a little wider. 'Vitali – are you okay?'

Trabant took his cue. 'Bluurrrggghhhhh…!'

'See!' continued Eva. 'He very sick. So, all okay I go?'

'Er, we look for… chase… er… oh, forget it! Muchas

198

gracias,' replied the officer, now losing the will to live. 'Adiós, señora.'

'Okay, adiós,' replied Eva, before softly closing the door, and waiting until the officer knocked on the next-door cabin before finally letting out her breath.

'You speak Slovakian too?' whispered Trabant, coming out of the bathroom.

'Only basic stuff, with horrendous pronunciation,' she whispered back. 'But I think it did the trick.'

She silently relocked the door, re-wedged the chair, then crept past into the bathroom to wash. Trabant followed and stood in the doorway.

'Great sound effects, Monsieur,' said Eva.

'Thanks. Even better thinking by you, and a great disguise.'

Eva smiled. 'He was looking for a French lady with long hair. All he saw was a soapy Slovakian, but how much time it will buy us I don't know.'

She patted her face dry, then took Trabant's hand and led him to the bed. 'Bristo, my plan from here is to telephone my team and get them to initiate an extraction.'

'Oh!'

'Don't worry, that's a good thing. They'll either stop the ship, or send a helicopter. Until then, let us remain positive and remember the facts – that we are together, and thanks to you, very comfortable in this cabin. So, may I now borrow your phone, please.'

'Sure,' replied Trabant, retrieving it from his jacket pocket.

'I'll contact my team. You kick off your shoes and get comfy on the bed.' Eva dialled Thierry's mobile and waited patiently for him to answer.

'No reply?'

'No. And now it's gone to voicemail,' she said with deliberate calmness, before trying Claude's number and again disguising

199

her frustration as his mobile gave the same response. This time she left a message.

V

Eva woke with a start. Bristo was still fast asleep, so she quietly rolled over and rechecked the phone, and was horrified that not only had it not rung, but that they'd been asleep for over three hours. It was now 5.42 p.m.

Why had the phone not rung? It had a signal. What were Thierry and Claude doing? She had specifically instructed them to call back and confirm the extraction plan. It was basic procedure. Damn it!

'Bristo, wake up!' she said softly.

'Hmmm?'

'I need to phone my team again, and also pop up on deck to confirm where we are. You stay here, but take the gun. If anyone attacks, you know the drill – aim at the biggest target.'

'But I thought…'

'It's just a precaution. I'll only be gone a few minutes. When I return I will knock on the door quickly then slowly, so you know it's me. Meanwhile, wedge the chair back beneath the door handle.'

Eva opened the cabin door, checked the corridor was clear, then made her way to the lounge area. There were still many passengers about: some drinking at the bar, some in window seats reading, but all seemed subdued, perhaps by the prospect of the many hours to kill until they reached their final destination. The question being – where *was* that destination?

She kept moving, with eyes low, avoiding interaction with anyone, especially the CCTV cameras, until finally she made it outside. The sea air that had made them both sleepy now brought her back to life, and just for a moment she allowed herself to enjoy the ruffle of wind in her hair. But something was wrong – very wrong.

She walked across to a young couple taking photos of the gulls hovering above. 'Er, excuse, you speaky the English?'

'Sure do, ma'am – Alabama's finest.'

'Ah, wunderbar!' she replied, in the worst dialect she could muster. 'It is that, er… my elderly mama, she want to know when we arrivey?'

'At the Galapagos? Around lunchtime tomorrow.'

'Oh, of coursey. Stupid me. Thankings you.'

With their destination confirmed, she stepped away and redialled, first Thierry's phone then Claude's, fighting her frustration as again both diverted to voicemail. She left another message then headed on towards a group of elderly passengers, hovering by the wall-mounted deck plan.

'Ciao, ladies,' she said. 'A pleasant journey so far, I hope?'

'Yes, thank you, dear,' replied the group leader. 'And you are?'

'Er, Deck Security… plain clothes today,' she quickly added, acknowledging her attire.

'Any success finding those two stowaways?'

Eva froze. 'So you've heard all about them?'

'The English guy with big ears, and the gorgeous French lady? But of course! We're doing as the Captain asked, looking everywhere too. Still, I'm sure his full passenger roll-call at 1800 hours this evening will winkle them out.'

'Y–yes, the one in… yikes – five minutes' time!' Eva focused on containing her horror. 'It most certainly will do.'

Eva hurried on, ignoring their further questions, sprinting once she'd turned the corner until back at the cabin door.

Knock, knock, knock… knock-knock-knock…

'Bristo, we have to move – fast!' she stated, quickly entering the cabin.

'What's wrong?'

'The crew are onto us. Can you swim?'

'Yes, sure. But why?'

'We have to jump ship.'

'JUMP SHIP!'

'Yes.'

'Eva, are you crazy?'

'Yes, very! Señora Loco, remember! We either jump or get captured.'

'But…'

'Bristo, we have no choice.'

vi

The officer on the ship's bridge didn't know what hit him. Eva burst through the doorway, flattened him with an almighty punch to the jaw, then turned towards the ship's navigation equipment.

'Okay, Bristo, we have perhaps two minutes to get off the ship.'

'You really mean it, don't you!'

'Yep. Now – take my gun and keep a lookout. I need to check our position.'

'We're on Deck Two by the bridge, aren't we?'

'Yes. I mean – where precisely in the ocean.'

'Oh, I see.'

The bridge was small and narrow. To the left stood a row of untidy, chart-strewn desks, overlooked by a wall of screens. Eva studied each screen in detail, looked back down to the desks and, at the third attempt, found the correct chart and weighed down each corner with a selection of desk-top junk. Grabbing pencil and ruler, she counted the longitude increments along the top, drew a vertical line then repeated the exercise horizontally until the two lines intersected. Then, with an intensity that almost burnt through the paper, she scoured the surrounding expanse of blue, until...

'Bristo!'

'Yes?' he replied, leaning in from the doorway.

'I've transposed the GPS coordinates onto this chart. We are... here, and our best chance is to get... here.' Eva tapped her finger next to a minute black dot. 'There isn't time to make another phone call, and we need to gather kit. If I call out the coordinates of the island we need to get to, can you text them to someone on your team?'

'Yes, of course,' he replied, fumbling for his phone. 'But there's hardly any battery power left. It'll die any second.'

'So might we if we don't get this info across. Are you ready?'

'Yes, go for it.'

'Message to read: "Myself and Eva Avante have escaped from Panama City. Please rescue us from the island with the following coordinates. 4 degrees, 9 minutes, 17 seconds north."'

'17 seconds north... okay,' repeated Trabant, tapping as fast as his keypad would allow.

'84 degrees, 3 minutes, 22 seconds west.'

'22 seconds, er... west.'

'Good. Now quickly send it. We only have moments left.'

Trabant scrolled through his contact list. *Agnes Armstrong, Aunt Rose, Azurite Dry Cleaners...* No good. Come on, where was Bravinger's number? *Babylon Chinese Take-Away, Balmoral Building Services, Bentley...*

'BENTLEY!' exclaimed Trabant. 'Personnel gave me his number.'

'Great! Use that.'

Trabant pressed 'Send' with all his might.

'Has it gone through?'

'Going... going... yes, sent.'

'And you'd better text MI6 HQ too.'

'Yes, of course. Vauxhall Cross Plumbers, come on… NO! Eva, the phone's died!'

'Don't worry,' she replied, grabbing the chart as she ran towards the door. 'Quick, follow me… no, wait! The cameras!'

Trabant followed Eva's eyes to the rectangular CCTV display above the door, showing images of all sections of the ship – in particular the rear of each deck. 'And there's the crew, only one deck below us now! Eva, what do we do?'

'Focus on disabling these cameras, or the crew will see us jump off!' Eva raced across to a computer screen, clicked the mouse, accessed the menu and scanned the list of options.

'A-ha: "Security Settings".'

Trabant ran to Eva's side. 'I can't read Spanish. Can you translate?'

'Yes. This menu says: "Camera Options", "Alarm Options", er…'

'Click on "Camera",' said Trabant. 'Now, is there a sequence or activation link?'

'Er… not that I can see. We have "Remote Assistance", "Image Finder"…'

'Oh, damn… what was it?' mumbled Trabant, looking up to the white tobacco-stained ceiling for inspiration. 'Enter 2-4, er…'

'Bristo, what are you thinking?'

'I had to test an MI6 security jamming program once. It won't last for long…'

'Neither will we if—'

'But it might just… GOT IT! Eva, is there a link called "Cameras"?'

'We're already in it.'

'Oh, okay. What about "Sequence"?'

'Yes… there.'

'Great! Right-click on it. Then on "Control", then click "Rotate". Now, in that long box type: 1-8-0. Now press the

Alt and F6 keys at the same time. Er, okay… now, in that same box type: 1-4-5-5-2-6-8-9-5-6-9 and press… ENTER!'

The cameras didn't budge.

'Perhaps the input code was 1-5-5-4-2-6-8-9-5-6-9. Or even 1-2-5-4-5-6-8…'

Eva turned in a flash towards the pole-axed ship's officer, and began shaking him by the collar. 'Señor, wake up! Turn the cameras off or I throw you overboard.'

'Huh?'

'Eva, what do the words "Cámara" and "subir" mean?'

'Camera… up. Bristo!' she exclaimed, dropping the man back to the floor. 'That's it!'

Trabant clicked the mouse repeatedly, then looked back to the cameras… and waited, but not for long… until all five shuddered in displeasure, then reluctantly raised up, until finally pointing directly at the clear blue sky; the glorious sight confirmed by each and every CCTV screen.

'Bristo, I love you!' exclaimed Eva, kissing him hard on the lips. 'You're not only gorgeous, but a computer genius too.'

'Well, I…'

The sound of voices ended their embrace. They ran outside, and peered over the railings to see seven, maybe eight crew members spread across like a police search-line, advancing towards the stern, passing amongst the lines of startled passengers, double-checking every face, probing every alcove.

'Eva, they'll soon be climbing the stairs.'

'Yes. So it's time for our swim. Quick – this way!'

vii

The upper deck was deserted. They ran across it, past the rows of empty sun-loungers to a small kiosk, which was closed.

Eva took the gun, covered it with a seat cushion to minimise the resonance, then shot open the lock. 'I'll grab supplies. Can you get us two life-jackets,' she said, nodding towards the dispenser on the railings.

'Sure.' Trabant ran across and opened the front. 'It's empty!'

'Never mind!' replied Eva, frantically stuffing supplies into a black holdall, itself grabbed from a shelf. 'Use this.'

They ran to the stern railings. Eva detoured to a red-and-white coffin-shaped container, bundled out the folded life-raft, closed the lid to cover their trail then immediately pulled the raft's ripcord. In a matter of seconds the raft took shape, as the internal gas cylinder rapidly exhaled.

'Okay, Bristo – put your jacket, shoes, socks and anything else heavy inside the holdall. My trainers too, please,' she added, frantically kicking them off.

As the flat rubber sheets of the life-raft began to fill out, Eva worked furiously, attaching two lengths of rope to the raft's nose ring – one leading to the black holdall, the other tied securely around her waist. 'Now, help me lower this over the back.'

Trabant did so, until the raft dangled over the edge, and the holdall balanced precariously on the outer ledge, with nothing else between them and the water but one almighty drop.

'We're not really going to…'

'Yes, we *are* really going to. Put on your buoyancy device, climb over the railings next to me, and when I say, jump as far away from the stern as possible. Keep your arms tight to your body, your legs closed, your head and body dead straight. Hold your breath as long as you possibly can, then breathe out very slowly, by which time you'll be back at the surface. Ready?'

'Not really.'

'On the count of three. One, two, three – JUMP!'

'Aaaaaahhhhhh…'

Eerie silence…

Even more eerie… splosh!

206

The surface was hard as ice. Over and over they spun in the washing machine of undercurrents, until the huge propellers finally despatched them to the great dark abyss beneath. Eva kicked with all her might to the surface, gasped for breath then immediately began looking for Trabant.

'Bristo?' she called, as loud as she dared with the *Cornelia Cortez* still so close.

No reply.

She began to pull the life-raft closer, and tugged on the other line as well, praying that the holdall was still attached; that the rope was strong enough to support it. It was. The line was taut. And the swells raised her just enough to see the hive of activity back on board. Crew members were running in every direction, but none had yet peered back down into the churning wake, which they would the moment the life-raft was discovered missing. But by then, Eva prayed, the line of the horizon would have mercifully intervened.

'Bristo?'

Still no reply.

She ducked her head beneath the surface and squinted through the blurry haze of plankton, but all she could see was the holdall's rope disappearing into the depths. She resurfaced, wiped her eyes then looked around again. Suddenly, over the peak of another huge swell, appeared the smiling brown-and-yellow face of a... giraffe?

'Huh?'

'Eva – I'm h-here!' he replied, clinging to the neck of the giraffe-shaped inflatable rubber ring Eva had pilfered from the ship's kiosk.

'Thank heavens! I thought I'd lost you.' She swam towards him, towing the life-raft, feeling the weight of the holdall hanging in the depths beneath. 'Are you okay?' she asked, now holding him close.

'Yes, but I think I've lost a cuff-link. How are you?'

207

'I'll be better once inside the raft. After you…'

'No, please – ladies first.'

'Such a gentleman.' Eva smiled then kicked hard, pulling herself up in one efficient movement. Trabant handed up the giraffe, watched it disappear inside, took Eva's hand and clambered up himself.

'Good work. Now, help me retrieve the holdall.'

They pulled on the rope with all their might, as if reeling in a monster game-fish, until at last – with one final almighty effort – they lifted the holdall up out of the water, and over the raft's lip.

'Gee, what's inside – gold bullion?'

'Things to keep us alive.' But Eva's eyes remained fixed on the slowly fading ship. 'Okay, if you can get these oars into position,' she continued, pointing to the two poles Velcroed to the floor, 'I'll check our bearing then we'll get rowing.'

'Where did you get that from?' asked Trabant, seeing the compass hanging round her neck.

'The ship's bridge.' She placed it flat on the body of the raft, waited until the arrow settled then aligned the bezel. 'The island is south-west, which is… that way,' she pointed, with assurance. 'We'll recheck our position every twenty oar strokes, to ensure we're on course. By my reckoning, we'll be there in two hours maximum, subject to the *Cornelia Cortez* not spotting us. So let's get rowing – fast!'

19

A Definition of Paradise

THE WINDS AND TIDES had been kind. Yet Eva and Trabant continued to row with all their might, not stopping until the *Cornelia Cortez* had finally disappeared over the rolling horizon.

'I thought she'd never vanish,' puffed Trabant.

'Me too,' replied Eva. 'Let's take a short break and catch our breath. Here, have some water.'

'Thanks.' Trabant swigged the bottle and passed it back. 'Are we on course?'

'Yes, definitely,' replied Eva, checking the compass bearing. 'It's straight ahead.'

They both peered ahead, scanning the blank horizon for the island they so desperately needed to reach.

'I've never seen so much water in all my life,' mused Trabant.

'A consistent, steady pace is the trick,' said Eva. 'And to drink lots of bottled water. We mustn't dehydrate.'

'Aye, aye, skipper. Any chance of a sandwich?'

Eva smiled. 'Afraid not. I didn't pack any, but I'll cook us a seafood special when we get there. Deal?'

'Deal!'

'Good. So, if you're ready, let's get going.'

They both heaved the oars into the water, and slowly, once again, the raft began to move.

'Land ahoy!' shouted Trabant. 'Gee, I've always wanted to say that.'

Eva turned in a flash. 'We made it!'

They shared a victory embrace, then savoured the view a moment longer.

'Two hours twenty-seven minutes,' beamed Eva. 'Not bad at all.'

'It's like a picture postcard.'

'Yes, our own desert-island paradise. Right, let's quicken the pace and cover the last short distance.'

The outline of the island grew larger with every oar stroke, and the atoll's dense cap of mangroves soon joined the parade of palm trees to form the warmest, lushest welcoming party either of them had ever seen. Barely ten minutes later, Trabant followed Eva over the side and into the refreshing turquoise water. They dragged the raft the last few metres, wading in from waist height, until finally the glistening sand scrunched beneath their feet, and the raft left a shallow graze across the virgin surface as they made for the cover of the mangroves.

'This looks promising,' said Eva, heading towards a small clearing now visible behind an overhang of branches. They ducked underneath, then dragged the raft the last short distance before finally setting it down on the far side.

'So, what do you think?' asked Eva.

Trabant looked around, like a weary traveller inspecting his hotel room after a long and arduous journey. 'I love it!'

With that, he walked across to a large rock, slumped down, closed his eyes and succumbed to the weight of exhaustion. And the sound of the lapping ocean quickly set to work, massaging away the tribulations of their harrowing escape, doing its best to instill calm where horror and dread had once ruled supreme.

Slowly he reopened his eyes and pondered the shimmering blue ocean, across which Eva had somehow navigated. And there she sat, on the rock opposite, running her fingers through that glistening black hair, every inch the seductive mermaid, every inch the most beautiful woman in the world.

'I don't know how you managed to get us here,' he said. 'You've been incredible.'

'Aah, you are the star, Bristo. But our work is not yet done. Night will soon be upon us, and we need to make a shelter, build a fire and eat.'

'Could we order a takeaway,' smiled Trabant. 'You know, under the circumstances…'

'No problem. We'll send smoke signals from the fire.'

'Thank you. But first, please tell me what's in the holdall. I'm dying to know.'

'Oh, nothing too exciting, I'm afraid,' she said, retrieving it from the life-raft and unzipping the top. 'Your jacket; enough bottled water to last three or four days, if we're careful; the chart I used to find this island, ruined but now far from enemy hands. For you: a Panama sunhat, bottle of factor fifty suncream – I know what Englishmen are like in the midday sun; a nice pair of blue beach shorts, a white polo-shirt, flip-flops for us both. And for me: sun oil, a black bikini, straw hat and this white summer dress which I simply couldn't resist.' She giggled, holding it up against herself. 'What do you think?'

'Very nice.'

'Thank you. We'll be the best-dressed couple in the whole Pacific.'

Couple? If only, thought Trabant.

'I grabbed this diving knife too,' she continued, wagging it in the air. 'Will be mighty useful. I lost my gun though; felt it slip from my garter when we hit the water after jumping

211

ship. Some crab is probably wreaking havoc with it as we speak.'

'Yes, they do say gun crime is everywhere these days.'

Eva laughed. 'Indeed it is.'

'I still have my water pistol though,' he added, retrieving it from inside his jacket pocket.

'Where did you get that?'

'From Gunboat's compound. I've never stolen anything before in my life, but as you say, under the circumstances…'

'Very resourceful.' Eva saw that Trabant was beginning to shiver. 'Okay, let's get out of these wet clothes and to work on our tasks.' With that she stood and pulled off her T-shirt to reveal a stomach so flat and toned it reminded Trabant of his mother's old washboard. 'By the way, how's the book?' she continued, now wriggling out of her skirt.

'Hmmm… what book?' replied Trabant, struggling to divert his eyes.

'*The Beginner's Guide To*—'

'Oh… *that* book. Let's see.' He withdrew the remaining contents from his jacket. 'Well, my phone is ruined, but the book… is thankfully intact. Must've been specially treated,' he added, blowing the pages apart.

'That's good to hear. Can't have a beach holiday without a good book. Okay, I'll hang our wet clothes out to dry, then go collect materials for our shelter. Could you make us a nice fire?'

'I'll try,' replied Trabant, speaking with false conviction as he watched her stride down the beach, her golden skin glistening in the sunshine, her black hair dancing in the breeze, her body curvy yet toned, strong yet graceful, supple yet resilient – and totally naked except for the skimpy black knickers and bra.

'Fire?' he mumbled to himself. 'How on earth do you make fire?' At that precise moment, he could barely even remember his name.

212

Eva slotted the final branches of the shelter together, then laid the deflated life-raft down neatly to make a bed.

'Voilà!' she said proudly. 'I always wanted a place by the sea.'

'It looks amazing,' said Trabant, looking up from his huddle of frustration. 'Have you done that before?'

'Not on a desert island. How's the fire going?'

'Not very well. I keep rubbing the sticks together, but can't get a spark.'

Eva knelt down beside him, rooted through the stash of wood and retrieved a flat piece, gently split it open to form a groove and inserted a clump of bone-dry vegetation. Next, she dug a shallow hole in the sand and placed the wood across it.

'It lets in more oxygen to feed the flames,' she said, answering the question in his expression. Then, she ran the tip of a pointed stick to and fro along the groove towards the clump of vegetation. 'Get the idea?'

'U-huh.'

Trabant took over, rubbing back and forth, praying for the lord of fire to make the appearance they so desperately needed.

'That's it,' said Eva. 'Keep going.'

Beads of sweat appeared on his forehead, but Trabant toiled… in the battle of wills… with the wood that offered zero promise of reward.

Back and forth… back and forth…

'How on earth… has mankind… survived all these years?'

'Don't let up now.'

Back and forth… back and forth…

'I don't think I can do this much—'

'Look – smoke!' exclaimed Eva, as the merest wisp rose from the vegetation. 'Now, quickly – blow on it, very gently.'

Trabant did so, and the smoke swayed, pondering its next

move, then, as instantly as a gas hob ignites, transformed into a ball of tiny flames.

'You've done it! Now add some more leaves.'

The flames lapped up their food like a nest of hungry chicks, and quickly doubled in size. 'Wood... I need wood!' said Trabant, all of a fluster.

'Here...'

'We did it, Eva!'

'You did it,' she replied, delighting in his sense of achievement and growing self-worth. 'Now, keep tending it. I'm off to get dinner.'

With his creation complete, Trabant sat back and allowed his eyes to wander along the beach. And there she was again – the most beautiful woman in the world, walking down to the water's edge, basking in her own reconnection with Mother Nature. She turned round and waved, as if feeling his eyes upon her. Trabant waved back, and in that moment realised – that paradise is defined not by where you are, but by whom you are with.

iv

The sun was beginning its descent as the two fish cooked gently on the fire, filling the air with a delightful aroma.

'Eva, what *are* you doing?' asked Trabant, calling back into the shadowy mangroves, perplexed at the sounds of chopping, pouring and hissing of liquids.

'Be patient, Bristo.'

Moments later she was back at his side, holding two glasses. 'Okay, there were a few more things in the bag I didn't tell you about.'

'Like what?'

'The vital accompaniments to any sunset – gin and tonic. Cheers.'

214

'Cheers! But how…?'

'There was more in the kiosk than I let on. Six mini bottles, one large tonic, two limes and two plastic glasses. But sadly… the ice cubes didn't make it.'

'Oh, Eva. I thought you were going to say something really bad then.'

'Gin and tonic without ice *is* really bad.'

They walked forward and sat shoulder to shoulder on a mound of sand, sipping the heady potion and basking in the warmth and comfort it gave. It had been the longest day, and now, with the deep orange sky reflecting across the ocean, they could finally relax and watch the sun swapping shifts with the moon and stars.

'It feels as if we're the only people in the whole world,' said Eva, dreamily.

'Perhaps we're not,' replied Trabant, looking over his shoulder. 'Perhaps there's an indigenous tribe lurking in the shadows.'

'Well, as long as they don't steal our gin and tonic, I don't care.'

'Yes, I hope not. This is delicious.'

'Hey!' exclaimed Eva. 'Maybe they'll have an ice machine.'

Trabant laughed. 'And coasters too.'

'Very good! Coasters, by the coast – I like it. Well, that's decided. We'll invite them over for dinner. Reckon they'll have had fish before?'

'Nah!'

She laughed. 'And talking of which…'

'Eva, before we eat, I just wanted to say, well… thank you, for everything.'

'I think we make a great team,' she replied.

Trabant looked into her eyes; those dark pools of milk chocolate that now sparkled with flecks of orange from the fire's gaze, and hoped, even just for now, that she meant it.

215

'So do I...' he replied.

Nature's dimmer-switch finally brought the day to a close, and as the sun went down as smoothly as the two fish they'd eaten, exhaustion could no longer be repelled.

Trabant followed Eva into the shelter, pulled the blanket of palm leaves up to their shoulders and cuddled up close behind. The sound of breaking waves filled his weary ears, then finally, mercifully, cast them adrift upon nature's lullaby towards the open waters of deep, delicious sleep.

Paradise felt good in his arms. Softly, gently, he kissed her goodnight.

20

As Hard as Roberto Durán

THE ISTHMUS OF PANAMA had never seen such fury.

The Learjet hurried to a standstill upon the runway of Aeropuerto Marcus A Gelabert, and Gunboat Charlie Chávez descended the steps then stomped across the moonlit tarmac towards the awaiting helicopter, with Enrique following close behind.

'Boz, please listen...'

'NO EVEN TALK TO ME, ENRIQUE!' bawled Gunboat, climbing inside then slamming the door so hard it almost broke its hinges. 'UP!' The rotors began to speed up. 'FASTER!'

The copter began to rise.

Gunboat shook his head in continued disbelief. 'One job... that all: keep the English pig lock up. And what do my wife and Raúl do: take him out dancing!'

The national flag of Panama also flapped, sharing the turmoil, as the helicopter quickly descended on Ancon Hill. And the moment it landed, Gunboat kicked open the door and marched across the rooftop of La Fortaleza.

'Boss, I so, so sorry,' whimpered Raúl, at the head of the twenty-strong welcoming committee.

'You gonna be!'

'I'm so angry with señor Trabant,' said Mrs G, also waiting in the porch entrance. 'I took him to the Abajo for lunch, and he just ran—'

'BUT WHY THE HELL YOU TAKE HIM THERE?' shouted Gunboat, walking straight past and into the vast chambers inside.

'Don't raise your voice to me, Charles. You're the one who invited him here!'

'IT WAS NO INVITE! I BRING HIM HERE TO…'

Gunboat cursed his way through the house until he reached the desk in his office. 'BAZOOKA – SCRAM! ENRIQUE – WHERE THE HELL ARE YOU?'

'Here, Boz.'

'Get on the phone. Call everyone – NOW!'

'Everyone?'

'Sí! Every human on this planet. Get them looking for the English pig. NOW!'

Raúl arrived in the office. 'Boss, I really am sorry. I was just choosing a burger, and then…'

Gunboat replied, with barely containable anger. 'Five of my men in hospital, a Panama City taxi driver needing jaw rewire, and captain ocean liner wondering how this beautiful Slovakian lady punch as hard as Roberto Durán.'

'But—'

'And me, EL CAÑONERO, facing biggest embarrassment of my life, because if the English pig no turn up at the rematch, I no only lose everything, but will also be laughing stock of criminal world! And all because of a burger, a couple of rum pintados and an earful of SALSA!'

'Calypso.'

'SHUT UP!'

'No way this going to happen – UNDERSTAND?' Gunboat smashed his fist down hard onto the desk, launching the trio of paperweights and accompanying clutter into the air.

'S-sí, Boss,' gulped Raúl.

'Boz, you want de ducks again?' asked Enrique. 'I've replaced de broken one from last time.'

'No, Enrique, I no want the ducks. I want you to RELEASE THE DOGS!'

Enrique Salvador Sánchez knew exactly what that meant. The dogs were a ferocious network of bounty hunters, who'd leave no stone or informant unturned in the search for their quarry, no matter how politically unsavoury the tactics needed to be. If anyone could find the English pig, it would be the dogs.

'No problem, Boz. I make the call right now.'

'FASTER!' shouted Gunboat, as he stood and walked out onto the balcony. Panama City looked calm. The lights of Casco Viejo twinkled beneath the moonlight, and a few cars crawled north along Avenue Justo Arosemena. But Gunboat looked further afield, across the glittering Pacific Ocean towards the horizon, which he knew held the answer.

'You out there somewhere, Gringo Loco,' he growled to himself. 'And no matter where, I gonna find you.'

21

A Glacier-Blue Conception

SUNLIGHT TICKLED BISTRO TRABANT'S eyes like a feather duster until finally they opened. Slowly he focused, at first on the charred remains of last night's fire, then further out through the mangrove branches to the golden sweep of sand.

'Breakfast!'

'Hmmm? Oh, lovely,' he replied, sitting up then wiping away the last remnants of deep sleep.

'It's fish again, I'm afraid,' said Eva, sitting down beside him. 'And small, sushi-sized ones.'

'Thank you. But I do feel guilty, you know.'

'How come?'

'Well, I have tropical fish at home. I might be eating their cousins.'

Eva contemplated his concern. 'I am sure they will appreciate the extreme circumstances.'

Trabant nodded in agreement, then took a bite.

'I also went to check out the island. It's only a mile in diameter, maybe less. We're so lucky it appeared on the chart.'

'It's a miracle. Any sign of our indigenous tribe?'

'No, we have the place to ourselves. As for our rescuers, they may arrive today, but most likely tomorrow, depending on where they're coming from. So let's make the most of our time. Fancy walking off our breakfast?'

Hand in hand they strolled down to the water's edge, and splashed their feet in the wash.

'Feels like our first day on holiday,' beamed Trabant.

'I think we deserve one. So, Monsieur Secret Agent, which way shall we go – left or right?'

Trabant looked both ways, at the identical sweeps of sand that disappeared behind the clumps of mangroves. 'Er... left.'

They continued on, wading through the water. A solitary bird circled overhead, then touched down on the tallest palm for a well-earned break in its marathon migration.

'So, what made you join the DGSE?' asked Trabant.

'You have my grandmother to thank for that. She was in the French Resistance, during the Second World War.'

'Wow!'

'Yes, she used to climb ladders in the middle of the night to snip phone wires, gather intelligence for the RAF, that kind of stuff. Her kitchen was the nerve centre, where she'd cook lovely chicken casseroles and plot against the Occupation.'

'My grandfather flew Hurricanes for the RAF in the Battle of Britain.'

'Really? He should have stopped by. He'd have been most welcome.' Eva smiled. 'My gran is ninety-three now. Never have I met a woman with such fire in her heart. When I was a child, she would say to me, "Eva, whatever you do, fight and protect your loved ones, your home, your values, and what is right." Once that seed was sown, I only had one destiny.'

Trabant smiled at the fondness of her recollections. 'So what's it really like being a secret agent?'

'Dangerous. Exciting. Rewarding. Most importantly, it gives me the opportunity to make a difference.'

'You're always so cool when there's trouble around.'

'The training is relentless, so things become second nature. Though sometimes it drives me nuts.'

'How do you mean?' asked Trabant.

'Well, for example: if I go to the supermarket, I find myself checking the sight lines; planning how to disable the man by

221

the frozen peas, or what to do if his dachshund suddenly turns on me?'

'Are dachshunds dangerous then?'

'A secret agent must be ready for every eventuality. That's how you have to be – ready to react to the unexpected, in an instant.' Eva clicked her fingers to emphasise the point. 'But I didn't do a good job in France. I should have driven you straight to Paris.'

Trabant shook his head. 'Eva, you saved my life! You were incredible.'

'But if I *had* driven you to Paris then this whole situation would never have arisen.'

'Ah, but then I'd never have had this wonderful view.'

Eva laughed. 'I guess not.'

Trabant pondered the tone of her reply. Whether she was playful or decisive, consumed with self-reproach or beating the living daylights out of an enemy, her French accent remained consistently, hugely sexy. And when she laughed – that wholesome, unaffected, almost childlike laugh – boy, she lit up the world; his world. In fact, surely everyone's world that she...

'What?' he asked, suddenly aware that he too was being inspected, but with a playful curiosity.

'You seem deep in thought.'

'Hmmm... Oh, yes, just er, thinking... that you seem, er... very good at fighting too. Bet you never got picked on at school.'

'Why, did you?'

He declined to answer. 'Have you done martial arts?' he continued, remembering Bravinger's exact same question, a lifetime ago.

'Yes. I took up judo when I was seven. It's a wonderful sport.'

'Are you a black belt?'

'Yes, fourth dan. I've represented my country too. I was very proud.'

'That's brilliant!'

'Thank you. Judo is hugely popular in France. I've trained in karate too, plus in the army they teach you—'

'You were in the army!'

'Yes, I've been around a bit. Not like that…' she quickly added. 'I mean, in a combat kind of way.'

'It must feel great to knock a man out with one punch,' said Trabant, looking to his clenched fist with yearning.

'I'll teach you how, if you like.'

'Would you – really?'

'Yes, of course. But first you have to close your eyes.'

'Okay. Now what?'

Eva's kiss was electric.

'I like you a lot, Monsieur Bristo Trabant. I did from the moment I met you.'

'I like you too, Eva,' he replied, savouring her kiss for as long as possible. 'My mother's name is Evonna. F-fancy that, eh?'

Eva smiled. 'Tell me more about your family, and your surname. I'd like to know.'

'Okay. Well, my family originates from Poland. When my grandfather came to England in 1940 to fly with the RAF, Grandma stayed behind with their twin daughters – Evonna, my mother, and my Aunt Rosalina, known as Aunt Rose, who I now live with in London. When the war ended, Grandpa sent for the family, but Grandma was too ill to travel and sadly passed away shortly after.'

'I'm sorry.'

'Rosalina went to England, but my mother and her childhood sweetheart Petr – my father-to-be – wanted to make the most of the new optimism and opportunities in post-war Germany. They relocated there, and had various jobs, one of the latter ones being in the Trabant factory in Zwickau, in the former East Germany.'

'Ah, yes. Your mother in the paint-shop, your father building the engines, right?'

223

'Yes, exactly. How did....?'

'You said before, when we were in the house in Biot. See – I was paying close attention.' Eva winked. 'I imagine it was a very busy factory.'

'Yes, it was a bustling time. The nation needed affordable transport. Lots of it. The Trabant fitted the bill perfectly. It became the people's car, and that's where my parents' respect and affection for it started.'

'And when were you born?'

'In 1979.'

'In Zwickau?'

'No. By then my parents had moved to Berlin – East Berlin – and were living behind the Berlin Wall. I was too young to know any different, but my mother tells me the oppression was awful.'

'I've only read about it. Must have been horrible.'

Trabant nodded. 'With each year I began to learn. My parents didn't want me growing up in the shadow of the Wall, with its armed guards and barbed-wire checkpoints, but you couldn't just leave. And then there were the spies and informants, making sure everyone toed the line. We had relatives in West Berlin we couldn't even wave to, for fear of getting into trouble.'

'That's crazy!'

'I know. The state wanted us to have zero contact. It had long been panicking over the numbers of East Germans fleeing to the West, and their answer – in 1961 – was to build a wall to stop them. In the following years it grew bigger and bigger. By the time I was born it was enormous. Those fleeing only wanted opportunity, and not to be forced into living under totalitarian rule.'

Eva nodded in agreement.

'It wasn't all bad in the DDR,' continued Trabant. 'Many prices were subsidised, and as a mechanical engineer my father qualified for one of the new-build high-rise flats. It's just that he would listen to the radio and watch television, and see all the goodies the West enjoyed, and become angry at the East German state for not allowing him to provide the same for us.'

'And the Wall, together with the secret police, was the physical enforcement of that ruling,' said Eva.

'Precisely. My father felt entitled to the right to choose where to raise his family, especially after he and mum had moved to East Germany to work in the first place. He simply wanted what *he* – not the state – considered the best for his family. With that choice taken away he began to rebel. He was quite outspoken, and it wasn't long before he drew the attention of the Stasi – the secret police. They'd already put his friend Hector in prison for three years for "speaking against the state". Mum told me it was only a matter of time before father ended up there too. He knew that, and so was constantly thinking of ways to overcome the Wall, for us to escape to the West side. He dug tunnels, built a catapult, even thought of hijacking a plane. None of his attempts worked. Then one day he and some friends bought a carpet delivery van. Me, my mother and father, and at least twenty others squeezed into the back. Someone else then drove it, at incredible speed, through a checkpoint.'

'Oh, my! What happened?'

'It never made it. The border guards opened fire, killing the driver. The van crashed into the Wall. Everyone fled. Mum picked me up in her arms and ran screaming. The border guards were in a frenzy, firing at everyone. Mum got me to safety, but Dad...' Trabant lowered his head, '... was shot dead.'

Eva quickly put her arms around him. 'Oh, Bristo, no! That's terrible.'

'He just wanted a better life for his family, that's all.'

'And you were how old?'

'Three. After that my mother vowed we'd leave East Berlin, but only when it was safe to do so. The memories were too painful to stay forever. She promised me that one day the Wall *would* come down, and we'd go to England to live with Grandpa, and *have* that better life, but to do so we both needed to learn English. So we did. We practised every day, in our tiny kitchen, looking out the window at that ghastly Wall, hoping that one day we would be allowed to pass through it. And finally, seven years later, that day came – 9 November 1989 – the day the Wall came down. We packed everything into the car. You see, Mum and Dad actually owned a Trabant car, and we set off; Mum driving, me in the passenger seat navigating, with all our worldly possessions, and about a hundred rounds of Käsebrötchen – cheese rolls. Maybe that's why I have such a pale complexion.'

Eva smiled, but with respect for the pain of Bristo's story.

'The roads were packed,' he continued. 'Trabant cars everywhere, many literally abandoned the moment people made it into West Berlin. People were dancing in the streets, families were reunited, while many other people headed on further towards places they'd been dreaming about for years – Greece, Holland, France. But my mother and I kept going, on through the night, and caught the ferry to England, to start that new life with Grandpa in the Cotswolds.'

'She sounds like a strong lady.'

'She is.'

'And did you settle in okay?'

'It took a while. Grandpa had lots of friends, but at school no one could pronounce my surname.'

'Why, what is it?'

'Travietzviesvielski.'

'Yes, I can see why,' replied Eva, warmly.

'So – because of the car – one of the teachers suggested we shorten it to Trabant.'

'I like it. Though Travie…vielski is nice too.'

'It made it easier for the other children at school to say,' replied Trabant. 'Looking back it was a natural choice; a sort of nickname. I guess as a family we stood out like a sore thumb, me being driven to school in our Trabant. No one had ever seen one in the Cotswolds before. Everyone seemed to own Mini Metros or Mercedes. To start with I felt a bit self-conscious – not in us having a Trabant, just that I stood out. "Oh, look – it's Bristo Trabant!" my classmates would say. I liked the name, but not that they also loved to tease me, because I was different, because of my ears, because of our car.'

'Some kids can be cruel.'

'That's what happens when you're different. Some people like to poke fun, especially at school.'

Eva gently held his hand. 'And I think that you, Monsieur, are the kind who takes it very much to heart.'

Trabant nodded. 'But in our car and the Trabant name, all I felt was pride, knowing what we went through to even get there.' He then began to smile, with an incredible fondness, as if recalling the very dearest of friends. 'Gletscherblau…' he said, dreamily.

'What's that?'

'The German word for the colour of our car – our Trabant. It means "glacier-blue". We still have it – a 601 model. The paintwork's a little faded, other than that she's good as new. I still maintain her. My mum has very strong feelings for that car.'

'Because of the connection with your father,' said Eva.

'Yes. And also because I was conceived on the back seat – in 1978, after a Sunday picnic overlooking Berlin's Spree River. So you see, I'm a Trabant through and through.' He wiped his eyes. 'I'm sorry. I guess it's just the emotion of the past few days.'

'You've been through too much.' Eva leant forward and kissed him tenderly on the cheek. 'Thank you for telling me your history. I like you even more now, Monsieur Bristo Trabant.'

Never before had words made him feel so good; so warm; so light-headed. She – the most beautiful woman in the world – liked him, and even more than 'a lot!' Wow!

His thoughts gained wings, and began to fly, towards the fantasy of marriage; of church bells and tumbling confetti.

'*Do you, Eva Marianne Avante, take Bristo Huckleberry Trabant to be your lawful wedded husband?*'

'*Oh yes, yes – get that ring on my finger!*'

'*And do you, Bristo Huckleberry Trabant, take Eva Marianne Avante to be your lawful wedded wife?*'

'*Too right.*'

'*Oh, Bristo…*'

'*Oh, Eva…*'

'*I now pronounce you man and wife.*'

(Cheers from the congregation.)

'*You may now kiss the bride.*'

Another kiss of electrical magic.

(Aaaaaahhhs from the congregation.)

And then his speech, which went down a storm, and—

'Earth to Bristo, receiving?'

'Hmmm?'

'Bristo, are you okay?'

'Y-yes. What is it?'

'You were miles away. Have you had too much sun?'

'No, we were just… I mean…'

Eva smiled. 'Did I catch you daydreaming, per chance?'

'A little…'

'I hope it was nice.'

Trabant smiled back. 'Yes, very, but…'

'But what?'

He looked into her eyes, her dark pools of milk chocolate, and saw everything he'd ever wanted. 'Nothing,' he replied softly, before looking away. 'As I said, it was only a dream.'

22

Just Love, That's All...

THE FOLLOWING MORNING THEY set off for another walk, only this time heading to the right, where everything was just as beautiful as the day before, only appearing in reverse order.

'I feel like we've checked into the ultimate health farm,' said Eva.

Trabant closed his eyes to savour her voice, knowing it wouldn't be necessary to hear the voice of every other woman in the world, for he instinctively knew that to him, it would be the most beautiful voice in the world.

'I'm sorry breakfast was fish again,' she continued. 'Gee, what I'd give for a boiled egg.'

'And soldiers?'

Eva laughed. 'I'll settle for the Royal Navy right now. They could rescue us.'

Trabant declined to answer, and Eva detected his dejection. 'Bristo, is everything okay?'

'Yes, I just didn't sleep well.'

'I know. You were tossing and turning all night.'

'Sorry. Did I wake you?'

'Only when you stole the covers,' she smiled. 'Here, come with me,' she continued, leading him by the hand up the beach to the mound of sand where they had savoured their gin and tonics. And as before, they paused to listen to the ocean wash upon the shore, and the gentle breeze ruffle the palm trees. 'This place is *so* good for the soul.'

Trabant stole a glance at Eva's eyes. The dark pools of milk chocolate were warm and alive as ever, but now in preparation for something she wanted to say.

'So tell me, is there a Mrs Trabant back at home?' she asked.

'Only my mum, in Chipping Sodbury.'

'I mean, do you have a wife?'

'Oh, right. No, sorry… I don't.'

'No need to apologise. I'm pleased. How about a girlfriend?'

'No.'

'Lover?'

'No one.'

'No lady at all?'

'Well, Aunt Rose's cat is very fond of me, if that counts?'

'Not really,' she giggled. 'So no one at all?'

'Nope.'

'Well, miracles never cease.'

'How do you mean?'

'Oh, come on. You are a very handsome man. I am sure you have plenty of admirers back home?'

Plural? Just one would be nice.

'It's okay,' continued Eva, playfully nudging him. 'You can tell me.'

'Honestly, there's no one. There was in the past, but not for a while now.' Trabant eyed her with suspicion. 'Why?'

'I'd just like to understand why on earth you are single?'

'I guess I'm not very, you know… good with women.'

'Why? Do you have a deep, dark secret?'

'No.'

'Then is it a confidence thing?'

'Perhaps,' replied Trabant, shrugging his shoulders.

'Because most women *do* like their men to be confident.'

'I rest my case.'

'But I, Monsieur Secret Agent, am not most women. For me, it is the soul that counts.'

Trabant offered a half-smile. 'Many people seem to find relationships easy. I guess I'm just not one of those people.'

'Perhaps the next lady will be the one.'

'Perhaps,' he replied, jabbing a stick into the sand.

'You have a very low opinion of yourself.'

Trabant jabbed the stick with greater intensity. 'And what about you?' he said. 'I bet there's someone in your life?'

Despite her silence he hoped she would answer. He needed her confirmation, to finally rid his mind of any foolish, lingering hopes.

'There is no one. I was married. He died. That is it.'

She grabbed a handful of sand, held it tightly then watched the golden grains cascade through her open fingers. Trabant contemplated the sudden pause in her joviality, and her obvious pain, then put down his stick, reached across and gently placed his hand on hers.

Eva looked up from the pyramid of sand, and their eyes locked. 'I think you are very special, Monsieur Bristo Trabant.'

Trabant felt the connection, but looked away, down the beach, across the rippling surface and far out to sea; giddy at the realisation of just how much he liked her…

… and in no doubt how monstrous the pain would be to love then lose the most beautiful woman in the world; a pain he knew would inevitably arise, and a pain from which he knew he would never recover.

Trabant shook his head. Pain was upon him again, his old adversary. He knew it too well. The loss of his father at the age of three continued to have a profound effect. Such a waste of the most wonderful life. And for what? The enforcement of a political ideal. Trabant scrunched his eyes. His mother had been robbed of her devoted husband. He'd been deprived of a loving father, and the bond to share through his formative years, and beyond. Not a day went past without him in his thoughts. Not an anniversary passed without the flood of tears

231

and despair. Yes, pain had done its worst; made Trabant the man he was today: distant, closed-off, and afraid to open up and pursue what he truly wanted, for fear of yet more pain, of which he'd had quite enough already.

'Bristo?'

'Hmmm…'

'May I ask a question?'

He nodded.

'What if there was a woman who really liked you, who wouldn't want to change a thing about you. A woman whose feelings were true, who needed you as much as you needed her. What then?'

Trabant shrugged his shoulders.

'Ah, come on. What would you do – seize the moment, or let it pass you by?'

'Er…'

'Shall I spell it out for you?' she asked.

'Might save some time.'

'Well, Monsieur Secret Agent, I am that woman. There, I've said it! So how about you and I getting together?'

Trabant scrunched his eyes once more.

Eva leant closer. 'I have made my feelings perfectly clear. I want to be with you, you know – as boyfriend and girlfriend. Is that plain enough?'

'You're crazy.'

'Señora Loco, remember? But seriously, I know what I like, and I like you.'

Trabant looked out to the horizon. A scattering of fluffy, cotton-wool clouds drifted without concern, urging him to embrace the same outlook.

'So, what do you say?' asked Eva.

Silence.

'If you don't answer I'll tell *every* intelligence agency that MI6's new recruit wears Rupert Bear boxer shorts.'

'Tell who you like. I don't care.'

'Bristo, I have no wish to be pushy, but in my line of work, well… I do not have the luxury of time. It is important to learn the lessons of the past, but also to live for *right now* and the *future*; to make happiness happen. That's my motto.'

'That's two mottos, isn't it?'

'Yes. I have many. But the point is, if I don't set the ball rolling, then I fear nothing will ever happen between us. So?'

Trabant looked into her eyes – those dark pools of milk chocolate into which he should dive headfirst and never resurface. 'Eva, with all my heart…'

'You'll hurt your bum sitting on the fence, so how about a straight *yes* or *no*?'

Trabant closed his eyes. 'No.'

The bird in the summit of the tallest tree shook its head in disbelief, then turned its back. And Eva's body slumped, and her eyes blinked as the word sunk in. 'Oh, I hoped…'

Trabant lowered his head, and instantly regretted the hurt he had caused. 'It's not you, it's me.'

'Are we so different?' she asked.

'Yes. You are champagne, and I am lemonade.'

'I think you have put me on a pedestal.'

'I couldn't help it,' he replied, apologetically.

'But I didn't ask for that. I'm just like everybody else, with needs too, and a heart I want to give to you – just you – right here and now. I have offered myself to you on a plate. If you do not wish to gorge yourself then there is not much else I can do.'

'Eva, you are far too nice to be gorged on.'

'Maybe I want to be gorged on, and devoured too. What's wrong? Aren't you hungry?'

'I'm starving.'

'Then tuck in!' she exclaimed.

'I'd love to.'

'But…?'

'I think too much of you to take advantage.'

'Alone on a desert island. Most men would try their luck.'

'But I'm not "most men". Eva, don't you see? You're an incredible woman,' he said, blurting out what he'd hoped to contain. 'And I'm just, well… me.'

Eva gave him a stern look. 'If you think you're no good, Monsieur, then you'd better think again.'

'Y-yes, okay,' replied Trabant hastily, like a naughty child promising to never do it again.

'I'd love to be with you, Bristo,' she continued.

Trabant rubbed his eyes, trying to dispel his turmoil. 'But it couldn't work.'

'Why?'

'I just think it's for the best.'

'Whose best – yours?' Eva turned away, then back again quickly, her eyes darting with emotion. 'How about loved? Am I too nice for that too?'

'No, you're perfect. As I say, it's me.'

She shook her head with confusion. 'Bristo, if you do not have the same feelings then just tell me, and I will totally understand.'

'Eva, I have huge feelings for you.'

'But not the same feelings?'

'Yes, okay, the exact same feelings.'

Trabant stood up, as he confronted the enormity of what he'd always wanted, and the absolute conviction that to finally grasp it was simply too big a risk. 'It's exactly that which…'

'Which is what? Tell me, Bristo, please.'

Eva stood and faced Trabant, with her back to the ocean, not understanding his resistance, her emotion swelling like the currents beyond. Couldn't he see his feelings were safe with her. He had nothing to fear, and if unworthiness was his only objection, then his argument was flawed.

'Just love, Bristo – that's all. No tricks. No catches. Please, tell me. What precisely is it you're afraid of?'

Trabant looked into her eyes, then to something moving beyond her shoulder.

'A boat!'

'You're afraid of a boat!?!' she exclaimed. 'What's that got to do with—'

'No, Eva, a boat – heading straight for us. We're rescued!'

ii

They ran to the water's edge and waved furiously. The landing craft was racing towards the beach, with one man on board, and the waves splashed high and wide across the bow, like sprays of celebratory champagne. Further offshore, waiting patiently, a larger vessel shimmered in the dazzling sunlight.

'Quick, let's collect our belongings,' she exclaimed.

They put everything into the black holdall and ran back down to the water's edge. The boat had already covered the remaining distance, and was now stationary a few metres from the shore.

'It's Bentley himself,' smiled Eva.

And so it was. The Priority Surveillance Unit's top field operative jumped into the water and strode onto the beach.

'Sorry to keep you. Got here as soon as I could.'

'Boy are we glad to see you,' said Eva, her dislike of Bentley temporarily diluted by the euphoria of rescue.

He stepped forward to shake Trabant's hand. 'Hello, we haven't actually met before. You've caused quite a stir around the world.'

'Yes, I'm truly sorry for all the trouble.'

Eva looked at Trabant and smiled.

'Well, if you're both ready,' said Bentley, gesturing towards the boat, 'let's get you back to mother ship. I think you'll be suitably impressed.'

The huge, white motor yacht sat patiently amid the rolling swells, its rows of tinted windows wrapping the craft like a pair of designer sunglasses. On the stern, the Panamanian flag danced within the warm breeze. And above, two men stood on the flybridge, deep in conversation.

'This is a lovely boat,' said Trabant, as the landing craft pulled alongside.

'Yes, I agree, she's a beauty,' replied Bentley, gesturing for them to climb onto the rear platform.

Trabant followed Eva up the stainless steel steps and onto the main deck. Bentley came up last then shuffled past, dropped their holdall to the floor, turned back and faced them again, leaning against the open doorframe.

'The last ship we were on was called *Cornelia Cortez*,' said Trabant. 'What's this one called?'

Bentley did not reply. Instead he just clicked his fingers, and immediately two men appeared through the doorway, dressed in black.

'Eva, w-why are they pointing guns at us?'

In that instant she understood precisely. 'How much is Gunboat paying you, Bentley?' she sneered.

'A damn sight more than the British Secret Service. Oh, come on, Agent Avante, don't act all surprised. I've been on Gunboat's payroll for years. Think about it. Could I afford houses in Monaco, Milan, and a brand new Ferrari on my MI6 salary? No chance. I've been a servant without proper reward for too long.'

Trabant backed away as his nightmare returned. As he did so, the gunmen intensified their aim.

'I'd stand perfectly still if I were you,' hissed Bentley. 'It's been a long journey, and my men are extremely bored. One more step and…'

'At least let us sit,' scowled Eva, her eyes darting towards the holdall, wondering if she could reach the diving knife inside.

'Very well. But with your hands on your knees.'

They both eased onto the cushioned deck-seats.

'Won't Bravinger be wondering where you are?' asked Eva.

'He lets me do things my way.'

'But the coordinates,' she countered. 'The phone records will show Bristo texting you our location.'

'Sure, but in my report I'll say you were nowhere to be seen. Perhaps you never made it. Perhaps Gunboat found you first.' Bentley shouted up to the flybridge. 'Skipper, you up there?'

'Yes, sir.'

'Set a course for Panama. Radio ahead. Tell them I have a cargo that will please Gunboat immensely. And tell them we'll be home in time for tea.'

'Yes, sir,' replied the skipper, enthusiastically.

From the bow area, a huge chain rattled as the anchor was retrieved. The great engines fired into life, churning the water into whirlpools of froth, before gaining power and digging harder into the dark azure.

'I am so sorry, Bristo,' said Eva. 'You cannot plan for betrayal.'

Trabant tried to reply, but he had no words. His eyes flicked from point to point, unsure where to settle until finally choosing the familiarity of his toes. Happiness had been theirs, just for a moment, only to be shattered by the wolf in sheep's clothing.

Slowly, dejectedly, he looked up to their captor. 'I thought you were supposed to be loyal,' he said.

'I am,' replied Bentley. 'To myself.'

23

The Snarling Contempt of Punta Pacifica

THE BRONZE STATUE OF Vasco Núñez de Balboa peered out across the glistening splendour of the Pacific Ocean; Spanish flag in one hand, sword in the other. At his feet, the great ocean lapped the rocky coastline, and behind – where in 1513 the densest of mangrove forests had once prevailed – stood the sprawling concrete jungle of Panama City, proud and defiant amid the searing afternoon haze.

ii

The skipper guided the huge motor yacht through the break-water entrance to the private marina, and up alongside the long, wooden jetty. The twin props bubbled their final revolutions, and once the crew had secured the ropes, he finally killed the engines.

At the icy command of an AK-47, Eva and Trabant walked down the gangway, along the jetty and on towards the awaiting helicopter. To the left, beyond the curls of razor wire, oblivious traffic hurtled along the waterfront. And to the right, perhaps twenty metres but seemingly a world away, lay an armada of pleasure craft, neatly moored on the safe side of the boardwalk.

With gun in hand and reward in mind, Bentley shoved the prisoners inside the helicopter, climbed in himself and nodded to the pilot. In no time they were rising, high above the metropolis beneath, and turning in an arc that brought them dead in line with Ancon Hill. Trabant lowered his head, disbelieving the hand dealt by the man sat in front. But he had no time to wallow, as Eva nudged him then gave a look of granite. Trabant instantly knew what it meant, that despite the odds, she would never, ever give in. And neither must he.

iii

The helicopter touched down on the huge G-shaped landing pad. And there he stood, on the balcony outside, the immense, smouldering outline of the man himself, Gunboat Charlie Chávez, dressed in customary garish Bermuda shirt.

Bentley beckoned the prisoners out with his snub-nosed gun, then on through the welcoming committee of armed men and inside La Fortaleza, down the two flights of stairs, along the corridor and out into the large open-plan office where, at the large desk, a bear-like paw drummed impatiently.

'At last!' scowled Gunboat. 'The card cheat and the interfering hostess. Bentley, you done me proud.'

'My pleasure,' replied Bentley, sneering at Eva.

'Enrique, you can call off the dogs now!'

'Sí, Boz!' Enrique quickly dialled his mobile. The dogs would understand, though not without a sense of dejection at being prematurely called to heel.

Gunboat turned back to the prisoners. 'So, you enjoy your desert island vacation?'

'Yes, thank you,' replied Eva. 'It was delightful.'

Gunboat eyed them both with flame-thrower intensity. 'You seriously think you could escape me, huh?'

'It wasn't exactly hard,' lied Eva, for all the Herculean effort it had taken.

'But I always gonna find you. No matter where you hide.

Your fate was seal when you interrupt in Le Club Maritime du Soleil.'

'I disagree,' said Eva.

'I tell you!'

'We'll see about that.'

Gunboat's face contorted in frustration. 'Why is it women always have to have last word? My wife is exactly the same.'

'That's because I'm right and you're wrong.'

'ENOUGH!' Gunboat slammed a huge fist down on the desk, launching the same traumatised paperweights into orbit. 'I *always* have final word. Tomorrow is Saturday, the day of the rematch. The running order is simple: I win the card game, and then you, señor Trabant, will die. But no by bullet or blade. Oh no, I devise *far* more gruesome and spectacular death; the kind that will leave my guests tremble.'

'"Trembling" you mean?' said Eva.

'Sí. Trembling. Señor Gringo Loco will die before our—'

'Sorry, who is this señor Gringo…?' asked Eva.

'That's me,' replied Trabant.

'Sí! He will die, then my good name and reputation will be restore, and everything get back to normal.'

Eva feigned a look of crushing disappointment. 'Oh, damn, I forgot. Bristo and I already have plans for Saturday. Terribly sorry.'

'Do we?' whispered Trabant.

'Yes,' replied Eva, loud enough for the room to hear. 'I'm taking you to see the Moulin Rouge, in Paris – remember?'

Gunboat glared at Eva. 'You will also pay the ultimate price.'

'No, the tickets were free. I have a friend who—'

'SHUT UP!' screamed Gunboat, jumping to his feet. 'YOU WILL DIE, BOTH OF YOU, THE PRICE FOR MESSING WITH ME – EL CAÑONERO, GUNBOAT CHARLIE CHÁVEZ!'

'We'll see,' smiled Eva, defiantly.

Gunboat slowly sat back down in his chair. 'Just who the hell you think you are, stopping me kill this man in front of my guests?'

'A normal decent human being,' replied Eva, 'with a clear sense of right and wrong, that's who. You should try it sometime.'

'I expect the DGSE to keep eyes on my affairs, but no to poke its nose and stir everything up.' Gunboat smiled at Eva's wide-eyed reaction. 'Oh yes, señor Bentley tell me *all* about your surveillance operation. I hope you found me interesting?'

'To be honest, you're rather boring.'

'Boring!?!'

'Yes.'

Gunboat turned to Enrique for reassurance. 'Am I boring?'

'No, Boz. She winding you up. You de greatest!'

Gunboat turned back to Eva with eyes like machete blades. 'Yeah, d'ya hear that? I the greatest, and you better remember it.'

'I admit, you *are* much bigger in real life.'

'You say I'm fat?'

Eva shrugged her shoulders.

'You can die right now if you want?'

'I'd rather not. My job is to put you behind bars, and that is exactly what I *shall* do.'

Gunboat laughed. 'Oh come on, Agent Avante. Me behind bars? Everyone know that will *never* happen.'

Eva appreciated the chilling degree of truth to Gunboat's words, but pressed on regardless. 'I'm speaking for the countless victims of the wars you fuel. My people will not stop until—'

'Both MI6 and DGSE will pretend the whole thing never happen,' replied Gunboat. 'You know that well as I do.'

Trabant shuddered that Gunboat knew both their real employers.

'But you cannot kill two secret agents,' replied Eva, 'and expect to get away with it.'

'You may be loss to your organisation, Agent Avante, but as for señor Loco? Come on, MI6 must really be scrape the barrel if he the best they could send.'

'He is not a full-time agent,' protested Eva. 'He's only a stand-in.'

'He certainly no look the part,' replied Gunboat. 'Especially with them big ears. And as for that book – *The Beginner's Guide To Being Secret Agent*. What a load of baloney that is.'

'We all have to start somewhere,' said Eva.

'And now I bring it to an end.'

'Yes,' agreed Bentley. 'He certainly has to die.'

'You can wipe that smirk off your face, Bentley,' hissed Eva. 'We trusted you.'

'Trust is for losers, and there's no better example of a loser than the man you're standing next to.'

'He's a better man than you'll ever be.'

'Ha! Don't make me laugh. He's just like his namesake – that horrible little East German car. Bland, ugly and completely unsophisticated.'

Enrique and Raúl laughed out loud. Gunboat, too, until stopped by a stark realisation. 'Eh! I no actually know much about the Trabant.'

'Let me enlighten you,' said Bentley. 'Produced during the Cold War era and sold throughout the communist bloc, Trabants were cheap, nasty and very simple.'

'I prefer uncomplicated,' countered Eva. 'And they're also reliable, dependable, and have a really cute shape.'

'Y-you really think so?' asked Trabant.

'For sure.'

'But they're made out of plastic!' laughed Bentley.

'Duroplast, to be precise,' replied Trabant. 'It's a fibre-reinforced plastic.'

'Yeah, reinforced with what – cardboard?'

'No! Cotton or wool, or glass fibres. And that was just the

outer panels. The monocoque was steel. Anyway, Duroplast was only developed out of necessity. The Soviet Union had stripped our country of industrial equipment, and the West had put a trade embargo on steel. We had to find an alternative.'

'Whatever!' laughed Bentley. 'Anyone who owned a Trabant had one aim in life – to change it for something else.'

'That's simply not true. It was the car of the people. They were loved, still are, *and* over three million were sold.'

'Rubbish!'

'Fact!'

'Eh, at last!' beamed Gunboat. 'Señor Gringo Loco got some fire in his belly!'

Trabant's eyes flickered with emotion.

'No stop now, señor,' continued Gunboat, 'I like the sound of this car. It rise up against the odds, like me. It keep going, like me. And also like me – it got balls! Continue...'

'Well, I just think Bentley should get his facts straight.'

'You tell 'em, Bristo.' Eva smiled, fully understanding his sentiment, and the enormity of the comparisons between car and man. The Trabant was a car defined by its history, by its part in a changing world, and by how it symbolised the hopes and dreams of a downtrodden people, standing strong, until finally, together, they had brought down the Berlin Wall, and triumphed against the most impossible oppression.

Eva could feel it – the energy of the underdog, and perhaps the Trabant had a more inspiring and heart-warming story to tell than any other car in history. Yet still it encountered this ridicule. Well, it deserved better than that. Bristo deserved better than that. For he too was defined by a history, of personal loss and hardship, yet despite that he too strived for better, and like the car, he too would never stand alone, for she would be with him, in his time of need, to ensure he triumphed against yet another Berlin Wall-sized predicament.

'Well, they also last for years,' continued Trabant, 'and represent hope, companionship and loyalty.'

'Yeah, qualities that you, Bentley,' added Eva, 'wouldn't recognise if they slapped you round the face.'

'Undeniably a very long life span,' scoffed Bentley, 'which clearly neither of you have.'

'Don't be so sure of that,' said Eva.

'Eh, no mock too much, señor Bentley,' growled Gunboat. 'It easy to mock when born with silver spoons in the mouth.'

Bentley ignored Gunboat's remark. 'The thing is, Agent Avante, I too am like my namesake: distinguished, luxurious, and with no expense spared, if you catch my drift.'

'The Bentley marque is wonderful. But you, Agent Bentley, are a disgrace to your country. You too, Gunboat.'

'SILENCE!' Gunboat leant forward and pointed his finger like a projectile missile. '*I* make the rules, and I'll have you know, the people of Panama love me!'

'I don't think—'

'ENOUGH!' shouted Gunboat. 'Enrique – take them to the aquarium.'

iv

The helicopter rose through the mangrove canopy, then turned east, following the coastline towards the snarling contempt of Punta Pacifica.

Eva looked closely at the peninsula, at its squash of million-dollar high-rises and hotels. And there, just beyond on the waterfront, stood the huge square building emblazoned with the bold red lettering, 'Panama City Aquarium'. It was a five-storey, glass-covered Rubik's cube of a building, with a curious silver dome upon its roof, and the ground-floor perimeter consisting of elaborate gardens and shark-shaped hedges. And

244

at the rear, a loading compound, enclosed by a twelve-foot-high, wrought-iron fence.

The helicopter touched down onto the public car park. Two dozen guards were already in position with weapons aimed. The head guard stepped forward and opened the door.

'Move!'

Trabant and Eva were ushered across the tarmac and through an opening iron gate, then up the short flight of steps and on past a never-ending line of men ferrying boxes marked 'Caviar' or 'Nibbles'. Finally the guard stopped outside a doorway opposite a staircase. The adjacent sign read: 'Stairs to Upper Level One and Conference Theatre.'

'Is that where the rematch will take place?' asked Eva.

'Sí, and it'll be a full house too. Now, get in here.'

Eva begrudgingly stepped inside, noting the thickness of the door, which way it opened, and the position of the hinges. Trabant followed close behind, and was barely inside before the heavy-gauge door slammed shut behind.

Their cell was like the inside of a cargo container, barren of anything except two chairs, a wooden table and a dangling naked light-bulb. Eva immediately set to work, feeling along each wall in turn, from floor to ceiling, for any avenue of escape.

'Any luck?' asked Trabant, inspecting the opposite wall.

'No. We'll need an explosive missile to break out of this place. Our only chance of escape may be in the morning, when they collect you for the rematch. Boy, I wish we still had the holdall.'

'Why, is it gin and tonic time?'

'I was thinking more of the diving knife. Come on, let's stand on the chairs and check the ceiling. We only need a few broken welds and we might be able to push through.'

As Trabant retrieved the chairs, the cell door opened and a guard threw a bag into the middle of the floor. 'Dinner.

Compliments of Gunboat,' he said indifferently, before slamming the door behind him.

Eva stepped forward and inspected the contents. 'Ooh, Chinese takeaway. Crispy aromatic duck; noodles, prawn crackers, and some water. You hungry?'

'Starving.'

'Okay, let's eat, then we'll formulate a plan. They think it's all over, Bristo, but it never is. Not until the fat lady sings.'

'Really?' he replied, with slight confusion. 'I didn't know Mrs G was in the choir?'

Eva smiled, broke a prawn cracker in two and gave Trabant half.

'Thank you,' he replied.

'You're welcome.'

'No, I mean thank you for everything. And I'm sorry about our conversation on the desert island. You know, the one where I said no to us getting together, as boyfriend and girlfriend.'

'Oh, that one.'

'Yes, that one. It's just that, well... I—'

'It's okay. I'm sorry for giving you a hard time.'

'You didn't.'

'I think I did, a little. It's my Corsican heritage. My father is from Ajaccio. We can both get a touch feisty. It's only because I like you, a lot.'

'And I like you, Eva.'

She leant closer and nudged his arm. 'I'll tell you something else, too.'

'What's that?'

'You can reject me as many times as you like, but you will never stop me caring.'

246

24

Mountain Goats and Capsules

FROM FIRST LIGHT, PRIVATE jets dominated the Panama City sky, homing in from far and wide to complete their final descent into Aeropuerto Marcos A Gelabert.

Once landed, the passengers quickly transferred to the awaiting helicopter shuttle service, which relayed them onwards to the car parks surrounding the Panama City Aquarium.

Enrique checked his watch and smiled. Phase One – the forty-five-minute window from first helicopter touchdown to last guest stepping into the reception area, had gone exactly to schedule; the whole process expertly synchronised by Aquarium Air Traffic Control, namely Nuña, Rico and his cousin Alhambra. Every guest had arrived. No one was late.

The guest list totalled three hundred and twenty-five, consisting of the world's top one hundred criminal elite, together with their entourages of advisors and bodyguards, many of whom were only hired as fashion accessories, not as necessary business tools.

Enrique updated his clipboard. Phase One – check. Now, Phase Two: the thirty-minute interval for socialising, also seemed to be progressing without complication, as old acquaintances hugged and reminisced down the well-trodden, yet shady cobbles of memory lane.

Sicilian Mafia chief Luca Canavelli divulged cookery tips to fellow Mafiosi from Serbia, Albania and Bulgaria. Infamous Spanish money launderer Allozo Tinto, star of the recent reality

TV programme *I'm A Maximum Security Prisoner, Get Me Out Of Here,* signed autographs and talked dollars with Brazilian financier Paolo Roberto Varienga. The Union Corse discussed student exchange with the Colombian drug cartels. The Neapolitan Camorra battled the Calabrian Ndrangheta at table football. Sergei Mischailov and his Russian mafia comrades traded diamond industry gossip with their Belgian counterparts. 'Double Tap' Hurunguru and his fellow African warlords drooled over the AH-64 Apache attack helicopter raffle prize. Señor Imran showed Anton Gizon, and a very nervous Frankie Fugazi, photos of his beloved new F-16 Falcon fighter jet. Azara Pampita Rázzon swapped holiday-home details with the heads of the New York Families. Nedho 'the Hook' Hamsho interrogated the aquarium staff about the varieties of triggerfish on show. The Jamaican Yardies discussed Chicago Blues with the men from New Orleans, and both the Chinese Triads and the Japanese Yakuza struggled to understand a single word the Irish mob were saying.

And all the while, Gunboat mingled, acting the perfect host, but with revenge firmly on his mind.

'Everyone seems to be making merry,' said Bentley, appearing from nowhere. 'In which case, I'll make myself scarce. Don't want anyone recognising me.'

'You can sit by de—' But Bentley had already gone. Enrique shrugged his shoulders, rechecked his watch then beckoned a guard over. 'Get de English pig ready. It time for Phase Dree.'

ii

The cell door opened with a slow, taunting creak. Three guards stepped inside, with AK-47s pointed. 'Okay, it's time to go.'

Trabant sat at the table, cradling his stomach, moaning incoherently.

'Get up! Put these shackles on,' barked a guard.

'He can't,' replied Eva, at his side, consumed with worry. 'He's sick. Can't you see?'

'I don't care. I have my orders.'

'Well, he can't move! Take a look yourself.'

The guard paced forward, huffing and grumbling, checking his watch. 'How long's he been like this?'

'All night!' she replied. 'I think it's food poisoning.'

'Hey, there's nothing wrong with señora Fang's local take-away.'

The guard shook Trabant by the shoulder, disconcerted by his limp response.

'Perhaps the other guards could have a closer look?' suggested Eva.

The guard beckoned his two colleagues. 'See what you make of this, boys.'

Trabant lowered his head to draw them closer still. The moment all three were in range, Eva exploded into action. Her forward kick was perhaps the hardest she'd ever delivered, knocking the first guard clean unconscious before he hit the deck. Vicious punches to jaw and groin felled the second. The third was barely quick enough to raise his gun, as Eva swung a clenched fist to his temple. The impact landed, but not hard enough. He fell, but grabbed Eva's arm in the process, pulling her down with him, but also squeezing the trigger, firing bullets in every direction. Trabant – halfway back across the room to help Eva – dived under the table for cover. The noise was deafening; the prospects for survival lessening by the second. And still Eva wrestled for control of the guard's gun – rolling, scrabbling, until finally the magazine emptied.

'Eva?' Trabant tentatively raised his head to see the other two guards lying motionless – one most certainly dead, the other groaning loudly. And there, mercifully, was Eva, punching the last shreds of consciousness out of the remaining guard's head.

'Your plan worked!'

'Yes... just,' Eva replied, before suddenly freezing at the sound of advancing footsteps. 'Quick – play dead. Now!'

Trabant threw himself to the floor, with arms and legs scattered best he could, in the seconds before the four guards from outside plucked up enough courage to peek around the doorframe and work out what the hell had just happened.

'Jeez, they're all dead!' said the first inside, with gun trained but eyes disbelieving. 'Gunboat's gonna go ballistic!'

'Just make sure,' said the next guard.

'How?'

'Like this...' The guard stepped forward and swung his right boot into Trabant's ribs.

'Ooeeeeerrrrrrrrrrrrrr...'

'See – still alive! Now, try the lady.'

The second guard wasn't fast enough. As he drew his foot back Eva swept his standing leg, grabbed his AK-47 and turned it on the disbelieving gathering... but seconds too late to negate the guard standing immediately to her left, who kicked hard into her jaw with crunching, brutal finality. She fell instantly.

'EVA!' screamed Trabant, turning through his pain to see her lying motionless. 'NO!'

The light in her eyes had been extinguished, yet he still wouldn't accept her vulnerability, that she *could* be hurt, until the guard stepped forward and kicked her hard in the ribs, then smiled at her lack of response.

'LEAVE HER ALONE!' shouted Trabant, crawling to be at her side. 'Eva, can you hear me? Please – wake up! PLEASE!' But she lay broken – the most beautiful woman in the world – her jaw gaping open, surely broken too.

Trabant held her in his arms and began to sob. This was all his fault, the direct result of his stupidity in Le Club Maritime du Soleil.

'Quick! Get the English pig upstairs,' shouted the head

250

guard. 'Gunboat will be fuming at the delay. And get him changed into that beige suit.'

'NO, YOU DON'T! GET OFF ME!' shouted Trabant, on the verge of hysteria, kicking and fighting with all his might as the grasping hands clamped onto him. 'GET OFF!'

'Quit fighting!' shouted the head guard, taken aback by the determination of the prisoner. 'If your girlfriend's not already dead, she soon will be.'

Trabant jolted at the guard's words. Girlfriend! That's exactly what she would have been, if he hadn't been too frightened to take her hand when she'd offered it. Trabant scrunched his eyes, pleading for the chance to turn back time; to re-enact every scene of the past seven days with the wisdom and hindsight he now so painfully possessed.

'Eva, I'm so sorry,' he cried.

'I said – GET HIM UPSTAIRS!' shouted the head guard.

Trabant wiped his eyes. The rematch was about to begin, and perhaps he really was a dead man. But Gunboat had been wrong about what he'd said in Le Club Maritime du Soleil. When you're a dead man, when you're pushed way beyond your limits, there *is* something else you can lose – fear!

A switch flicked inside, one Trabant didn't even know existed; one pressed by the strongest human instinct to protect one so loved. Yes, loved – for that's exactly how he felt, and he didn't care for subduing it a moment longer. His eyes continued to stream, and the pain of the loss of his father returned; the pain that hurt so deeply every single day. To lose a loved one was unbearable. He simply would not allow the same to happen again.

Trabant turned, with raging eyes. 'Don't you dare hurt her – not my Eva!'

'It's too late for both of you,' sneered the guard. 'Get moving. NOW!'

'No.'

'Don't make me hurt you.'

'You can't. Not anymore,' hissed Trabant.

'Okay, let's see about that.'

Crack.

The gun's butt punched the breath from Trabant's stomach. He dropped, but the guards supported his weight, shuffled to get a better grip then dragged him out of the cell.

'Faster!' shouted the head guard. 'Get him upstairs.'

'What about the lady?' shouted the last remaining guard.

'Take her down to the basement. Put a bullet in her head.'

'N-O-O-O-O...' screamed Trabant.

iii

The guests filed through the doors into the conference theatre. Stewards checked tickets and guided the criminal nobility to their soft, padded seats; the rows of which reached high up to the gods. Upon each seat lay a copy of Trabant's hand-written apology letter, perfectly visible amid the glare of the powerful spotlights. And there, in the centre of the stage, stood a solitary table draped in green baize, set with a carafe of water, two glasses and a pair of fate-deciding decks of cards.

The house lights dropped like an axe.

Whistles and waving Zippo lighters soon pierced the darkness. Then a lone spotlight appeared, aimed at the far left corner of the auditorium, which revealed a pair of black curtains. For a moment – nothing, then the black curtains parted and Trabant appeared, shoved out into the lion's den, dressed in his beige suit.

The crowd released their contempt, closely followed by the under-seat plethora of rotten fruit and vegetables, which rained down from every angle with commendable accuracy, to splat home on the prisoner's head.

'Keep moving, gringo,' ordered the guard, from beneath his umbrella.

Trabant shuffled onwards, the weight of the shackles heavy upon his wrists and ankles; the immovable glare of the spotlight almost burning the tips of his ears. Finally he reached the stage and climbed the five steps; his head held low until he came to a standstill behind the ominous, impassive gaming table. Warily he looked up, and dared to focus on the hideous blur of bad sentiment.

The crowd hissed back, a panorama of vultures perched on the edges of their seats. And the MC leant closer and chuckled in Trabant's ear. 'Now you know how the Christians felt.'

Trabant remained impassive.

The axe of darkness fell again, yet this time the spotlight resisted, prolonging the moment, cranking up the drama until, finally, the music began.

First the horn section played a descending scale, and soon the drums followed to build a thunderous crescendo, which faded almost as soon as it had arrived, to leave the string-section to float the auditorium through the darkness, within the moment of theatre… until the horns returned, and then the drums, to bring another booming crescendo.

Up in the control room, the tension had become unbearable.

'One minute thirty-one, thirty-two, thirty-three…' Mauricio (Director of Music) counted as the music continued, then signalled to Fernando (Head of Lighting) to get ready.

'Thirty-five, thirty-six, thirty-seven… NOW!'

Fernando yanked down hard on the black metal switch, and prayed to the gods of theatrical goodwill that illumination would be granted.

The gods were merciful.

The spotlight came back on, far brighter than before, and

now focused on the immense bulk of Gunboat Charlie Chávez, standing in glorious profile, to soak up the immediate screams of adulation.

'One minute thirty-nine, forty... come on, music, where the hell are you?' pleaded Mauricio, glaring down into the orchestra pit.

'What music you waiting for?' asked Fernando.

'"Mountain Goats and Capsules".'

'Eh? Don't you mean "Montagues and Capulets" from *Romeo and Juliet*?'

'NO! Gunboat insisted, despite both my and the conductor's combined fifty-six-year experience of classical music, that "Mountain Goats and Capsules" was, and always had been, the correct name for the piece. And that even señor Prokofiev – the very gringo who wrote it back in 1935 – had also named it incorrectly.'

Fernando nodded profusely. 'Well, if Gunboat say it about mountain goats and capsules, then it about—'

'... mountain goats and capsules. Precisely! But why they no play—'

Suddenly, as if by divine intervention, the Panama City Young Offenders Philharmonic Orchestra began to play the next section of Prokofiev's masterpiece, the stomping, pounding section that always reminded Gunboat of a Russian army, marching relentlessly through the harshest of winters. And onwards he now marched, in time to the music, down the walkway, waving to the crowd, shaking hands, followed by a twenty-strong entourage amid a dazzling criss-cross of spotlights, and a million-piece shower of ticker-tape that spiralled down from the ceiling, to lie in a shimmering carpet of silver and gold.

'GUNBOAT... GUNBOAT... GUNBOAT...'

He climbed the steps, jogged forward to centre stage and began punching holes in the air. The crowd screamed. The house lights blazed back on, and the Master of Ceremonies, a large man with receding hair and bulging stomach, raised his microphone to address the crowd.

'Señoras y señores. It's here, it's now, it's – SHOWTIME!'

The crowd cheered with delight.

'We welcome you all to – the Panama City Aquarium.'

Another big cheer.

'In association with Big–Time–Charlie Promotions, we are proud to present – the MAIN EVENT! A special one–off clash; a grudge rematch requested by public demand; a true battle of wits to be played out in a one–chance–only, sudden–death game of – S–N–A–P!'

The crowd roared.

'The first person to correctly shout the word "S–N–A–P" will be declared – the W–I–N–N–E–R!'

An effusion of whooping.

'Señoras y señores, without further ado, let me introduce – the C–O–N–T–E–S–T–A–N–T–S! In the blue chair, from London, England: an MI6 spy, a cheat and a very loco gringo. Señoras y señores, put your boos together for the completely despicable – B–R–I–S–T–O T–R–A–B–A–N–T.'

'B–O–O–O–O–O–O–O–O–O–!'

The MC waited for the second wave of rotten fruit to subside, lowered his umbrella then continued, ramping up the drama in his voice.

'And in the red chair, weighing in at two hundred and ninety–five pounds; from El Chorrillo, Panama City; the true, undisputed, h–e–a–v–y–weight champion of the underworld... the one... the only...

EL CAÑONERO HIMSELF...

G–U–N–B–O–A–T C–H–A–R–L–I–E...

C–H–A–A–A–V–V–V–E–E–E–E–E–E–E–E–Z–Z–Z–Z...'

'GUNBOAT... GUNBOAT... GUNBOAT...'

'Señoras y señores, let's get ready – for WAR!'

Delirium had now claimed the auditorium. Both men sat down, shuffled their seats closer to the table, then wiped their hands on the conveniently positioned towels. The shackles were unlocked from Trabant's ankles and wrists, and Enrique inserted an extra-large Havana cigar neatly between the first two fingers of Gunboat's right paw, lit it then shuffled back to stage-right.

The MC began to address the two players. 'Okay, señores, I want a good clean game. No low blows, and definitely no cheating.'

'Yeah, d'ya hear that, Gringo Loco?' hissed Gunboat. 'No cheat!'

Trabant stared back – beyond fear, beyond rationality – with his paraffin anger ready to ignite.

'You both know the rules,' continued the MC. 'When I give the command, play to the best of your abilities. And may señor Gun... I mean, may the best man win.'

The MC tossed a coin high into the air. 'Señor Gunboat, heads or tails?'

'Head,' he growled. 'Trabant's!'

The coin landed, bounced once then settled.

'It is tails. Señor Trabant to turn the first card.'

The crowd grumbled its disapproval.

'Señoras y señores – let the game C-O-M-M-E-N-C-E.'

The croupier shuffled each deck of cards with scalpel precision, placed one in front of each player then stepped back. Trabant reached for his first card, but then paused, as his mind searched for Eva throughout the basement corridors of the aquarium. Could she somehow still be alive? He had to end this game quickly and find her.

'Señor Trabant, please lay your first card,' urged the croupier.

Trabant obliged.

Six of Hearts.

'SNAP!' shouted Gunboat immediately.

'No, señor Gunboat,' replied the croupier softly. 'We need *two* cards for there to be a possibility of *snap*.'

Gunboat glared back, then turned his first card.

Eight of Diamonds.

'SNAP!' he repeated.

'Six of hearts and eight of diamonds is not *snap*, señor.'

'It is if I bloomin' say it is!'

A murmur of unrest circulated through the crowd.

Nine of Spades.

Gunboat eyeballed Trabant, transmitting a just-you-dare warning from the inferno within, then turned his next card.

Queen of Spades.

Trabant continued with gritted teeth, just as Eva would have done, but something made him look to the left, to see Enrique standing in the wings, wearing an ear-to-ear smile of such immense satisfaction that Trabant couldn't help but wonder why?

And then, in another moment of horrific clarity, he realised... and his soul staggered... as if dealt the fatal blow himself. But the blow had been dealt to someone else, someone so cherished, and Enrique's expression left him in no doubt as to whom. Trabant lowered his head in crushing disbelief, for in that moment he knew...

... he just knew...

Eva was dead.

'Señor Trabant, your next card, if you please,' said the croupier.

'NOOOOOOO!'

'Señor, you have to. It's the rules of the game.'

Trabant clutched the table, anchoring his body amid the flash-flood of despair.

'Last chance!' continued the croupier. 'If you refuse to continue then you forfeit the game.'

'I don't c-ca...'

But now he did care, more than ever before in his life. And through the mist he heard the words Eva had said only the previous night in their prison cell, when he'd asked how she always stayed so strong.

'*I transform anxiety into positive energy, to use to my advantage.*'

'*Like a turbine harnesses the wind?*'

'*Yes, exactly like that.*'

Trabant took a deep, wind-turbine-like breath. He had to play on; to continue the work of the most beautiful woman in the world; to try and land the blow to finally shatter the foundations of Gunboat's empire – irreparably. To win again at cards, with the world's criminal elite watching, would surely end the reign of El Cañonero. He glared back across the table at Gunboat, then flipped over his next card.

Nine of Diamonds.

'SNAP!' shouted Gunboat.

'They do not match!' exclaimed the croupier.

'Hell!' cursed Gunboat, as he tentatively laid his next card.

Ace of Diamonds.

Trabant quickly laid his next card, with the word of victory poised on his lips.

Three of Spades.

Gunboat blew a mouthful of cigar smoke straight into Trabant's eyes, then quickly despatched his next card beneath the spreading blanket of Cuban fog.

Two of Clubs.

'SNAP!'

'No, not snap... and señor Chávez, please refrain from distracting your opponent.' The croupier turned to Trabant. 'Señor, are you okay?'

'No! I'm not okay,' he replied, blinking hard to regain his vision.

'Are you able to continue?'

Trabant nodded, then laid his next card.

Queen of Hearts.

Gunboat released his next card with such force that it slid across the table, over the edge and down onto the floor. The croupier retrieved it from the carpet of ticker-tape, then with a huff of disapproval, placed it firmly back on the table.

Four of Diamonds.

'Señor Gunboat, that is your second violation of the game,' said the croupier. 'I have no alternative but to issue you with – a yellow card!'

The crowd began to jeer.

'Yellow card – you joking?' pleaded Gunboat.

'Do I look like I'm joking?' continued the croupier, waving the custard-coloured card high in the air.

'No, you look like a man who soon gonna be dead.' Gunboat stood to confront the croupier.

The MC rushed forward to intervene, in a voice deliberately low. 'Señores – calm down! Like we agreed, the game must appear to be fair to have the desired effect. Gunboat, please… sit back down.'

Gunboat reluctantly did so.

'Señor Trabant, please… lay your next card,' instructed the croupier.

Trabant took another deep breath, then flipped his next card.

Four of Diamonds. FOUR OF DIAMONDS!

Exact match to Gunboat's card! And it stared back, daring him to say the word, to claim the victory yet again.

'*Whatever you do… don't play him at cards!*'

This time he knew better. Trabant looked up across the table. Gunboat's face was slowly blossoming with the same realisation. It was now or never – for the memory of the most beautiful woman in the world.

'S-s-s-n-a… AAARRRGGGGHHHH!'

A juggernaut of pain crashed into the small of Trabant's back. His head and body twisted, and his lungs scrambled for the air that had been punched clean out. In the moments before he collapsed forward onto the table, Trabant turned to see Enrique standing close behind, wielding a sinister black cosh in his right hand. A single blow had done it, cleverly disguised yet delivered with such ferocity it had not only stolen his word, but destroyed the back of the chair in the process. And now, from across the table, came the crushing resonance of Gunboat's word, shouted loud for the whole world to hear.

'S-S-S-N-N-N-A-A-A-A-A-A-P-P-P!'

The crowd erupted.

'SNAP, SNAP, SNAP, SNAP, S-N-A-A-A-A-A-A-P-P!' continued Gunboat, taunting Trabant across the table.

'Indeed, it is snap,' shouted the MC, raising the victor's clenched fist high into the air. 'And I declare that the winner is – G-U-N-B-O-A-T C-H-A-R-L-I-E…
C-H-A-A-V-V-E-E-E-E-E-E-E-E-Z-Z-Z-Z…'

V

Trabant remained slumped across the table, with head in hands, fighting the pain from the blow that had almost broken him clean in two. Yet the pain of failing to claim victory for Eva hurt far more than any physical injury ever could.

Gunboat grabbed the microphone from the MC. 'Señoras y señores, colleagues from the real world of commerce – I am the winner! Justice is done, and normal order is restore. Yet my victory should be of no surprise. Because I no actually lose to this English pig in the first place. Oh, yeah, that right! Back at Le Club Maritime du Soleil in Cannes, this gringo here CHEAT!'

Gasps of manufactured horror rained down from the gods.

'Sí, it true. And you all know there is no thing I hate more than a card cheat.'

Scowling boos joined in from every angle.

'Señor Gringo Loco set out to poison the world against me; to crack the foundation of the empire I have so painstaking create, and for that, in a matter of moment, he pay the ultimate price.'

The crowd began to cheer.

Gunboat turned to his guards waiting in the wings. 'Okay, take him to you-know-where.'

As Trabant was dragged away, Gunboat stepped forward and raised his paw to reclaim silence. 'Señoras y señores, before the English pig meet his end, I have more to say. I am product of the street. I have been given no handout or free lunch. I make my own path, and battle up to the summit of criminal greatness through combination of hard work, determination and brutal, unrelenting greed. I build my empire with these bare hands, brick by brick. And though many of those brick have been stolen, the same principle still apply – that in life, we get what we deserve.'

The crowd stood to applaud.

'This is my world, my rules. And what I say goes. Got it?' The crowd nodded, as one, under no illusion as to the truth of his words.

'Corruption, intimidation, extortion and refusal to kneel at anyone feet have been cornerstone of my success. And that success benefit you all. My umbrella of protection has wide reach. Every single one of you here today has step beneath it, taken shelter from the elements of political hypocrisy, and enjoy the countless benefit I offer. We have run our enterprises and scams together. We have all become rich, and you enjoy protection from police *and* rival organisations simply through your association with me, EL CAÑONERO! So you agree – it far better to live as my amigo than to die as my enemigo.'

261

'We love you, Gunboat!' shouted a voice from the darkness.

'Muchas gracias,' he replied, but his scowl remained firm. 'The majority of you support me, and for that I offer my gratitude and continue friendship. But there are some of you who no only doubt my ability to continue, but also demand this rematch. By doing so, you bite the hand that feed. You know who you are, and very soon, so will I. Until then, rest uneasy, my disloyal amigos, for I shall visit you in your nightmares. And then, when I ready, and after you have sweat sufficiently, I will visit you in person.'

Sections of the crowd exchanged glances like missile tracer.

'But right now, it is time for the English pig to die.'

'YEEAAYYYYYYYYYYYYYYYYYYYY!' cheered the crowd.

'So, señoras y señores, I ask you now to follow me out the auditorium, and along to the specially designed luxury observation window, to witness the gringo's death, at the hands – or fins – of the Panama City Aquarium's latest and greatest display.'

Gunboat stepped down from the stage and forced his way back along the aisle towards the rear exit, then out into the corridor. In less than a minute, he was beside the cinema-screen-sized observation window.

'Is everyone here?' asked Gunboat.

'Sí, Boz,' beamed Enrique. 'Over to you.'

With all the guests in position, and feverishly speculating about what could possibly be lurking behind the enormous pair of dark-red velvet curtains, Gunboat stepped up onto the adjacent platform, and raised his arms once more to the crowd.

'GUNBOAT… GUNBOAT… GUNBOAT…'

'Señoras y señores, there are few creatures in the ocean as perfectly evolve and awesomely deadly as the one who now swim behind these curtains. And it only fitting that I, the world's apex predator, should enlist the services of the ocean's equivalent to finally rid this planet of señor Gringo Loco.'

The crowd strained, desperate to see the menace lurking beyond the velvet. Gunboat slowly pulled the drawstring, and watched the curtains part.

The crowd gasped.

'Look at the teeth on that!' screamed a voice from the front.

'It's huge!'

'It's massive!'

'Señoras y señores,' beamed Gunboat. 'I give you *Carcharodon carcharias* – the Great White Shark.'

25

The Guns of El Chorrillo

'STRAIGHT AHEAD, LADY, AND no funny moves,' barked the guard, jabbing the tip of his AK-47 into the small of Eva's back.

An intermittent line of fluorescent tubes ran overhead. Eva continued along the basement corridor, with hands held high, and ribs throbbing from the guard's savage kick. Only her clenched teeth had prevented her jaw from breaking, which she waggled best she could to bring it back to life.

'Left here,' instructed the guard, pushing her through another fire door.

'Where are you taking me?'

'You'll see.'

Eva stumbled on, thinking, focusing, energising. 'You know, the lighting… in this place… is really… terrible,' she said. 'And—'

A muffled roar came seeping down from upstairs.

'What's that noise?' she asked.

'The crowd enjoying Trabant being eaten alive.'

'WHAT! Where's that happening?'

'Upper Level One. Now, shut up and keep walking.'

Eva's mind went into overdrive. She had to get upstairs, but with the guard's assault rifle pressed in the hollow of her back, there was zero margin for error.

'Think about what you're doing,' she pleaded.

'Killing you means nothing to me.'

With every footstep her edginess increased. If she could just build a small gap, enough to—

'I'm going to enjoy killing you,' laughed the guard.

'And I think I'm going to be sick.'

'Shut it!'

'Seriously, I need to... stop, just for a...'

The AK-47 dug in again.

'Ouch! Okay, I'm moving!'

'Turn left, at the end,' ordered the guard.

'Is that w-where you'll shoot me?'

'Yes, as soon as we turn the next corner.'

'Where – here?' asked Eva, speeding up.

'No, round the corner, I said! And slow down!'

Eva did so, then sped up again.

'Don't play games, lady.'

'Sorry.' Eva slowed, then instantly reversed – with all her might. In the split second before the guard crashed into her back, her left arm came sweeping down in a vicious arc, knocking the tip of the gun away from her back. Total surprise muddied the guard's reactions, but Eva's momentum continued, as she spun on the balls of her feet, powered forward and drove her open right hand hard into the guard's face. The crunch sent him sprawling backwards, and his gun tumbling to the ground. As he cradled his broken nose, Eva pressed home her advantage, kicking hard to the groin then punching into the exposed ribcage, before dropping his lumpy frame to the ground with a trademark leg-sweep.

She stepped back, her body poised in karate stance, ready for round two. But the guard lay beaten. Yet Eva's eyes retained the shock-blast of intensity, for there was still so much to do. She scooped up the guard's AK-47 and ran for the stairs, to get to Upper Level One... but paused... her head momentarily charged with the painful recollection of events back in Cannes. She sprinted back to the guard, lined up her foot and kicked him hard in the ribs.

Crunch!

'And that's for busting up my Alfa Romeo.'

'Aaaaarrrggghhhh! But that wasn't me!' winced the guard.

'To me, you are all the same.'

ii

Another cheer filtered down from Upper Level One.

Eva ran back along the corridor, praying the guard's information would be accurate. Up the staircase two steps at a time, she quickly passed the access doors for Sub Level Two, One and Ground Floor, until finally Upper Level One appeared.

With gun butt into her shoulder and eyes focused through the sights, she burst through the door, scanning high and low for any resistance. The coast was clear, but again the muffled sound of cheers taunted her. But from which direction? She battled her indecision then ran to the right, along the corridor until thankfully the volume became louder, finally peaking right outside a door marked 'Staff Only – Do Not Enter'.

The handle was locked. She stepped back, aimed the AK and unleashed hellfire, then barged onwards, kicking aside the remnants of splintered wood. A short, winding corridor led her to a floor-to-ceiling wall of glass, perhaps six inches thick. Through it she could see (about three metres below) a huge expanse of water. One of the aquarium display tanks? Yes, beneath the surface of which lurked a huge, dark shadow, circling ominously. And to the far side, on an observation platform, stood Enrique, Raúl, Ramón... and Gunboat himself, who was angrily prodding a long broom-handle at another man; a man precariously teetering his way out along a plank of wood, the end of which bounced just above the centre of the pool.

But it wasn't just any man, it was – 'BRISTO!'

She had to get to him, but how? To shoot the glass would startle him, and send him toppling in.

'Damn it,' she cursed, in frustration, then began to scour her surroundings for inspiration. On the far side, behind another observation window, she could make out the blurred faces of all the guests. And then, immediately to her left: a drinking-water dispenser and a wall-mounted tannoy system, complete with microphone. She ran to it, scanned the list of extension numbers, flicked the 'ON' switch and immediately heard the drone of pumps and gushing water through the speaker.

'Yes!' she exclaimed. She now had contact with the shark enclosure, but, more importantly, she could also hear the voices from inside. But what could she say to make Gunboat listen? Or, at least, to delay him?

She quickly poured a glass of chilled water from the dispenser, half-filled her mouth to disguise her voice, readied herself at the microphone and prayed for a moment of divine inspiration.

iii

The shark's dorsal fin continued to slice through the water. And another jab from the broom-handle pushed Trabant further out towards the end of the plank.

'Señor shark's a beauty, huh?' beamed Gunboat.

'Yes, l-lovely,' whimpered Trabant.

'I dink he lovely too,' smiled Enrique. 'And what better way to kill de English pig! I very impressed.'

'Muchas gracias, Enrique. The Great White is an evolutionary masterpiece, perfected over four hundred million year. We should marvel at ultimate creation of nature. Ruthless, all powerful, and very hungry! Bet you regret messing with me now, eh, señor Gringo Loco?'

'Y-yep!'

'It a dog-eat-dog world, and it me who has the sharpest teeth.'

The shark quickly resurfaced, begging to differ.

'I a simple man, señor Trabant,' continued Gunboat. 'Mess with me and I mess with you. Then again, be nice to me and I still mess with you. You try to ruin my reputation, and now you pay the price. So go on – jump in.'

Trabant looked down at the churning water, at the monstrous beast circling beneath. 'You m-may o-own an aquarium, Gunboat, but you d-don't know much about sharks.'

'WHAT?'

'H-humans… we're n-not their natural diet.'

'I SAID – JUMP IN!'

'Fat chance!'

'DID YOU SAY FAT?'

'No, I meant not enough… wo, wo… aaaaaah!'

Trabant fell, but down onto the edge of the plank, to which his arms and legs instantly clamped, with all their might.

'If you no jump, I shoot you off that plank,' scowled Gunboat, drawing his Colt .357 Magnum from its holster.

'But h-humans are too bony. Sharks want to eat seals, for all their nutrient-rich blubber.' Trabant looked back to the shark, certain it was nodding in agreement.

'Oh, shut up!'

'But it's true!' pleaded Trabant. 'Of course sharks can be dangerous, but the reason for most attacks on humans, which incidentally are extremely rare, is mistaken identity. But even so, they're p-persecuted because of man's misconceptions, and the sensationalism of the gutter press.'

Gunboat rolled his eyes. 'Eh, Enrique – señor Gringo Loco's on his soap-box again.'

'But it's true, Boz,' replied Enrique. 'I no like de English pig, but I have to agree wid him on dis one. Also, hundreds of dousands of sharks are killed every single day, predominantly for shark-fin soup. Many species face extinction. It's shocking! Dey have far more to fear from us.'

'Do they?'

'Sí. *And* dey a keystone element in marine ecosystems. Take dem out and de w-h-o-l-e system come crashing down.'

'Is that a fact?' exclaimed Gunboat.

'Yes!' replied Trabant. 'You of all people should k-know that.'

'Well, muchas gracias for the marine biology lecture,' said Gunboat, as he aimed his gun. 'Señor Loco, quit stalling and get in. My audience is getting impatient.'

'STOP!' blurted Eva through the microphone, literally as the shark's head broke the surface, with its jaws gaping.

Raúl's jaw also dropped, but in utter disbelief. 'Holy Santa María! D'ya hear that, Boz – a talking shark! That'll pull in the punters!'

'Yeah, and multi-lingual too,' added Ramón. 'It's got a French accent. Shall I contact Ulrika in marketing? This is liquid gold!'

'FOR CRYING OUT LOUD!' shouted Gunboat. 'Sharks can no speak! No English, no French, no *any* language. Got it?'

It was a once in a lifetime moment that Eva simply couldn't resist. 'Oh, yes we can!'

'Oh, no you... What the...!?!'

'You should be... (gargle)... ashamed of yourself, Gunboat.'

'NEVER! I no ashamed of no any thing I ever did.'

'Well, you should be. Traumatising Monsieur Trabant like this. A real predator would admit... (gargle)... defeat and let him go. After all, he beat you at cards fair and—' Eva paused as the shark dipped back beneath the surface.

'HE NO BEAT ME – HE CHEAT! AND I AM REAL PREDATOR!' shouted Gunboat. 'AND ANYWAYS, I BEAT HIM IN REMATCH!'

The shark reappeared. 'Then all is equal,' she continued, in her best aquatic monotone. 'So let the small fry go.'

'NO! It bad for business,' replied Gunboat, looking to his frustrated guests beyond the window.

The shark resurfaced once more. 'Señor Gunboat, if you don't let Monsieur Trabant go, you will have a... (gargle)... mutiny on your hands.'

'No make me laugh!'

'Oh, for sure – you will not laugh, when I... (gargle)... speak to every fish, shark, octopus, penguin and crocodile in your aquarium. And together, we shall rise up against you on a wave of revulsion.'

'I NO SCARED OF NO ANYONE!'

'You will be outnumbered a thousand... (gargle)... to one.'

'BRING IT ON!'

'It will be an aquatic bloodbath!'

'SO? I WILL REPLACE YOU ALL. THERE PLENTY MORE FISHES IN THE—'

'Ah! But I will speak to them too. Word travels... (gargle)... fast underwater. Every time you dip your toe in the ocean, a greeting party will be waiting to bite.'

'Sounds nasty, Boss,' said Ramón. 'What we gonna do?'

'FIGHT!' replied Gunboat, turning back to the tank. 'YOU NO THREATEN ME, SEÑOR SHARK – I AM EL CAÑONERO!'

'Boz,' interrupted Enrique. 'It no a señor shark. It a señorita. Look – it ain't got no claspers!'

'What the hell are they?'

'De two little sausage dings under its tummy dat show it a boy and no a girl.'

'Really?' Gunboat peered closer, then shook his head clear of the distraction. 'Enrique – shut up! Trabant, jump in – NOW!'

'No!'

'No make it any harder for yourself.'

'How can I possibly make it any harder for myself?'

270

'I warning you, if you no—'

'Señor Gunboat,' cut in the bubbling, sloshing, almost-hypnotic voice. 'If Monsieur Trabant falls in the... (gargle)... water, I will not bite. I will simply flip him back... (gargle)... out with my nose, to safety.'

'EAT HIM!'

'NO! Us sharks are sick and tired of... (gargle)... you humans failing to consider things from our point of view. We are mercilessly hunted for shark-fin soup. And as for attacks, more people get killed each year by falling... (gargle)... coconuts, or hippos, than sharks. But are they vilified in the same way? No!'

'YOU SAY EL CAÑONERO LOOK LIKE A HIPPO?'

'Yes, a little. But more importantly, I'm saying to all... (gargle)... humans: get educated and learn the real facts. Don't hate sharks – understand sharks, then you might even grow to love sharks! Don't fear us, fear for us!'

Gunboat clenched his fists in frustration.

WHOOOOOOSHshshshshshshshshshsh...

'What the hell was that?' asked Ramón, instinctively ducking beneath the rumbling thunder.

'Harrier GR9,' replied Gunboat, matter-of-factly. 'Question is – what it doing flying overhead?'

'Must be from that aircraft carrier,' mused Raúl.

'What aircraft carrier?' exclaimed Gunboat.

'The one in the bay.'

'WHY YOU NO TELL ME?'

'Sorry, Boss. I forgot to say. You and Enrique were so busy with the rematch, and I didn't think it important.'

'NO IMPORTANT!' shouted Gunboat. 'On the day the world's criminal elite are here to watch me feed MI6 agent to a shark, you no consider the arrival of a twenty-two-thousand-tonne aircraft carrier on our doorstep to be important?'

'Well, if you put it like that...'

'AAAARRRGGGGHHH...!' screamed Gunboat, with frustration. 'Enrique, Ramón – come with me to the Crow-Nest. Raúl – get Trabant off that plank and bring him too.'

'But what about the guests?' asked Enrique.

'Tell them I have postpone the show till after this little aircraft carrier has been dealt with. Okay?'

'Sí, Boz. Whatever you say, Boz."

'And anyway, I must see the English pig die with my own eyes.'

'Sí, Boz. Of course, Boz.'

iv

'Hmmm... it a British Royal Navy *Invincible*-class aircraft carrier,' grumbled Gunboat, peering intently through his binoculars from the Crow's Nest, the level just below the aquarium roof. 'Two hundred and ten metre long; four Rolls-Royce Olympus gas-turbine engine giving her top speed of thirty knot; crew of approximately one thousand; operating both rotary and fixed-wing aircraft plus whatever else they can cram inside. Total cost: just over three hundred million pound, yet still only available in battleship grey.'

'Such a boring colour,' said Ramón.

'Reckon dey're selling de ship, Boz?' asked Enrique.

'Not on this occasion, which is shame as I have definite buyer. Nope, I think they want their agent back.' Gunboat bit down on his cigar. 'Enrique, get a message to them, that unless they move from my harbour immediately, they will have to change their name from HMS *Indomitable* to HMS *Seabed*. Got it?'

'Sí, Boz.'

Enrique scampered away, and Gunboat returned to his examination of the vessel of war, sitting ominously just a few miles offshore. 'Hmmm...' he grumbled. 'And it no just one ship, there's a whole bloomin' taskforce – a Royal Navy destroyer, a supply ship and an assault ship with landing platform dock capability too. Just like the Department of Taxation, they never come alone.'

Moments later Enrique returned, panting like a husky. 'I spoke to our contact, Boz; got de ship's... (puff)... telephone number, and rang it.'

'And...?'

'Just as I dought, Boz. Dey've requested we hand de English pig over. What shall I say, Boz?'

Gunboat lowered his binoculars. 'Enrique, give them this very simple reply. Tell them to bog off!'

'Bog off?'

'Sí, with a capital *Bog*. They understand.'

'O-okay, Boz.'

Minutes later, Enrique returned, ashen faced.

'What did they say?'

'You correct, Boz. Dey fully understand, and in reply, dey say dey're gonna send de Royal Marines to rescue Trabant.'

'So, they got the balls to take me on, huh?'

'Sí. Boz. Dey're crazy!'

'Well, let us no disappoint them. Enrique – scramble the troops.'

Enrique licked his lips. The troops were the GOEC – The Guns of El Chorrillo – Gunboat's private army of mercenaries, cut-throats and hoodlums, who'd be busting at the seams to repel the invaders.

'You mean who I think you mean, Boz?' he asked, knowing full well but longing to hear Gunboat's thunderous battle cry.

'Sí, Enrique, I do. The time has come – TO FIRE THE GUNS OF EL CHORRILLO!'

26

Eighty-Ninth-Minute Winner

EVA RAN BACK DOWN to ground level and along its corridor, trying every door to gain access to the shark tank. But each time she only found a storage cupboard or dead end. She continued on to the next corner, but suddenly halted – at the sound of voices fast approaching, barely metres away.

She peeked round to see the motley crew of Gunboat's guests streaming towards her, escorted by numerous GOEC soldiers.

'Damn British Royal Navy, gatecrashing our party,' grumbled one of the guests.

'Yeah, I've never seen a shark attack before, and was *so* looking forward to it.'

The adjacent fire-exit door recess was her only chance. She dived into its shadows and flattened her body best she could, willing the huge procession to change direction. But it didn't. It approached, ever closer. There was no way they could miss her. She turned her head away, to hide the whites of her eyes, but unwittingly squeezed the release bar. The doors broke open and tumbled her out into the bright daylight. She frantically closed the doors behind, and through the crack she watched, holding her breath, with rifle at the ready. But, mercifully, the procession passed by, showing zero interest in the narrow beam of daylight that pierced the darkness inside.

Eva gave a huge sigh of relief, then slowly opened the door to step back inside.

'Stop! Drop your weapon.'

She froze.

'I said – drop your weapon.'

Eva did so. And in her peripheral vision she saw two men approach, but spaced a couple of metres apart. She turned slightly to her left, ready to strike. They'd soon be in range. Both had blackened faces, wore military fatigues, *and* carried SA80 A2 assault rifles – standard-issue of the British Royal Marines! She turned further to see another two men, dressed the same; then further down the beach, a RIB – a rigid-hulled inflatable boat – waiting patiently, manned by another three men, themselves staring back with bated breath.

'My name is Eva Avante, of the French Secret Service. I'm here to rescue MI6 Agent Bristo Trabant.'

'I'm Scott and he's Spike. We're Royal Marines from that huge taskforce out in the bay, and here to do the same.'

'Excellent! Then follow me inside. I think I know where he is.'

'Not until I check you out further.' Spike whispered into his Bowman headset. 'Alfa Two Seven to Ridgeback. Over.'

'Go ahead.'

'Apprehended a lady claiming to be Agent Eva Avante of the French Secret Service. Request further information to confirm identity. Over.'

'She's still alive! Fantastic! Just a minute, let me ask someone. Over.' They waited. 'Okay, Alfa Two Seven, ask what type of biscuits the French Prime Minister had at Number Ten. Over.'

'Well?' asked Spike, turning to Eva.

'Windsor Shortbread slices. About twenty of them.'

'That's spot on,' replied the voice. 'Now, just to be sure, ask the second security question.'

'But we haven't time!' protested Eva.

'Sorry,' said Spike. 'We have to be certain.'

'Very well, but please hurry.'

'Okay. Who scored the winning goal in the 1979 FA Cup Final?'

'What kind of question is that!?!'

'The kind set by Agent Bentley barely an hour ago.'

'Well, let me tell you, Agent Bentley is a—'

'Please,' interrupted Scott. 'Just answer the question.'

'Okay, okay! It was Alan Sunderland, for Arsenal, in the eighty-ninth minute, against Manchester United.'

'Not Liam Brady?'

'No! Monsieur Brady burst through from midfield, passed the ball out left to Graham Rix, who crossed to the far post, where Monsieur Sunderland slid in to score. It was a wonderful move *and* finish. Perhaps the most dramatic conclusion ever to a cup final.'

Scott shook his head. 'How on earth did you know all that, being French?'

'My friend's cousin played for Arsenal. They are my English team. Now please,' continued Eva, bending to scoop up her AK-47, 'let's get back inside to rescue Bristo.'

'Put her on, would you? Over,' crackled the headset. Spike passed it over.

'Hello, Agent Avante. Delighted you're still in one piece. Please confirm Agent Trabant's status and position.'

'Alive, and last seen dangling over a shark tank.'

'How long ago?'

'Ten minutes.'

'What about Gunboat and the GOEC?'

'Limbering up for a fight. So we need to get moving. Over.'

'Message understood, but I'm afraid you'll have to come back with the reconnaissance team.'

'No way!' shouted Eva. 'I have to save Bristo.'

'I'm sorry, ma'am,' said Scott. 'All non-Marine personnel are to be escorted back to Ridgeback. It's for your own safety.'

'No, I'm going back in.'

'Alfa Two Seven to Ridgeback. Agent Avante is refusing to come with us. Over.'

'Agent Avante, that's a direct order from me also,' replied a different voice, which Eva immediately recognised as that of her boss, and head of the DGSE Intelligence Section, Gérard Depouis.

'Eva, I know how you feel, but I must insist. We need you to relay intelligence of the building's layout, strength of the enemy and so forth. Over and out.'

Her head dropped in dejection. Marine Spike stepped forward and placed a hand on her shoulder. 'Don't worry, we'll get him out. You've done your job.'

'No, I haven't,' she cursed, her eyes wild with fury. 'That's the whole point.'

ii

HMS *Indomitable*'s radar continued to scan. On her flight deck sat two Harrier jump jets, and a third rose up from the hangar on the lift. Voices barked through the piercing intercom; air handlers readied themselves, and pilots made their final checks. The great lady of war was almost ready.

The RIB pulled up midships along the starboard side. The lead seaman secured the winch to the central A-Frame, gave the thumbs-up and sat back as the motors lifted the boat up out of the water, higher and higher, then guided it into her little alcove three-quarters of the way up the hull. Eva immediately clambered out, nodded cordially to Scott and Spike, then followed the waiting officer past the armed guard, through the doorway and along the blue-floored, grey-pipe-lined passageway. They climbed the first ladder chain up to Two Deck, then continued along to Planning Room Four.

The ship's layout was familiar to Eva, as she had spent many months at sea on special ops. She knocked, waited, then stepped inside.

Rows of Royal Marines, dressed in combats, sat facing the large video screen. A tall man with brown hair and barn-door shoulders stepped forward to introduce himself. 'Ah, Agent Avante, welcome aboard. I am Commodore Speed, in charge of this taskforce.'

'Thank you, sir,' replied Eva, nodding. 'Pleased to meet you.'

'Likewise. And I think you know Colonel Bravinger, Jones, and of course your superior, Monsieur Gérard Depouis.'

'Yes, sir, I do. Gentlemen…' She nodded again, concealing her surprise at seeing Bravinger at the business end of an operation.

'Great to see you alive,' said Depouis. 'We've been worried sick since your disappearance from the DGSE surveillance flat.'

'Yes, I am sorry, sir. There was little time to react once I saw Bristo at La Fortaleza. But I did phone Thierry and Claude from the ship that we boarded. Are they okay? They did not return my calls.'

'Thierry and Claude were kidnapped, and only found this morning, locked in the basement of a house in El Carmen.'

Eva's face flooded with concern. 'Are they okay?'

'Yes, thankfully. Just shaken up. Their car was run off the road near Tocumen International Airport. They were taken at gunpoint.'

Eva shook her head in disgust. 'That explains it.'

Commodore Speed shared her anger. 'I'm just about to finish the briefing, Agent Avante, so if there's anything you'd like to add?'

'Only one thing, sir – but with regret. I must inform everyone that Agent Bentley is actually working for Gunboat.'

'Rubbish!' scoffed Bravinger. 'He's our top man. How dare you insinuate—'

'It is not insinuation, it is fact. Agent Trabant and I escaped from Panama to a remote desert island, the coordinates of which we texted only to Bentley. He came to rescue us, but instead of bringing us to safety, he delivered us straight back to Gunboat.'

'I don't believe you,' snapped Bravinger.

'What I say is true. Ask yourself this: did Bentley inform you we'd made contact? No. Did he say he was going to rescue us? No.' Eva stepped closer. 'I have travelled halfway across the world to save Bristo, only for your so-called top man to betray us. And I'll bet it was he who kidnapped Thierry and Claude, and assisted in disarming your Vienna unit too. The fact is he's a traitor, and if cornered inside the aquarium, will kill without hesitation.'

Bravinger's face boiled. 'These are very serious accusations, Agent Avante.'

'Which is why I insist you check Agent Bentley's mobile telephone records to corroborate what I say.'

Commodore Speed stepped in. 'Colonel Bravinger, I suggest you do precisely what Agent Avante says. However, right now, I must finish my briefing.'

'Absolutely, sir,' said Eva.

Bravinger also nodded in agreement.

Commodore Speed addressed the room. 'Okay, gentlemen, let's recap why we're here – to rescue this man…' Speed tapped the photograph on the screen. 'Bristo Trabant, MI6 agent, captured a week ago after a failed surveillance operation on this man, Gunboat Charlie Chávez. The last sighting was by Agent Avante…' Eva nodded, 'of him dangling over a pool containing a very large shark.'

'Bull—' coughed Bravinger.

'No!' snapped Eva. 'I assure you it is true.'

'Forgive me, Agent Avante,' replied Bravinger. 'I was enquiring as to the variety of shark. Is it a Bull Shark?'

'No, a Great White, and about four metres long.'

'What's the difference?' asked Jones.

'Never mind, never mind,' replied Speed. 'It really doesn't matter. What's important is that at 11.27 Gunboat refused to release Trabant. Hence our imminent action.'

'When do we set off, sir?' asked a Marine.

'In precisely fifteen minutes. We agreed to that time delay, to allow Gunboat's guests to clear the building.'

WHOOOOOOSHshshshshshshshsh…

Planning Room Four shook beneath the deafening thunder clap.

'What the blazes was that?' asked Bravinger.

'The second Harrier taking off,' replied Speed. 'Wonderful sound, isn't it? Never fails to put a lump in the old throat.'

The room shared the moment, drifting on a cloud of love for their beloved close-air support assets, the lifeline for many a Marine under fire.

'Anyway, where were we?' continued the Commodore.

'Talking about Agent Trabant, sir,' replied a Marine at the front.

'Oh, yes. And I'd now like to hand over to Royal Marine Sergeant Johnson, who is in tactical command and will therefore continue the briefing.' Johnson – a tall, hard and wiry man – stepped forward.

'Okay, men, as the Commodore says, the key to this mission is that Agent Trabant remains alive. So we need to be quick and efficient. Get in, grab him, then get out again.'

Planning Room Four nodded in agreement.

'Do as little damage to Gunboat's building and personnel as possible. Only engage if fired upon. And remember Agent Avante's warning: be cautious if you encounter Agent Bentley.'

The room grumbled its disgust at the potential of a traitor.

Johnson rapped his knuckles on the table. 'Now, I draw your attention to this satellite image.' A hazy black-and-white photograph of the Panama City waterfront appeared on the screen. 'Here is the Panama City Aquarium, where Agent Trabant is being held. A team from the Special Boat Service were deployed overnight from HMS *Nautilus* to secure the area. They made it ashore undetected. All they encountered were the smells of barbecued chicken and the gentle tones of salsa wafting from a small open window. At first light they radioed back to confirm a) that the shore was secure, and b) the best places for us to land. We will therefore use three LCVP MK5 landing craft.'

Eva nodded in agreement. She knew the craft well: the type first used in the Second World War; ideal for shore landings and, in its modern-day format, capable of twenty-five (admittedly bone-jarring) knots. She'd deployed from one herself with her platoon; had crouched low, with rifle in hand and kit on back, until the bow ramp dropped, and then it was 'Go, go, go!'

'Each will hold thirty-five Marines,' continued Johnson. 'The three craft – named A, B and C – will be driven across from HMS *Warrior* to us here, where you will board via the starboard aft accommodation ladder. The craft will then set off in formation for the shore. Landing crafts A, B and C – you will land here, here and here.'

Planning Room Four nodded in agreement.

Johnson continued. 'There will be two RIBs close by for emergency purposes. Tides have been treble-checked, and the sea level will be high. The bottom composition is rocky, full of big black boulders, some hidden just beneath the water surface, so lead seamen must be very aware when driving the last ten metres or so. Men, once disembarked, the distance to the aquarium building is about fifty metres. Take care with your footing, the surfaces will be jagged and slippery. Make your way up across the grassy area, and gain entrance as soon as you can. Group A is to attack the north face and main entrance; Group B, the south face and main entrance; Group C, the east face and loading bay. Harriers from 800 Naval Air Squadron will provide cover. Naval gunfire support, if needed, will come from HMS *Defiant*. Yes?' said Johnson, pointing towards the raised hand.

'What kind of resistance can we expect?'

'Plenty. Gunboat's men will be armed with AK-47s, perhaps rockets, even grenade launchers. Who knows.'

'How about fire from above?' asked another Marine.

'Our Sea King MK7 Airborne Surveillance helicopter has confirmed no sightings of any air, surface or vehicle threats as yet. And they've been scanning the landscape since before we all edged into position. Special Boat Service have reported no signs of roof-mounted artillery, but you never know. Rest assured that both teams are ideally placed and will continually update the command team. Any other questions?'

'Yes. What's inside the large silver dome on the roof?'

'Your guess is as good as mine. Expect the worst and hope to be pleasantly surprised'

Another Marine raised his hand. 'And once we're inside?'

'Take one level at a time. Agent Trabant could be anywhere. Any other questions?'

'Yes, sir,' asked another Marine. 'What if Agent Trabant isn't grab-able, so to speak?'

'Commodore?' said Johnson, passing the question onwards.

'Then I will try to negotiate,' replied Speed. 'The British Government has lined up a plethora of juicy incentives as a last-gasp measure to try and appease Gunboat, the details of which you'll understand I cannot divulge.'

Johnson stepped forward. 'Okay, men, our call sign for this mission will be Echo Four Seven. As you know, HMS *Indomitable*'s call sign is Ridgeback. Keep your radios on at all times, and keep all communication brief but regular. It's imperative we know how our other groups are doing. And good luck!'

iii

Once Aquarium Air Traffic Control confirmed that the last guest had flown the building, Gunboat grabbed the microphone of the PA system, cleared his throat and addressed his own troops.

'Men, this is your leader. We are now about to be attack by British Royal Marines. Their boats will soon land on the beach. You know what to do. Defend at all cost. Take no prisoner. And remember – the ideals of law and order have no place in our world of criminal excellence. Repel the intruder, kick ass, and bathe yourselves in glory. And whatever happen – remember that defeat is simply no an option. Got it?'

'SÍ, BOSS!' cheered his men, at the ready, just inside the rear-exit doors.

The Guns of El Chorrillo were ready too.

iv

The three landing craft set off from HMS *Indomitable*, skimming their way across the Bay of Panama at breakneck speed. Another three, bone-jarring minutes later they landed at their respective points, dropped the bow ramps and released the groups of Marines across the rocky, slippery terrain towards the aquarium.

The GOEC responded immediately, piling out through the back doors of the aquarium with guns blazing – the signal for the Marines to return fire. The two sides collided head-on upon the once tranquil grassy picnic area. Round after round of ammunition whistled overhead and tore large chunks out of the surrounding palm trees. Marine Group Leaders shouted commands like American football quarterbacks, despatching runners down the flanks to outmanoeuvre the opposition.

283

GOEC reinforcements appeared through the back doors, but Marine Group A had already split, the forward half taking the entrance, the remainder helping Group B to finally push back the opposition.

'There's hundreds of them!' shouted Gunboat, looking down from the Crow's Nest.

'And dey'll soon be inside,' added Enrique, surprised at how quickly the enemy had advanced.

'They already are – look!'

Enrique turned to the bank of CCTV screens to see the hazy black-and-white figures now advancing along the numerous corridors. 'Boz, dey're also on Upper Level One.'

Further explosions shook the floor, and grew louder as the enemy advanced.

'NO!' screamed Gunboat, with hands on head, peering at another screen to witness the Caribbean Octopus Display explode into a billow of water and glass. 'THEY GONNA PAY FOR THIS! ENRIQUE – OPEN THE ARTILLERY CUPBOARD!'

'Great plan, Boz. And what about de English pig?' replied Enrique, nodding towards Trabant lying on the floor. 'You still need to kill him.'

'Yeah, I do need to kill him. And I'm sure the guests will understand.' With that, Gunboat quickly withdrew his nickel-plated hand cannon and took aim.

'N-no...' whimpered Trabant.

'Should have done this back in Cannes. Would have saved *all* this bother.'

'Yeah, please,' said Bentley, stepping out from the shadows. 'Just do it. You really must kill Trabant.'

'And where the hell you been?' growled Gunboat

'Watching the scuffle outside. Your men are getting their arses kicked.'

'SILENCE!'

Boom!

'Aaaaaaaah…!' yelped Trabant, in anticipation of the bullet… but it didn't come!

'Dat was another grenade, Boz,' said Enrique. 'De whole building's shaking.'

'They must be just along the corridor,' said Gunboat.

'GOEC command to Gunboat, over,' crackled the radio.

'Go ahead,' replied Gunboat.

'There are too many Marines… they've secured all lower levels, Ground Floor and now Upper Level One. But we keep on fighting. Over.'

'Sí, keep at it! And remember – no ever surrender! Over and out.'

'For crying out loud,' exclaimed Bentley. 'Will you please just kill Trabant.'

'Oi! Watch your mouth! Remember who you talk to.'

'Sorry, it's just that I'd, er… hate for you to miss your chance.'

'Hmmm!' grumbled Gunboat, while re-aiming his hand cannon.

Ring, ring!

'It's de telephone, Boz,' said Enrique.

'I KNOW THAT! ANSWER IT!'

Enrique ran to the receiver. 'Hola… u-huh… sí, sí, señora. Un momento. Boz,' he continued, covering the mouthpiece. 'It's señora Chávez.'

'Tell her I just a little bit busy.'

'But she say it really important.'

'Too important to stop me blowing this gringo's head off?'

'Sí. Apparently so.'

'I don't believe this,' grimaced Bentley.

Gunboat waddled over and snatched the phone, glaring at Enrique as if it was all his fault. 'Yes, sweetie?'

He listened intently, hanging on every word, until finally his jaw flopped open.

'Boz, what is it?'

No reply.

'Boz?'

A delicate, starry warmth began to replace the usual coal-blackness within Gunboat's eyes. Slowly, deliberately, he placed the receiver back in its cradle, leant against the adjacent wall, lowered his head and began to cry.

'Boz, what's wrong?' asked Enrique, in utter bewilderment. 'Is señora Chávez okay?'

'Sí, she fine,' sniffled Gunboat, wiping his eyes. 'No ever better.'

'Then for heaven's sake – shoot Trabant!' said Bentley.

Gunboat looked up through tear-filled eyes. 'That have to wait.'

'Why? Is it bad news, Boz?' asked Enrique.

Gunboat's face began to radiate sunshine. 'No, my loyal Mexican amigo, it the most wonderful news imaginable. I gonna be a father!'

'Oh, Boz!' gushed Enrique. 'Let me be de first to congratulate you.'

'Muchas gracias, Enrique. I can no begin to tell you how happy I am.'

Enrique smiled, then turned towards the prisoner. 'And what do you dink, English Pig? Hey – where *is* de pig!?!'

The space on the floor was empty. Bristo Trabant had gone.

27

A Fireball of Disgust

TRABANT RAN FOR HIS life, down the long internal staircase that led all the way to the basement. And still the building shook, amid the thunder-clap of military conflict.

Finally 'Ground Floor' appeared. He peered through the access door window, down the corridor of fish tanks and to the distant shards of light. Was he safe, at last? There was every chance, but first he had to find Eva, to be with her, no matter what. He continued down the next flight of stairs, not knowing what state they would have left her in. He couldn't bear to think, so ran ever faster, propelled by the most awful desperation; so fast he could barely keep synch with the harsh concrete steps.

'TRABANT – STOP!'

He recognized the voice instantly, coming from deeper in the stairwell.

Bang. Bang.

Two bullets tore at the ceiling, barely inches from his head. He ducked beneath the clouds of brick-dust, turned and ran back up the stairs. But his assailant's feet moved quicker, scaling the concrete steps maybe three at a time. He hurried onwards, consumed with panic, until mercifully 'Ground Floor' reappeared.

Trabant launched himself through the door and back inside the main complex. The shards of light were still twinkling, and ahead he saw the flash of gunfire. It *had* to be the Royal

Marines. He ran on towards them, praying they'd intervene in the nick of—

'I SAID – STOP!'

Bentley was homing in like an Exocet missile.

Trabant sped up, his feet now beyond the point of adhesion, slipping and clattering his way through another set of doors. Nearly there, perhaps just fifty metres—

Bang.

Another bullet whistled past. Trabant kept going, but Bentley was too fast; too fit…

'HELP!' shouted Trabant, calling to the kaleidoscope of shadows ahead, but Bentley's freight-train rugby tackle slammed him hard to the floor.

'Gotcha!' he hissed, quickly back to his feet. 'And now you're mine.'

Trabant lay face down and badly winded, yet with enough resolve to raise a bleary eye to his assailant, who was now tapping furiously into his mobile phone. But why not drag him straight back to Gunboat? It didn't make sense, and neither did the – ouch! – sharp edges digging into his chest. Were they fragments of brickwork? No, he remembered! One was *The Beginner's Guide To Being A Secret Agent*, and the other – his water pistol.

He manoeuvred his fingers inside his jacket, around the pistol's grip and slowly withdrew it. The reservoir was still full of the drinking water they'd been given last night. Eva's insistence he fill it had proved so wise, and the zero interest shown by the guards presented him with, perhaps, his only chance of escape.

Trabant muttered a silent prayer, then rolled onto his back as quickly as the torrent of pain would allow.

Squuiirrtt!

His aim was good – direct into Bentley's left eye.

'Aaarrrggghhh…'

As Bentley reeled, Trabant dived into the space behind, and scrambled onwards. In no time he was two metres back down the corridor, moving as fast as his bruises would allow. But Bentley was quick to regroup, and charged after him, again too fast, and this time to deliver a short, hard punch to Trabant's jaw, and finally quash the rebellion.

'Shut up moaning,' scowled Bentley, stamping repeatedly on the water pistol before kicking hard into Trabant's ribs. 'I have a couple of quick telephone calls to make.'

Bentley retrieved his mobile phone from the floor. 'What?!? Damned battery is flat!' He scanned the surroundings then hurried over to a wall-mounted telephone. 'This'll have to do,' he grumbled, in a voice revealing the first traces of stress.

Trabant remained horizontal, fighting the pain as it shot through his body.

'Come on, pick up, you lazy... Ah, Conda? It's me, Bentley... Yes, yes everything's fine... Yes, I used my real name, there's no need for disguises now... No, Gunboat didn't kill Trabant, so I'll do it myself... Yes, right now, and don't worry, I'll make it look like Gunboat did it so we can frame him... Yes, we're still on. So get moving... Phone all the contacts I gave you, right now. Explain Gunboat is about to get arrested. I'll call you in two hours.'

Bentley hung up then instantly dialled another number, ran his fingers through his hair while the line rang, then spoke quickly. 'Hello, Reuters? Great, I'd like to inform you of the murder of an MI6 agent. His name? Bristo Trabant... Yes, that's right, as in the car... Oh, the name of the murderer? Yes, I do happen to know. It's the notorious Panamanian arms trafficker Gunboat Charlie Chávez.'

Trabant shuddered. Death was upon him again, but this time from totally left field.

Bentley ended the call then turned back to Trabant. 'Does the name Oscar Conda mean anything to you?'

Trabant's eyes flickered in recollection of what Eva had said, way back in the DGSE safe house in Biot. *A huge turf war broke out… everyone died, all except one man, Oscar Conda, who fled and is rumoured to still be alive… but no one knows where… Gunboat still sees him as a threat.*

'Ah, I see Agent Avante *has* filled you in,' smiled Bentley. 'Gunboat wants Conda dead more than anything, but just can't find him. I knew all along,' laughed Bentley, '*and* that Conda would literally jump at the chance to claim what he feels is rightfully his.'

'Which is?' grimaced Trabant.

'The arms trade, you fool. Conda has the desire, but lacks both the intelligence and the balls to grab it for himself. That's where I come in. I've spent the past two years setting this whole thing up. Everything's in place. All we had to do was wait for the right opportunity to come along to get rid of Gunboat. And it finally did when you beat him at cards.'

'But h-how did that help?'

'Because we knew he would kill you. And the moment he did so I would inform MI6, get him arrested and out of the way, thus leaving the path clear for Conda to step in and take over. But you kept escaping, which was *very* annoying,' added Bentley, kicking Trabant once again to underline his point.

'Aaaarrrggghhh…'

'First with Agent Avante's intervention in Le Club Maritime du Soleil, then her preposterous idea of a rematch. That really played havoc with my plans. And then you both escaped to that desert island. Not only did I have to locate you, but I also had to ensure none of Agent Avante's colleagues got to you first. So I traced all calls from your phone, saw she'd called two of her team, negated them accordingly, and then hey-ho – you texted me. Happy days! That's why I brought you back to Gunboat, to give him another opportunity to kill you. But oh no, the stupid fat oaf couldn't even do that right. And so, after everything, it's me who has to administer the final deed of death.'

'I d–don't understand.'

'Don't you see, dumbo! Getting Gunboat arrested is the key to all this. I will make it look as though your death is down to him, and Reuters will spread the story to every newspaper in the world. MI6 will simply *have* to act. And the government will tumble like a house of cards, many others too, once the bloodhound press get their teeth into the story.'

'B–but everyone is frightened of Gunboat,' winced Trabant. 'What difference will my death make?'

'Because for the first time the public will know what's really been going on. It will be the scandal to end all scandals; a can of worms so wriggly and deep-rooted that the countless ministers, senators and dignitaries up to their neck in brown envelopes and clandestine pay-offs will *have* to be seen to be doing the things they were always supposed to be doing – locking up the bad guys.'

Bentley smiled as the last flecks of colour drained from Trabant's face. 'So, loser, they'll act all right. And with Gunboat out of the equation, Conda will get his revenge and the arms trade, and I get an even bigger percentage. Everyone's happy, right? Well, except Gunboat.'

'He'll kill you.'

'He'll never know it all stemmed from me. MI6 will believe every word I say, and once you're found dead, Gunboat will spend the rest of his life in some dirty, stinking cell. His supremacy will be over. And you, Mr Bristo Trabant, in the last few moments before I take great pleasure in killing you, must surely agree that I am indeed a genius.'

Trabant shook his head in revulsion. 'You're a disgrace to MI6; to the country; to—'

'I'm a disgrace!?!' laughed Bentley. 'You couldn't even complete your surveillance op in Cannes.'

'But I d–did relay some info.'

'Maybe, but not enough. You saw Solomon "Double Tap" Hurunguru talking with Gunboat?'

'Yes, and I texted his name to HQ.'

'Remember another man, Vincent Enezama, being there too?'

'No. Who's he?'

'The CEO of Walvis Aid, a bogus charity set up by Gunboat to facilitate the delivery of arms into the Central African Republic. They were meeting, right under your nose, to reschedule Hurunguru's deliveries. How do I know? Because it was me who set it all up.'

Trabant trawled his memory of Hurunguru's file. 'But there's no record of weapons being delivered.'

'Of course not. Because Gunboat's Ilyushin IL-76 cargo plane is registered to Walvis in Namibia, from where it flies to Liberia once a week, loaded with humanitarian aid. All above board. Only it diverts mid–flight to the Central African Republic, and beneath the boxes of medicines and vaccines lie cases of AK-47s and grenade launchers. The authorities never look because they're all on a bribe. Radar is woefully inept and unable to keep track. It's one of Africa's most fluid trafficking routes, and how, despite the UN's best efforts, Hurunguru's militia stays so well equipped, and ferocious. Slick, eh?'

'No. Repulsive.'

'Well, flight V5-AHO has paid for my villa in Sorrento many times over, so I beg to differ. Only its registration number had to be changed. Gunboat explained everything to Hurunguru in Cannes. It's now V5-GRS. And in a month it'll change again, as will the charity's name, just to keep one extra step ahead.'

Bentley kicked out again, just for the hell of it. Trabant winced under the blow, cradling his ribs. 'V5-GRS... Namibia to Liberia... V5-GRS...' he repeated, over and again, desperate to focus his mind and repel the incoming fog of unconsciousness.

'Ah, come on, don't worry!' taunted Bentley. 'I'll make your death quick. But first, you must tell me – did you score with Agent Avante? I admit, she was a looker, but boy did she love herself. Reckoned herself something special.'

'S-she *was* something special.' Trabant screwed up his eyes, now sinking beneath the weight of Eva's loss.

'Aah, bless! Had a crush on her, did you?' taunted Bentley. 'Well, let me tell you, she wasn't special at all. She was a bitch. An arrogant, rude, self-centred bitch!'

'No…' protested Trabant.

'Arrogant, stuck-up BITCH!'

Crunch!

Another vicious kick tore into Trabant's side, hard enough to now crack the same ribs, but also to reignite the paraffin anger inside.

'Women like her don't want losers like you,' continued Bentley. 'They want someone like me – a *real* man, an alpha male. Anyway, I'm glad she's dead. Just wish I could've done it myself.'

Trabant began to tremble; his anger now too volatile for his body to contain.

'Yeah, Eva Avante,' continued Bentley. 'The silly French tart. Her ex-husband had it right – used to knock her about. That's exactly what I'd have done.'

Trabant shuddered in realisation, at why she'd been so evasive on the desert island. How could anyone do that to her? His paraffin anger flared into a fireball of disgust, for her pain, for her loss, for everything that had happened.

'Bitch, bitch, bitch, bitch, bitch…'

'Shut up!' Trabant began to cry – an animal call to the woman he'd give anything to see alive again; to hold, to kiss, to say sorry to. The woman whose love he should never have declined, which he would seize unhesitatingly if given a second chance. But there could be no second chance, because of his own stupidity, and the greed and treachery of the man now standing over him.

'Bet she stunk of garlic too,' added Bentley, with glee.

'I like garlic,' growled Trabant.

'Tart. Whore.'

'Don't you dare talk about Eva like that!'

'What you mumbling about?' mocked Bentley, now screwing a silencer into the end of his gun.

Trabant looked up. Was he going to let this despicable man insult the memory of the woman he loved? And would he allow the sacrifice his father had made, all those years ago, to ultimately come to nothing?

NO WAY!

It was time, for him – Bristo Trabant – to take on that baton of righteousness, and wage it against the powers of evil that bore down upon him, and others, from every angle. His father and Eva had had the guts. Now so would he.

Bentley turned away to attach the silencer to his gun, merrily humming a victory tune to himself. As he did so, Trabant rolled onto his side and retrieved *The Beginner's Guide To Being A Secret Agent* from his inside pocket. The book flicked open at the beginning of 'Chapter 19: The Complete Novice's Guide To Throwing A Punch'. Trabant read as quickly as he could.

> **Step One:** Stand at forty-five degrees to the target.

He rose to his feet.

> **Step Two:** Curl fingers and thumb into a fist. Squeeze as tightly as possible for maximum impact.

294

Okay…

    Step Three: Bend forearm.

U-huh…

    Step Four: Twist away from target as far
                as possible. Refocus on your
                posture, then spin back as
                quickly as possible to land
                fist hard on the target's jaw,
                halfway between chin and ear.
                Follow through, as if playing
                a tennis shot.

Trabant had the anger, and now he had the tools. Abhorrence coursed through his veins like a tidal wave, bolstered by the pain of every tease and jab of ridicule he'd endured throughout his entire life. And before him stood the symbol of everything bad in the world.

Trabant coiled his body then tapped upon Bentley's shoulder. 'Hmmm…?'

As his assailant turned, the dam of revulsion blew wide open. … two, three, four – BOSH!

Bentley's head jerked away on impact, and the momentum carried Trabant headfirst into the glass of the Mediterranean Octopus Display. But it didn't shatter, and he looked back in time to see Bentley's eyes adopt separate orbits of surprise and confusion, before his legs finally caved and dropped his loathsome, contemptuous body down to the floor.

Trabant looked from his fist to Bentley then back again, barely believing what he'd just achieved.

'That's from Eva!' he roared at the man pole-axed at his feet. But it meant a lot more too. He'd struck another blow for the

295

oppressed. The fight-back was on, and his own tide had turned – forever.

'Hang on, Eva,' he cried, turning back towards the stairs. 'I'm coming for you.'

The shards of daylight from the end of the corridor continued to beckon, but Trabant wasn't interested. He would never leave without her, no matter what, but he needed to be quick. The GOEC were still active. And of more immediate concern, Bentley was now beginning to stir.

28

Gentle Lapping Waves

FROM THE BRIDGE OF HMS *Indomitable*, Eva looked fixedly through her binoculars, scanning the battle scene, peering between the plumes of smoke billowing up from the aquarium building into the mid-afternoon Panama City sky.

Jones walked up and stood beside her. 'Red Leader has just reported in. All levels in the aquarium are now secured, except Upper Level Three and the Crow's Nest, where Gunboat is still holding out strong.'

'Thank you for keeping me—'

Suddenly, to the left, a movement. Eva turned her binoculars to a small back door – a fire-exit perhaps – that led directly onto the grassed areas outside. The door opened slowly. Eva zoomed in as close as she could, to see a man wearing a beige suit poke his head outside, scan left to right, then step out into the open.

A beige suit? The one she'd given him way back at the DGSE safe house?

'BRISTO!' she exclaimed.

Eva looked closer still; saw the dark hair, saw him running forward across the grassy area straight for the water, navigating the debris of the ensuing conflict. Delight surged through her body. 'I've seen Bristo!' she repeated, as loud as possible. 'He's escaped!'

'Whereabouts?' asked Jones, raising his own binoculars.

'Just exited the aquarium, and now he's running down towards the boats. See him?'

'Yes... yes I do. Sir, come quick!'

Bravinger joined them in a flash, and snatched Jones's binoculars to look for himself.

'I see him too,' added Commodore Speed. 'It's a miracle. Get him to safety – quick!'

ii

The RIB waited patiently, bobbing up and down in the wash, its huge outboard motors chugging away on standby. Eva watched intently as he continued onwards, negotiating the obstacle course of rocks and crevices that led to the beckoning Marines. She imagined his joy, his overwhelming relief—

'Where's Trabant now?' asked Jones, returning with a new set of binoculars.

'Almost at the water.'

'Ah, yes, I see him. Boy, he can certainly run fast. Look at him go!'

The tide was slowly going out, and now the tips of jagged rocks broke the dark ocean surface. Dodging the dips and puddles had been hard work, but he was nearly there.

Twenty metres, fifteen metres...

The water twinkled in the afternoon sunshine, like a sheet of jewels calling his name.

'Come on, Bristo! Come on!' shouted Eva, cheering him on like a racehorse about to triumph against all the odds.

Twelve metres, ten metres...

He ran faster; only the final straight then salvation was his. Eight metres, five metres...

Almost touching distance now, almost—

Crack.

His body shook like a rag doll's, then fell face down at the water's edge – lifeless and twisted beneath the harsh resonance of gunshot. Birds scattered into the skies and the boat crew dived for cover, but then silence claimed all – a total silence – ominous, uncaring, and one that echoed with only the most sincere promise of finality.

'N-O-O-O!' screamed Eva, quickly lowering her binoculars to double-check with her own eyes.

Bravinger, Speed and Jones stood rigid too, stunned into disbelief. The body lay limp, moved only by the soft, gentle, lapping waves. Despite the presence of a Royal Navy taskforce, two elite intelligence agencies and the crack troops of the Royal Marines, a single bullet had done the job. One moment life, the next – death?

'Ridgeback, Ridgeback, this is Echo Four Seven. We have a man down at the water's edge. Repeat, we have a man down at the water's edge!'

Reality shattered the walls of Eva's composure. Her heart screamed out, looking all around, pleading for someone to tell her it wasn't so. But they couldn't, and with nothing left to cling to, her true feelings rose to the surface for everyone to discover.

'B-R-I-S-T-O!'

Tears burst out and down her quivering cheeks. 'Please save him, please let him live,' she cried. She would care for him, mend him, be there for him every inch of the way, no matter what. Just please, let him live.

'Ridgeback, this is Echo Four Seven... receiving? Over.'

'Go ahead. Over.'

'It's the worst news, sir. Man confirmed as dead. Repeat, man confirmed as dead, but sniper may still be active. Request air support to see him off. Over.'

299

The bridge became numb. Eva held tighter to the rail in front – her knuckles white and head held low – fighting the jabbing, thrusting pain with gritted teeth.

'Wilco Echo Four Seven. Message received and understood. Over.'

Within minutes, two Harriers had swooped down from the clouds and made a fly-past; their weapons systems scouring the coastline for the assailant, itching to unleash a devastating retribution, but there was no one to be found.

Optimism squeezed Eva's hand and urged her to be strong. She wiped her blurry eyes then refocused the binoculars, in the hope that somehow there was a different view, a different explanation; that by some miracle…

But the body remained still.

Her mind raced with everything they had been through: Le Club Maritime du Soleil, the DGSE safe house, the airport, the world security mobilisation, Calypso Abajo, the *Cornelia Cortez*, the desert island, the rebirth of the man before her eyes… then the betrayal, the look of defeat in his eyes that she just couldn't remove, the rematch, and now, finally – the end?

She clung to hope with everything she had, and watched as the Royal Marines worked feverishly with every ounce of care and expertise they possessed. But their heads were low, and the body limp, and she knew…

… she just knew

… he was dead.

iii

A second bullet had not been necessary, yet the birds still circled high above, riding the thermals as if to admire the marksmanship. Eva scanned the surrounding buildings again for signs of movement – a closing window, a glint of sunlight on the rifle's sights, anything. But there was nothing, not even a glimmer.

The sniper had gone.

Eva lowered her head again, this time in shame. If only she'd protected him. She was the highly trained secret agent, the one supposed to be experienced in the ways of the dark world he'd been thrown into. And she could feel the guilt already, rising like a dark smothering cloak; guilt she would carry for the rest of her life. But she wasn't alone. Someone else had a far greater responsibility.

She turned towards Bravinger, her eyes molten with anger. 'It's also your fault.'

'I beg your pardon?'

'You… you sent him to his death.'

'Agent Avante, may I remind you you're addressing the head of the British Secret Service.'

'All I see is a man with blood on his hands.'

'How dare you.'

'The truth hurts, huh? Bristo should never have been sent to Cannes in the first place. An innocent man thrust into a world he neither understood, nor was prepared for; who paid the ultimate price for your catastrophic error of judgement.'

'You're emotionally involved, Agent Avante.'

'DAMNED RIGHT I AM!' she shouted. 'That's the whole reason I signed up for the DGSE in the first place. Because I care. Because I have emotion. Because I want to do the right thing.' Eva scowled at Bravinger, beyond caring about the consequences of her words. 'Maybe if you cared too then none of this would have happened.'

'Agent Avante, you must calm down,' interjected Gérard Depouis.

'I'm sorry, sir, but Bristo was exposed, betrayed and let down. This whole situation is rotten to the core. And so, Mr Bravinger, are you!'

301

'Eva, calm down,' pleaded Depouis.

'No, sir, I won't. This is his fault,' she continued, pointing directly at Bravinger, her words breaking with emotion. 'He had it in for Bristo from the word go. Making cheap remarks, laughing behind his back, and I insist you do something about it.'

'You're upset,' replied Depouis.

'Of course I'm upset! But the question still stands, sir, right here and now: are you going to do anything about Bravinger?'

'There will be an enquiry, of course. But...'

'Fine. If you won't, I will.'

Eva moved towards Bravinger, but Depouis quickly stood in her way. 'Agent Avante, don't do anything foolish. Please, leave the bridge. That's an order.'

She shook her head in disgust. 'I haven't finished with you yet, Bravinger.'

'Eva, please...' said Depouis, 'just go.'

'I can do better than that, sir. Have my resignation too. If this is what being a secret agent has come to, then I want no further part in it.'

iv

The sniper had waited five hours for the man's head to appear within his rifle sights. From his vantage point all exits had been covered, all eventualities accounted for. Through the cross-hairs he'd watched the back door open, watched the man in the beige suit step out then scramble his way down towards the water's edge and smile at his fellow countrymen. The sniper had tracked his every footstep, awaiting his moment, treble-checking the target's features until totally satisfied it was the right man. And then, without emotion, his finger had softly squeezed the trigger and shot out the lights of the man he did not know.

Galeocerdo Cuvier's work was done. The Tiger Shark had secured his prey.

29

A Nice Cup of Tea and a Buttered Scone

'I DINK YOU'LL MAKE an excellent father, Boz.'

'Muchas gracias, Enrique,' replied Gunboat, wiping the tears of joy from his eyes. 'We been try for months.'

'So dat sexy lingerie really do de trick, huh?'

'What sexy lingerie?'

'You know, dat señora G buy just after you return from Cannes.'

'Yeah…' replied Gunboat, with a twinkle in his eye. 'Mother Nature work in funny way, and—'

Boom.

An almighty explosion rocked the aquarium building. Gunboat ran towards the bank of wall-mounted CCTV monitors in the Crow's Nest. 'LOOK – THEY EVERYWHERE!' he shouted. 'Must have crept up while we talk babies. See, I going soft already!'

Every image on the cameras was the same – clouds of smoke, lapping flames and a maelstrom of Royal Marines and GOEC beating the living daylights out of each other. And there, just one floor below, on Upper Level Two – a dozen or so Marines were carefully advancing along the dimly lit corridor.

'Gunboat to GOEC Command – you receiving? Over.'

A few seconds later the reply came crackling back. 'GOEC Command receiving. It kicking off big time down here, Boss. The Marines have secured Sub Levels One and Two, Ground Floor, and Upper Levels One and Two. Over.'

'Have they taken any prisoners?' asked Gunboat.

'Yes, about twenty men.'

Gunboat rechecked the monitors. 'Jeez, they right beneath us now.'

'What we going to do?' asked Enrique.

'FIGHT!' Gunboat hurried over to a wall of cabinets, tore open the doors and began handing out the AK-47s stored inside. 'It what I done *all* my life.' He beckoned his men closer. 'Enrique, Raúl, Ramón, follow me down the back staircase. We head them off at the Tropical Frog Enclosure.'

ii

The patter of army boots echoed from round the next corner. Gunboat signalled for his men to take up position: Enrique behind a large tank housing a thoroughly disinterested Caiman Crocodile; Raúl amongst the shadows of the mock-Amazon picnic area, and Ramón flat on his belly, invisible against the slithering, hissing background of the Boa Constrictor Display. Each man set his trigger finger to ready and awaited Gunboat's command.

The shadow of advancing Marines grew taller on the opposing wall. Gunboat waited in position just round the corner, with AK-47 poised and piggy ears straining to ascertain just how far away they now were.

Five metres, maybe less?

Boom.

Another explosion rocked the building, covering everything beneath in yet more dust and debris. A dart frog leapt for cover, but the wrong way, out of its tank and straight onto Enrique's shoulder.

'AAAAAH! GET IT OFF ME!' he screamed, jumping to his feet and revealing his position. Raúl and Ramón rushed to his

305

assistance, and the Marines hit the deck, with guns aimed – ready for action.

'Q-U-I-C-K... F-I-R-E!' shouted Gunboat, unaware of the frog distraction occurring behind him; launching himself round the corner with total commitment, to unleash the hellfire of his AK-47. Round after round of devil's breath tore at the brickwork, fluorescent tubes and an intricate overhead box junction of pipes, which burst and gushed water down on all those beneath. Yet the Marines stayed low, waiting until the magazine had finally emptied.

'Everybody okay?' called out the lead Marine.

Saturated but positive replies worked their way back up the line.

'I think it's fair to state, sir,' added the Marine second in line, realigning his helmet, 'that Gunboat's not happy.'

'Agreed. And I've never seen so many bullets miss so many targets in all my long military career. Quite astounding.'

'Do you think he's out of ammo?'

'Wait...' replied the lead Marine, seeing Gunboat's shadow disappear back round the corner. 'Listen...'

Tap. Click. Click-click.

'Get ready, men. He's reloaded.'

iii

The fresh banana-shaped magazine awaited its command, but Gunboat was momentarily distracted by the need to berate his men.

'Where were you? I was out there on my own!'

'Sorry, Boss,' replied Raúl, 'but those dart frogs are very poisonous. One bite and—'

'They no bite. They—'

Clack. Clack. Clack.

Short bursts of fire returned from back down the corridor.

'NO! MY BABIES!' screamed Gunboat, looking on in horror as the huge tropical fish tank just behind him erupted into a billowing gush of shattered glass and terrified inhabitants. 'No worry, Papa's here. Quick, Enrique – GET A NET!'

'Yes, Boz.'

'Raúl – grab that puffer fish!' yelled Gunboat. 'And be careful he no—'

Pop.

'Oops, too late!' replied Raúl, as the fish in his hands inflated to the size of a football. 'Wow, they really *do* puff up!'

'I puff you up in a minute. Put him in one of the smaller tank next door, and get that electric eel.'

'Okay!'

Zzzzzzzzzzz…

'YE-OW!'

Ramón joined Gunboat down on all fours, frantically grabbing at the shoals of fish streaming past on the torrent of aquarium water. Enrique quickly reappeared at their side, twirling a net like a fencer's sword to expertly flip the terrified fish up through the air and into a hastily grabbed bucket.

Boom.

'Bloody foreigners, come here and destroy my aquarium. Well, I show them…' snarled Gunboat, as he manhandled an armoured sucker-mouth catfish into the place it really didn't want to go.

'Gunboat, can you hear me?' cackled the megaphone.

'Dat's the Royal Marines, Boz,' said Enrique, wiping his brow. 'Must be just round de corner.'

'Yeah, they are. Wanna know how I know that? Because I the only one to face them. You were too busy tarting around with Kermit frog.'

'But I hate reptiles, Boz.'

'They no reptiles – they amphibians! And anyway, you—'

'I repeat – Gunboat, can you hear me?' called the Marine.

Gunboat's eyes narrowed. 'Enrique, make sure you get every last fish. I be back in one second.' He picked up his AK-47, waddled back to the edge of the corridor and peeked round.

The smoke and dust had almost cleared. Only random speckles remained in the air, creatively illuminated by the few remaining ceiling lights. The walls were peppered with a thousand bullet holes, and sheets of plasterboard hung from the ceiling like stricken infantry, about to drop at any moment.

'No one mess with El Cañonero. No one,' he grumbled to himself, then edged closer still, with the next six-hundred-and-fifty-rounds-per-minute instalment of merciless contempt awaiting the command of his trigger finger.

'For the third time – Gunboat, can you hear me?'

Gunboat turned the corner and sprayed bullets everywhere, squeezing the trigger so tightly it almost broke off in his hand, until finally the second wave of hellfire ceased.

Tap. Click. Click–click.

'Gunboat – please listen! We only came to get Bristo Trabant back before you killed him. We didn't want all this trouble.'

'You should know better than take me on. And he should no cheat at cards then, eh? Embarrass me like that in front of all my amigos.'

'We appreciate the slur against your name, and the British Government wishes to make an official apology.'

'It too late for that. I decided – it time for me to reveal the deep dark secrets in my little black book.'

'Now, now, let's not be hasty! There's no need for you to do that.'

'I think blowing up my aquarium is plenty reason to do exactly that. And for your information I no even have Trabant no more. He run away about twenty minute ago.'

'We know. He was shot dead outside the aquarium.'

Gunboat exhaled deeply, allowing a huge breath to wheeze past his battle-ready tonsils. 'So?'

'So this situation is now global.'

'How come?'

'The story has been leaked to Reuters by an unknown source. And right now there's countless television crews outside, from all over the world, wanting to know why a British MI6 agent was shot dead on the rocks, and why a Royal Navy taskforce is positioned just offshore.'

'That's your problem. No mine.'

'True. Except that this unknown source also told Reuters it was you who killed Bristo Trabant.'

'I NEVER! He deserve it, for sure, but it was no me who kill him.'

'Well, given these accusations, and with the whole world seeing these images, you must understand that the British Government has to be seen to be doing something about it.'

'Ah, so this all about saving face, huh?'

'In a nutshell – yes.'

Enrique hurried to Gunboat's side. 'Boz, we could do really well out of dis,' he whispered. 'Let's turn dis to our advantage.'

Gunboat nodded in agreement, then shouted back to the Marine. 'So what precisely you have in mind?'

'Well, my commanding officer, together with the British Prime Minister, has come up with an ingenious solution.'

'Can no wait to hear it.'

'Okay. Well, before I say it, you must promise to open your mind like never before. And remember to think of the bigger picture.'

'I open, so come on... hit me with it.'

'Well, we were wondering, in a round-about kind of way, if you wouldn't possibly mind... and remember, it's

only for the TV cameras... if you would consider, er...
surrendering?'

'ME, EL CAÑONERO – SURRENDER!?! NEVER!'

'It's only pretend, until—'

'BOG OFF!' shouted Gunboat. 'I no kill your loco agent,
and I no surrender to you, or no one – no ever. Got it? You
want me, you come here and get me!'

'Yeah, and me too!' shouted Enrique.

The lead Marine retreated a few steps. 'Echo Four Seven to
Ridgeback. Receiving? Over.'

'Go ahead,' replied Commodore Speed.

'Sir, we have a situation. Gunboat is refusing to surrender.'

'Oh!'

'What shall we do? Over.'

'Hang fire, Echo Four Seven. Wait for further instructions.'

The Marine returned to his megaphone. 'Okay, Gunboat.
I'm awaiting further instructions. Would you mind hanging on
for a mo...'

iv

The floor of the Rainforest section now resembled a giant,
sprawling Malawi lake, and though the main surge of water had
finally relented, it had spread far and wide. Gunboat painstakingly
rechecked the terrain, picking through the jagged fragments of
broken glass and rockery for any remaining life forms. Raúl and
Ramón continued their shuttle-runs, transporting the injured
fish to the makeshift fish hospital Enrique had hastily created
out of bricks and a large tarpaulin sheet.

'What the injury count?' asked Gunboat, peering over
Enrique's shoulder.

'Dirty-five dead, and rising. De injured are still coming in.
We must get de aquarists up here immediately.'

'Leave it to me.' Gunboat placed a monstrous, reassuring hand on Enrique's shoulder, then waddled back to the edge of the wall by the corridor. 'Oi! Señor Loco Megaphone – you still there?'

'Yes, señor Gunboat.'

'We have many casualty here. They need urgent attention. I gonna get our medical team up here, to transfer them to our in-house intensive-care facility.'

'Okay, that's fine with—'

'I no ask you – I tell you! Just like cards: I no ask people to play me, I t-tell…'

Gunboat jolted at his own words; at the sudden realisation that slapped him across the face; the sudden realisation that playing cards was his one weakness; a weakness his enemies had exploited to the max by engineering this whole damn loco rematch in the first place.

'Boz, you okay?' asked Enrique, as Gunboat's expression turned from surprise, through horror, to teeth-grinding fury. 'You need de ducks?'

'NO!'

'Good, because de aquarists are now here.'

The five medics stepped out of the lift and made their way along the corridor. Dragging behind them was a single trolley supporting one giant plastic bathtub of water, together with boxes of medical supplies, piping, cable-ties, fish food and a curious blue sports bag hidden beneath a tea-towel.

Gunboat contained his fury and beckoned the medics onwards through the uneasy stand-off, then turned back to Enrique. 'Well done with the fish. You did all you could.'

'Muchas gracias, Boz.'

'Now tell me, how much ammunition the aquarists bring?'

Enrique smiled. 'Five dousand rounds, plus two hundred grenades, all inside dat blue sports bag.'

Gunboat's face lit with a deathly smile. 'Excellent. And with the television cameras outside, we gonna give the world

311

a show they no ever forget. Now listen – I want maximum exposure.'

'Yes, Boz.'

'And do I look okay? Or should I go change my suit?'

'You a bit dusty, Boz, but dat's good. Dust convey to de outside world de shocking injustice bestowed on you by dese horrible invading forces.'

'Excellent selection of words, Enrique.'

'Danks, Boz. I be practising.'

'Excellent.'

'So tell me, Boz, what's de plan?'

'You will see. Come on, follow me.'

V

The aquarists made their way back past the soaked huddle of Royal Marines, carefully pulling the trolley and bathtub of three hundred and ninety-eight fish casualties.

'Raúl, Ramón, come here,' whispered Gunboat, beckoning them over. 'Me and Enrique are going up to the roof to create a spectacle.'

'Are we?' asked Enrique, bubbling with excitement.

'Oh, yes! You two stay here and hold off the Marines long as possible. There's extra ammo in this bag, plus food and beer. Give these gringo locos a picnic they no ever forget, eh?'

'Sí, Boss. It be our pleasure.'

Gunboat shook hands then turned, waddled up to the lift, pressed the button marked 'Roof' and waited with scowling impatience.

Enrique stood respectfully alongside. 'Boz, what kind of spectacle you dinking of?'

'The kind that win us this battle psychologically.'

'Wow, dat also a big word, Boz.'

'Sí. I be practising too.'

Enrique smiled, then thought of another question. 'Boz, can I ask someding else?'

'Sure, go for it.'

'If *you* didn't kill de English pig, then who did?'

'Enrique, life is full of mystery.'

'Oh, come on, Boz, don't be like dat. You can tell me.'

Gunboat just winked, then stepped into the lift.

'Come on, Boz,' continued Enrique, following him inside. 'Everyone's expecting you to kill him.'

'Since when I ever worry what people think of me?'

'But de card game, Boz… de rematch… your reputation?'

'Enrique,' replied Gunboat, watching the floor numbers count up on the illuminated display board. 'I come to realise that Trabant actually do me a muchas big favour.'

'How's dat?'

'He make me realise that lose at cards is my Achilles heel; one that people take full advantage of. And a man in my position can no afford to have slightest weakness. So, from now on I will no ever, ever play cards again – and will therefore become INVULNERABLE! And that important if I going to be a father, eh?'

'Sí,' replied Enrique. 'Sure is, Boz.'

The lift doors opened, and Gunboat and Enrique stepped out onto the roof. To the right, out to sea, the ominous presence of HMS *Indomitable* and co remained. To the left, the skyscrapers of Panama City smiled back. And far below, down on the ground, the last scatterings of GOEC and Royal Marines continued their battle, like prizefighters slugging it out in the final rounds.

Ahead, and dominating the roof, the huge silver dome glistened in the heat haze; its surface highly polished and patterned with countless hexagonal indentations akin to the appearance of a golfball.

'Quick – this way!' said Gunboat, beckoning Enrique to follow. He lumbered up to a large control box, flicked up the lid and pressed a button. Motors leapt into action, and through a cacophony of whirring and whining, the giant dome began to revolve on its axis and disappear into the hollowed-out recess beneath. As it did so, it began to reveal a long horizontal spike, then a nose, a cockpit, a body and wings, until finally – a tail.

'Like phoenix from the flame!' beamed Gunboat, almost beside himself with pride. 'The media will love this – you and I to take off in Hawker Harrier Jump Jet.'

'Wow, she beautiful!' gasped Enrique.

'Sure is, and she a special two-seater training model. So come on, let's get in.'

Gunboat climbed the ladder and unceremoniously stepped inside, wedging himself down into the cockpit. Enrique followed, comfortably slipping into the seat behind.

'Right, let's go,' said Gunboat, putting on a leather pilot's helmet and goggles.

'Boz, you ever flown dis before?'

'Nope. But it can no be that hard.'

'I no so sure, Boz. Dere an awful lot to—'

Click. Click.

'Damn! She no starting. Enrique – get the booster pack!'

'Where you keep it, Boz?'

'I don't know. Look around you.'

'Dere ain't no booster pack here, Boz.'

'Then get out and give me a push!'

'Sure ding, Boz.' Enrique stood and turned, but then suddenly froze. 'Boz, look back at de lift!'

Gunboat turned to see that countless Royal Marines had taken up positions on the roof, with their assault rifles aimed and ready.

'Raúl and Ramón no hold out very long, huh?' he growled.

'I dink dese Marines came from de other entrance, Boz. Over de far side of de roof.'

314

Gunboat turned towards the gathered enemy. 'EH – WHY YOU FOLLOW US UP HERE?'

'Just procedure,' a Marine replied.

'I thought I no accused of no anything?'

'You're not.'

'Then why you point guns at my head?'

'Just a show for the news crews. Take a look above.'

Gunboat diverted his eyes to the sky, and saw at least two helicopters hovering, with cameras running. He then saw a Royal Navy Sea King helicopter approaching, packed full of yet more Marines.

'What'll it be, Gunboat?'

The Marines held their breath as another puff of cigar smoke wafted up from the cockpit and away with the warm afternoon breeze.

'I NEVER SURRENDER!'

'Okay, forget surrendering. The British Government would like to invite you on board HMS *Indomitable* for a chat over a nice cup of tea and a buttered scone. No harm in that, right?'

'Are you deaf? I say – NEVER!'

'At least think about it?'

Another large cloud of cigar smoke took to the air.

'He's smiling,' whispered one Royal Marine to another. 'Fifty-three of us up here pointing weapons of annihilation at his head, and all he can do is puff his cigar and smile.'

Gunboat took a final draw on his cigar, flicked it into orbit then turned to Enrique. 'Well, my loyal Mexican amigo, it time to see what these gringos are made of.'

'I wid you, Boz. Just give de word.'

'As soon as I stand, open fire.'

'Will do, Boz.'

With that, Gunboat placed his hands on the sides of the cockpit and pushed down, to lift his massive frame.

Nothing.

He tried again.

'Boz – you all right?' asked Enrique.

'Rrrrrrrrrrrrrrrrrrrrrrrrggghhh!'

'Stand up, Boz. I right behind you.'

'I no can… rrrrrrrrrrrrrrrrrrrrrrrrrrr,' replied Gunboat, crimson-faced.

'Why not, Boz?'

'Because, Enrique – I stuck!'

30

A Message for Colonel Bravinger

EVA COULD HARDLY LOOK as the RIB finally docked alongside HMS *Indomitable*. And a tear began to fall at the sight of the black body-bag laid out on the deck, silently cradled by the crew, in acknowledgement of what should never have been.

'Sir, the body is now being lifted aboard.'

'Thank you, Jones,' replied Commodore Speed. 'Colonel Bravinger, Agent Avante, shall we…'

'No,' replied Eva, softly. 'I don't want to see him like this. Perhaps when he's, you know… at peace. You go. I'll be on the flight deck.'

'Okay, if you're sure?'

'I am.'

ii

The Officer of the Day saluted the limp body as it was hoisted aboard, transferred onto the waiting stretcher and then quickly moved through a twist of corridors to the lift. Sickbay was square, bland, and situated on Five Deck, five decks below the flight deck. Its sterile white walls were lined with wires that linked the machines and scanners. On the other side of the door stood a double sink, and on the wall opposite a clock stating it was now 16.41 local time.

A team of seven ran the unit. Doc Robson – the man in charge, with the face of a field-mouse and the fingers of a pianist – greeted the body with a solemn, respectful nod, before directing the stretcher carriers towards the bed.

Commodore Speed took up position just inside the door.

'Okay, Doc, get straight to it,' said Bravinger, walking towards the opposite wall. 'I want to ascertain the exact cause of death.'

'Well, Colonel Bravinger, taking a wild guess, I'd say it was down to that bullet. Wouldn't you?'

'Yes, of course, but I need specifics for the paperwork. So, if you don't mind…'

Doc Robson gently unzipped the body-bag. The face stared back, bereft of colour. The skin was smattered with sand, and a small piece of seaweed lay entangled amongst the short locks of black hair. As the zip continued downwards, the beige suit was revealed, sodden and stained, and complete with the dank smell of seawater.

With the zip fully open, the doc spread the bag out flat until it formed a large plastic sheet upon which the body lay. He then turned to one of his team. 'Dobsey, check the pockets for belongings, would you.'

'Sure.'

The man set about his work, and another member of the team began to remove the sodden dark-brown shoes, placing them neatly inside a see-through plastic bag. Next off were the black socks, revealing pale white feet.

'This is all I found,' said Dobsey, passing a book to Doc Robson.

'Hmmm… *The Beginner's Guide To Being A Secret Agent*. Recognise this, Colonel Bravinger?'

'Yes I do. Standard field issue for all new recruits.'

'Didn't do him much good though, did it?'

'No,' he replied, grimly. 'Can you see where the bullet entered yet?'

'Well, his face is intact, so it must be the back of the head.'

318

'That makes sense,' added Jones, loosening his tie. 'Bristo was running away from the aquarium and surrounding buildings where the sniper must have been positioned.'

'Agreed. But where on earth's the exit wound?' The doc carefully turned the head and looked even closer. 'Well, I never. The bullet has remained lodged inside. I can see the tail end.'

'You're joking!' exclaimed Jones.

'No. In fact, I think I can even get to it.'

Bravinger stretched an eye. 'Well, at least Trabant's features are unspoilt for his mother's eyes. And he will be remembered as a good-looking man who—'

'He was never *that* good-looking, sir,' cut in Jones, peering more closely at the features, his voice laced with shock.

'What do you mean?'

'Sir, this body – it isn't Trabant!'

'Then who the hell is it?' asked Bravinger, finally stepping nearer.

Jones took a deep breath. 'It's Bentley, sir!'

Bravinger looked closer still. 'Well, I'll be damned, so it is.'

'Give me a hand, Jones,' said the doc. 'I want to turn the body right over.'

Jones obliged, helping to gently roll Bentley onto his front.

'The sniper must have been waiting for Trabant but shot Bentley by mistake,' mused Bravinger.

'Yes, I can definitely reach the bullet,' added the doc, manoeuvring carefully. 'Ah, yes… a curious stubby design, enough to kill but not to come hurtling out the other side. Incredible. Perhaps the weapon itself was of lower velocity. Anyway, yes… here comes the bullet… and, ooh… hmmm, interesting… there seems to be a word engraved on the side.'

'What does it say?' asked Jones.

'Not sure yet.' The doc walked over to the sink and ran the cold tap. 'Well, it's more than just a word. It's someone's name carved into the casing.'

319

'We've seen this before, sir!' exclaimed Jones. 'Remember two years ago, at that anti-arms trade convention in Prague? Remember the chief whistle-blower was a man named Pablo Aktar.'

'Yes, what of it?' replied Bravinger.

'Aktar had promised to expose Gunboat's connections with certain political figures. But just as he stood to deliver his speech, a single bullet was fired through the stained-glass window, straight between his eyes.'

'Yes, I do remember,' replied Bravinger. 'He died instantly.'

'That's right, sir. And when the bullet was recovered, it was found to have his name engraved on the side.'

'Proving what, Jones?'

'That Aktar's murder was pre-meditated, sir, and that he was the intended victim. It was a message. It was the same when the Greek shipping magnate Paphos Chistadoulos-Dolopolos was assassinated.'

'Ah, but on that occasion he was shot twice.'

'Only because his surname was too long to fit on a single casing. It was the same outcome – the death of a man making a stand against Gunboat. He was about to reveal how he'd been approached to smuggle huge quantities of arms concealed within the hollowed-out bodies of life-sized Jurassic dinosaur replicas, bound for the Natural History Museum in Qatar. Then suddenly – bang, bang – he's dead too. We could never prove it, but the coincidence is too great to ignore.'

'What about the hit-man – any leads on him?'

'No, sir. He vanishes like the wind. We haven't the first clue to go on. All we *do* know is that his preparation and, forgive the pun, execution are exemplary.'

Bravinger rolled his eyes. 'Ah, but Jones, on this occasion the hit-man *did* get it wrong.'

'Sir, with the utmost respect, if the name on the bullet matches the head it is embedded in, then Bentley was, without doubt, the intended victim.' Jones turned back to the doc. 'Can you make out the name yet?'

'Indeed I can,' he replied. 'And young Mr Jones is right. It's not Trabant's name on the bullet. It's Bentley's.'

For a long moment the room fell silent.

'But I don't understand…' said Bravinger, scratching his head. 'Bentley's a national treasure.'

'He'll soon be buried treasure, sir.'

'That's just not funny, Jones.'

'I'm sorry, sir, but it's true. And I'll tell you something else that's true.'

'What?'

'With Bentley dead, Bristo Trabant may still be alive!'

Commodore Speed quickly grabbed his radio. 'Ridgeback to Echo Four Seven. Come in. Over.'

'Echo Four Seven receiving. Go ahead, sir.'

'The man shot on the beach was not Agent Trabant. I repeat, it was not Agent Trabant; it was Bentley. That means Trabant may still be alive, somewhere inside the aquarium. Please look everywhere. Over.'

'Wilco, sir. Proceeding immediately. Out.'

iii

Sickbay waited with bated breath, while Bravinger fought his own personal swirl of confusion. Had Agent Avante been right all along? Was Bentley really on Gunboat's payroll? And if so, just how many secrets had he sold; how many operations had he compromised? How many more agents had he betrayed? And if Gunboat had actually killed him, then what act would be so severe to warrant snuffing out what would doubtless be a highly valuable information source?

321

'Echo Four Seven calling Ridgeback. Over.'

'Go ahead,' replied Commodore Speed.

'Great news, sir. We've located Agent Trabant. Over.'

'Excellent work. Where was he?'

'Locked in a broom cupboard, sir.'

'Is he alive?'

'Yes, but in a bad way. He's been shot twice. Over.'

Sickbay fell silent.

'Okay, Echo Four Seven, message received and understood. Evacuate casualty to Ridgeback as soon as possible. Over and out.'

'Wilco, sir. Out.'

iv

The RIB wasted no time returning to HMS *Indomitable*. Trabant lay unconscious on the deck, wrapped in a blanket and beneath the protective armed guard of the four-man crew. Overhead, even more helicopter TV crews hovered and swooped, but they saw nothing specific.

The lead seaman docked without fuss at *Indomitable*'s port accommodation ladder, and the awaiting medical crew quickly held up a large tarpaulin sheet, behind which they lifted Trabant aboard. As the RIB put back to sea, Trabant was quickly transferred to a stretcher, put in the lift and whisked down to Sickbay, where Doc Robson's eager team transferred him onto the now-vacant bed and descended on him like a Formula One pit crew.

'Bentley's body is in the mortuary, in case you wondered,' said Doc Robson to Bravinger and Jones, as he searched for a gap, then dived into the melee.

'You'd better inform Bentley's next of kin,' said Bravinger.

'Not sure he has any,' replied Jones, glumly.

'Well, I'll be damned!' exclaimed Doc Robson, after cutting through Trabant's jumper. 'A bulletproof vest, that's what saved him. And look...' he continued, forcing his way out of the scrum with his hand open. 'Here are the two bullets lodged inside it.'

'But what on earth was Trabant doing wearing the GOEC uniform?' asked Bravinger.

'That's for you to figure out,' replied Doc Robson. 'All I know is he's a very lucky man.'

The doc cleared a space amongst his zealous colleagues and began to cut through the straps of the thick, armoured, sleeveless jacket, then carefully lifted it off Trabant's body.

'Aaaarrrggghhh...' groaned Trabant.

'Sorry, old chap, didn't mean to hurt you,' said the doc, his eyes drawn to the two nasty bruises on Trabant's chest, directly beneath where the bullets had impacted the vest.

'Look! He's coming to,' exclaimed Jones, hurrying closer. 'Bristo, can you hear me?'

'Eva?'

'No, it's me – Jones.'

'I-I've got to be with her!' Trabant exclaimed, trying to sit up. And then the tears began to stream, and his head lowered. 'She's dead!' he sobbed. 'And it's all...'

'All what?' asked Jones.

'... all my fault!' Trabant lifted his head again. 'Bentley... where *is* Bentley? He tried to k-kill me, and ...'

'Hey, relax... sssssssh, don't worry. You're safe now. Bentley is dead.'

Trabant's eyes held Jones's – searching, disbelieving, until finally comprehending. 'But Eva... is dead... it's my fault. Please, I must see her.'

'Just relax, Bristo. Eva's fine,' replied Jones softly, his hand gently restraining him. 'She's safe, on board and really looking forward to seeing you. We'll get her down here soon.'

'But I saw the look on Enrique's face,' said Trabant, his eyes wide with confusion. 'The guards took her away to...'

'You've been through a horrific experience. I don't know what you saw, but what I do know is she's very much alive.'

'Honestly?'

'Yes,' smiled Jones, reassuringly. 'And gorgeous as ever.'

Trabant eased back, and gradually caught his breath. 'She's alive...' he whispered, over and again, to convince himself of the miracle. 'T-thank you so much.' And slowly he began to drift, upon a wave of unimaginable relief.

Jones smiled and turned to walk away, but upon seeing Bravinger in deep consultation with Doc Robson, he turned back. 'Bristo, sorry to disturb you, but there's something else you must know.'

'W-what's that?'

'As I say, Eva is fine, but she resigned.'

Trabant's eyes opened in a flash.

'Yes, I know,' continued Jones. 'It was all heat-of-the-moment stuff, and I'll let her fill you in on the detail. But just remember, no matter what you read, no matter what the official reports say later, this whole rematch plan to save you was her idea. Not Bravinger's – no matter how much he will try to take the credit. Not mine, not anyone else's. All hers.'

Trabant's jaw flopped open. 'But she said both governments...'

Jones shook his head. 'She thought of it, masterminded it, moved heaven and earth to implement it. We all just acted on it – MI6, the DGSE, the CIA, Interpol. The list goes on.'

'Wow!'

'And it was only her lightning-quick intervention once you'd disappeared in Vienna that saved your life in the first place.'

Trabant blinked as another painful memory returned.

324

'Raúl was standing over me, aiming his gun. And then the phone rang, and after a brief conversation he said it was my lucky day; that Gunboat now wanted me brought back alive.'

'Eva orchestrated that. She's an amazing woman.'

'I agree.'

'And I'll tell you something else,' winked Jones. 'I think she quite likes you, you know.'

'Really?'

'U-huh! Anyway, here comes Lord Almighty…'

'Ah, Trabant!' said the head of MI6 in a voice far too loud for the circumstances. 'Good to see you alive again.'

'Hello, sir. Really sorry about all this mess. I didn't mean for it to happen. I just got a bit carried away.'

'If you feel up to it, can you tell us what happened?'

'Well, sir, I was in Le Club Maritime du something, and the cards were just going my—'

'No, no, no, man – what happened in the aquarium?'

'Take it easy on him, Bravinger,' cut in Doc Robson. 'He's very fragile.'

'You're telling me! Sorry, Trabant. Listen – do you know any reason why Gunboat would want Bentley dead?'

'No, sir. Though Bentley was definitely on his payroll.'

Bravinger looked to Jones. 'Yes, that's exactly what Agent Avante said too. Hmmm… okay. Now, tell us how you got shot and ended up in that broom cupboard?'

Doc Robson stepped in front of Bravinger and looked Trabant warmly in the eye. 'Are you sure you're up to these questions, lad? If not, just say and I'll tell these nice gentlemen to come back later.'

'No, it's fine, honestly.' Trabant winced a half-smile, and turned back to Bravinger and Jones. 'I was in this room with Gunboat and Enrique – the Crow's Nest I think they called it, and the telephone rang. Gunboat answered, Enrique turned

325

away to listen, and I took my chance to escape through the fire-exit.'

'Good thinking,' said Jones softly, urging him on.

'I was running down the stairs to find Eva. I got as far as the ground floor, but then Bentley caught up with me. I squirted him with my water pistol, but he punched me to the floor then started to make some telephone calls.'

'Who to?'

'One to a man called Oscar Conda. He said: "Yes, we're still on. So get moving." The second was to Reuters, telling them I was dead, and that Gunboat had committed the murder. Bentley then began to screw the silencer onto his gun. He was in a foul mood, and being unbelievably rude about Eva. So I punched him, then tried to escape again.'

'You punched Bentley?' gasped Jones.

'Yes, sir. Knocked him over too. There's a really excellent chapter in *The Beginner's Guide To*—'

'Never mind all that!' barked Bravinger. 'What happened next?'

'Bentley caught me again. We had another fight but this time I lost. H-he was standing over me, and kept on boasting about his great plan to replace Gunboat with Conda.'

Bravinger rubbed his eyes with irritation. 'We need hard evidence to back this up.'

'I-I don't have any, sir. Only my word. But, before I forget, I did learn of a weekly arms delivery made by Gunboat to the Central African Republic.'

'To Solomon "Double Tap" Hurunguru?'

'Yes, sir. Bentley bragged all about it. And I recited the details endlessly, to stop myself from passing out. It seemed to work.'

Bravinger stood aghast. 'So what exactly *have* you learnt?'

'That each week an Ilyushin IL-76 plane flies from Namibia to Liberia. Only it secretly diverts en route, and hidden beneath the humanitarian aid are cases of weapons. It lands, unloads, then continues to Liberia. The plane is registered to a front-company called Walvis Aid. It's registration number is V5-GRS. Previously it was V5-AHO. But best act quickly, sir. Gunboat changes the number regularly.'

Jones was already on his mobile phone. 'U-huh... okay, thanks.' He turned back to Bravinger. 'It checks out, sir. Walvis Aid are a registered charitable organisation. Their plane makes the journey every Wednesday. Nice one, Bristo. Excellent detail retention. Precisely the intelligence we need. Your mission is bearing some very tasty fruit after all.'

'Yes, good work, Trabant,' added Bravinger, reluctantly.

Trabant felt a tingle inside, not of self-congratulation, but of finally being able to help the cause.

'The question is,' continued Jones, 'how do we stop that plane taking off without Gunboat suspecting? If he learns of our intervention we'll have another crisis on our hands.'

'Sabotage?' suggested Trabant. 'My father used to put sugar in the fuel-tanks of the Volkspolizei vehicles, back in East Berlin. Worked a treat, or so my mother tells me.'

Jones smiled, then turned to Bravinger. 'Shall I contact the SAS, sir? They're also full of ingenious ideas.'

'Yes. And see if either they or the Marines have a unit nearby. Stop that plane taking off and we'll potentially save hundreds, if not thousands, of lives.'

As Jones returned to his phone, Bravinger returned to more immediate matters. 'So, Trabant, getting back to where we were. You said Bentley was standing over you, and revealing his plan to depose Gunboat.'

'Yes, sir.'

'And then what?'

'He pointed his gun at my head.'

'And shot you?'

'He made us swap clothes first.'

'Why!?!'

327

'He said he didn't want to get caught wearing the GOEC uniform, and that it would dirty my name if I was found wearing it. He did, however, say I could keep my Rupert Bear boxer shorts.'

'Rupert Bear?'

'Yes, sir. You know, the famous—'

'I know who Rupert the flippin' Bear is! Just tell me how you came to wear the bulletproof vest?'

'Bentley kept shouting at me to get dressed quickly. We could both hear voices approaching, English accents I mean, so it must have been the Royal Marines. Bentley kept looking back down the corridor. He didn't notice me slip the bulletproof vest on beneath the jumper.'

'A jumper, in the tropics?' asked Jones, as he ended his call.

'Yes, sir. It can get very cold by the Emperor Penguin Display.'

'Fair enough. So then what?'

'Once we were both re-dressed in each other's clothes, he punched me a couple more times. He seemed to really enjoy doing that, sir. He then led me to a nearby broom cupboard, shoved me inside and pointed his gun at my head.'

Sickbay again fell silent.

'His aim looked perfect. I thought that was it, sir. But just as he squeezed the trigger, about six Marines came running down the corridor. They were calling my name. Bentley became very agitated. He looked towards them, just long enough for me to huddle up into a ball. By the time he looked back I had my hands raised to protect my face. He had little to aim at, but still fired twice. It was like being hit by a hammer. I c-can—'

Tears began to well.

'Okay, Bristo, take it easy…' said Jones, placing a hand on Trabant's shoulder.

'Colonel Bravinger, I must insist!' shouted Doc Robson. 'This man is too traumatised to be interrogated like this.'

'Sorry, Trabant. Please – just tell us the last bit, in your own time.'

Trabant wiped his eyes, took a deep breath and continued. 'After Bentley shot me, he slammed the door closed, and that's the last I saw of him.'

Jones turned to Bravinger. 'Must have been moments before we picked him up in our binoculars, running across the rocks. And then he was shot.'

'And is that all of it?' asked Bravinger.

'Yes, sir. That's all. Would it be possible to see Eva now, please?'

Knock. Knock.

The Communications Petty Officer stepped into Sickbay and stood to attention. 'Message for Colonel Bravinger, sir.'

'Go ahead.'

'Sir, as requested, I am delighted to confirm that Gunboat Charlie and his associate Enrique are now on board ship, flown in by Sea King helicopter.'

Trabant immediately tensed up.

'Excellent news,' said Bravinger. 'Thank you. So how did we capture him in the end? Was it a glorious shoot-out?'

'Afraid not, sir. He was wedged solid in that plane of his. We had to cut him out with an angle grinder.'

'Oh, I see. And where precisely is he now?'

'On his way down here to see you, sir. He's not happy.'

'Oh!' Bravinger turned to Jones, the tumult of real fear circulating in his beady eyes. 'In that case, perhaps it's time I made myself scarce. Jones, you stay here and—'

'Remain exactly where you are, Colonel Bravinger,' said the strong assertive voice, 'until you've been officially relieved of your duties.'

'I beg your pardon!' Bravinger turned to the officer, but the voice had come from over the man's shoulder. The officer then stepped aside, and through the open doorway appeared the outline of another man – tall, slim, and poised like a racing whippet; his ageing frame dressed in the finest English tweed, and his parliamentary head capped by a dashing sweep of silvery-white hair.

Bravinger's jaw hit the deck. 'P-Prime Minister!'

'Indeed it is, gentlemen. Indeed it is.'

31

The Bridge that Spanned the Crystal River

'WHERE IS HE? I WANT KILL HIM – RIGHT NOW!'

All eyes turned towards the doorway, as Gunboat's thunderous voice grew louder, from down the ship's corridor.

'Okay, get out!' ordered Cuthbert Hanlon. 'I'll talk to you later.'

'Thank you, Prime Minister.'

'No, not you, Trabant. I meant Bravinger.'

'But it's me he wants to kill!'

'This whole affair needs to end, once and for all,' replied Hanlon, as he watched Bravinger scramble out through the side door. 'I can handle Gunboat.'

Trabant harboured the gravest of doubts. 'If it's all the same, Your Highness, I think I'll be off.'

'Stand firm, son. Think "Bulldog spirit", and don't call me Highness. I'm not royalty, you know.'

'WHERE IS HE?' shouted Gunboat, now forcing his way in through the main door.

'Sorry, sir,' said the Communications Petty Officer, following on close behind. 'But as Gunboat isn't technically under arrest, I couldn't stop him wandering around.'

'TELL ME WHERE HE IS, OR I TEAR THIS SHIP APART, DECK BY DECK!'

When no one answered, Gunboat turned and locked his coal-black eyes on Trabant. 'And as for you, señor Gringo Loco. You…'

'But, please, I—'

'… are off the hook.'

'But… I'm innocent! And… oh! Did you just say—'

'Sí!'

'H-how come?'

'I come to that in minute. But first, tell me where—'

'Bravinger's gone,' cut in Hanlon, with every ounce of calmness he could muster.

'Well, well – señor Prime Minister. How are you?'

'Could be better. And you?'

'NO GOOD! SEEN MY AQUARIUM – IT RUIN!'

'Colonel Bravinger has been relieved of his duties.'

'Why?'

Hanlon looked Gunboat straight in the eye, knowing that only the truth, the whole truth and nothing *but* the truth would now work. 'For sending Agent Trabant to watch you in Cannes in the first place. And because of the magnitude of this situation, it is only fitting that I – British Prime Minister – draw it to a satisfactory conclusion. So, anything you have to say, you can say to me.'

'You been on this ship all the time?' asked Gunboat.

'No. I arrived half an hour ago. The Royal Air Force flew me down specially.' Hanlon turned to Doc Robson and his team. 'Gentlemen, may I respectfully ask you to leave the room. I need to speak privately with Gunboat.'

'Our pleasure.'

'You too, Communications Petty Officer… er… Walsh,' he continued, reading the man's badge. 'But Jones and Trabant, you stay.'

Hanlon waited till the door had closed behind, then turned back to Gunboat. 'Your man, Enrique – where is he?'

'Talking missiles with the helicopter crew.'

Trabant's eyes narrowed, certain it was Gunboat's number two who'd actioned the plan for Eva's death.

332

'Eh, señor Gringo Loco, you relax, man,' said Gunboat. 'You *and* your girlfriend are both off the hook, so forget about bad feeling for Enrique, or anyone.'

Trabant gently nodded, and savoured the monumental gush of relief that followed. But it couldn't be complete, not until he knew exactly why they'd been given their underworld royal pardon.

Hanlon cleared his throat. 'Gunboat, I am under intense political pressure to maintain the status quo. Trabant remains alive, which is all we ever wanted. And, as a bonus, a traitor within both our camps has been exposed.'

'You mean Bentley?'

'Yes, regrettably.'

'But how you know?' asked Gunboat suspiciously. 'You only just taken charge of this mess.'

'Any trust I had in Bravinger deteriorated long ago. So I had Jones keep me updated on developments. Which compels me to ask – how long *was* Bentley on your payroll?'

'Oh, l-o-n-g time,' beamed Gunboat.

Hanlon closed his eyes. 'Well, to nail the details of his betrayal to the wall; you know, for everyone to see, I need a greater insight into—'

'Take this,' said Gunboat, retrieving a large brown envelope from his jacket pocket.

'What is it?'

'A large brown envelope.'

'I can see that. What's inside it?'

'All the proof you ever need, about secrets Bentley sell; arms deals he initiate; contacts he nurture. There's documents, photos, bank accounts – all very incriminating, though of course, amended to keep me well out of picture. There plenty you will never know about my business.'

Trabant lowered his eyes, desperate for his face not to reveal the intelligence he'd gained about Gunboat's weekly delivery to the Central African Republic, which he prayed the SAS could now stop taking off.

'I no normally help you people with stuff like this,' continued Gunboat. 'But I want the Bentley reputation destroyed the same way his life has been.'

'Didn't think paperwork was your thing?' continued Hanlon.

'For me – no. But Enrique love it. He like one of your little English dogs. What they called?'

'A poodle?'

'No, no. A strong, animal kinda dog. The name sound like mine, you know – terrifying!'

'Terrier?' suggested Trabant.

'Sí! A terrier. He one of them. He relentless. He keep note of everything. And I say this morning, Enrique – give me that envelope, just in case, because Bentley always a man to handle with caution.'

'How do you mean?' asked Hanlon.

'He greedy. He betray British Government by selling secrets to me. Once that line crossed, it's muy easy to do it again, and to anyone. He try to cross me, and got everything he deserve. This envelope was my insurance policy, just in case.'

'Very wise. And do you know who killed him?'

'I no know,' winked Gunboat.

Hanlon didn't dwell. 'You mentioned Agent Trabant is off the hook. What made you change your mind?'

'He make me realise that lose at cards is my one weakness. Stop playing and I become INVULNERABLE! Honestly, I can no ever thank him enough for bring it to my attention.'

Trabant smiled, nervously. But Hanlon refocused on his primary objective – to appease the legendary temper of Gunboat Charlie Chávez.

'Well, with regards to Bristo Trabant, we have two choices,' he continued. 'We either prosecute you for his kidnap and attempted murder…'

'No make me laugh!'

'… or drop all charges and forget this whole affair ever happened. And when considering the opinions of the political community, the second option – to everyone – is the far more favourable. Agreed?'

'Maybe.'

'Gunboat, you hold all the cards with that little black book of yours.'

'I know.'

'So what'll it take to keep it closed?'

'You can rebuild my aquarium for a start.'

'Granted.' Hanlon kept his face impassive, while his heart jumped for joy. Gunboat's acceptance of compensation meant that the whole calamitous situation was now, finally, salvageable. 'What else?'

'You no seem to understand. It also about damage to my reputation and good name.'

'I anticipated you'd feel that way. And so, during my long flight out here, I took the liberty of preparing a statement, which will clear your name of any wrongdoing.' Hanlon produced a hastily scribbled-upon sheet of Ten Downing Street notepaper. 'Would you like to read it?'

'No. I trust you, señor Prime Minister. But any tricks and you know what will happen.'

Cuthbert Hanlon nodded. 'Jones, get this circulated to every news agency and TV channel in the world. Insist it gets broadcast in precisely fifteen minutes' time. We can then all watch it right here on television.'

As Jones hurried out through the door, Gunboat raised an eyebrow, not yet finished. 'What about my injured men and fish?'

'All will be awarded full military honours.'

'My suit? Those Marines cut it to pieces with that angle grinder.'

'I'll have my own personal tailor flown out straight away.'

'Good,' said Gunboat. 'We make progress, señor Hanlon. Now, while we wait for press release to be broadcast, there something else I want.'

'What's that?'

'Ten minute alone with Trabant. Just him and me – in here.'

'You know I can't allow that.'

'I say he off the hook. No anything happen to him.'

Hanlon peered deeply into Gunboat's coal-black eyes, searching for the motives behind his unusual request. 'I'm sorry. That is out of the question.'

'But, Prime Minister, it no ever was a question.'

Hanlon lowered his head. 'Very well. Trabant, I'll be right outside if you need me.'

'But, Prime Minister, I'd much prefer it if—'

The door closed softly, and Trabant backed as far up the bed as possible.

'Relax!' smiled Gunboat. 'Six hours ago, yes, I want to wring your neck, but now I want shake your hand. Come on, put it there…'

'OW!'

'Becoming a father has amazing effect on me. Make me see whole different light. And that is muchas gracias to you.'

'I–is it?'

'Sí! Been trying for a child for ages. No luck. Then you come along with your blatant cheat in that first card game. My doctor reckon the anxiety you cause make me extra fertile. Next thing – wham, hey presto – señora G is expecting.'

'But that was only a week ago. Surely that's too soon?'

'No argue. Women work in mysterious ways. Perhaps the other night make the difference. The point is she in the club and I reckon it down to you.'

'Not personally. Honestly, I didn't… I mean, while you were away I… please, she's an attractive lady of course, but I…'

336

'Oh, shut up!' groaned Gunboat. 'The fact is she pregnant, and in your own small, annoying little way, you help. So leave it at that. Okay?'

'Yes. Happily. But your guests… w-won't they still be expecting you to kill me?'

'Since when I worry 'bout what people think of me? And anyway, sparing life of MI6 *and* DGSE agents will give me muchas extra bargain power too. Far more than if I kill you. But there even more to my decision than that.'

'Really?'

'Yep. No think I no appreciate what you do for me. I very grateful.'

Trabant shook his head in confusion.

'Want me to explain, to prove I fully appreciate the length you go to?'

'Please.'

'Okay. Well, there two things. Firstly, because you cheat, Bentley expose himself as a traitor. And believe me, I hate traitor far more than card cheat. And second, you hand Oscar Conda to me on a platter.'

'D–did I?'

'You know you did. So you see, señor Gringo Loco, you have done more for me in one week than I have struggle to do in years. So the least I can do is let you live, huh? In fact, what I should *really* do is offer you a job.'

Trabant began to shiver. Strengthening the position of the world's most notorious criminal had certainly not been the goal of his mission. 'But how did I do all that?'

Gunboat smiled. 'Okay, I play your game a minute longer, then I get Prime Minister Hanlon back here to continue appeasing me.'

'O-okay.'

'Right. You gave me telephone numbers – remember? Well, I call your office. I pretend I am you, and once I give the nice

337

señora the codes she ask for, I find I now have MI6 level five security access.'

'L-level five?' stuttered Trabant, knowing that related directly to his own department – the Priority Surveillance Unit.

'Sí. So I decide to check up what else Bentley involve with, 'cos I no ever trust him much. The señora mention another active assignment – the protection and nurture of MI6 informant Oscar Conda.' Gunboat winked. 'As you can imagine, I absolutely delight! And it also confirm that Bentley was a liar.'

'Did it?'

'Yeah, because I ask him a hundred thousand million times if he knew where Conda was hiding, and he said he no did. And all the time he lining him up to take over from me – the lying, deceiving dog. That reason enough to kill him. Anyway, while on the phone to señora Muy Helpful, I push my luck further, and no only did she give me the exact location of Conda's guano farm in Borneo, but also guaranteed times of when he gonna be there.'

Trabant's jaw flopped open, aghast at how easily the details had been gained. 'I heard Bentley telephone Conda from the aquarium,' he added quickly, to pre-empt what Gunboat would inevitably say next.

'So did I. Despite all the explosions and gunfire, I see the little red light appear on my telephone console. I thought: that funny – someone dialling out, what with everything going on. So I listen in, hear them talk, hear them say exactly what they plan to do.'

'Y-you must have been livid!'

'It confirm what I already know.' Gunboat leant forward, his eyes intense but unnervingly warmer. 'You help me, señor Trabant, and that act alone save your life. And the man who shot Bentley is now on his way to Borneo to kill Conda, or so I hear,' he winked. 'Within space of few hours, the two weakness in my armour will both be dead. Plus I never, ever play cards again. So you see, my new best amigo, I have muchas to thank you for.'

Trabant's head begun to spin. Both men had died because of the telephone numbers and security access codes he'd given Gunboat. But when? And how!?!

Gunboat smiled. 'I no believe you forget. They were written on that piece of paper, the one you leave inside your jacket pocket, way back in Le Club Maritime du Soleil. Remember? When you try to escape and Raúl grip your jacket, and you slip down and out of it. Well, we search it. The piece of paper was wedge in the pages of that book, *The Beginner's Guide To...*'

Trabant jolted. The damned piece of paper! The one Bravinger had ordered him to destroy; the one he'd fretted over losing then subsequently forgotten all about; the one that had fallen into Gunboat's hands, to inadvertently sign the death warrants of the two men.

'No worry,' winked Gunboat. 'That piece of paper – it be our little secret. And no look so worried. You lose an enemy and gain a friend. And believe me, I a good friend to have.'

Trabant closed his eyes in horror. 'C-can I go now?' he asked, weary from the revelations.

'Sure. Your troubles with me are over!'

Could they ever be? Trabant levered his legs down onto the floor, and inserted his feet into a pair of Royal Navy slippers. His gut reaction was compelling – to distance himself from the man who'd threatened their lives time and again.

The thought of Eva re-energised his spirit. He had to be with her, and witness the miracle of her safe passage through this whole terrible episode; to see her smile, the sparkle in her eyes – and to ask the question he really wanted to.

Gunboat studied Trabant with curiosity as he shuffled across to the door. 'Eh, señor Gringo Loco, you still have muchas on your mind, huh?'

Trabant didn't answer.

'Well, she upstairs… on the flight deck.'

'W-who?' replied Trabant, without raising his eyes.

'Agent Avante – the French señorita.'

His head turned in a flash. 'Is she?'

'Yeah. Up the bow end, by the ski jump.'

'That's the pointed end, right?'

'No so much on an aircraft carrier, but yeah – the front.'

'T-thank you.'

'She really like you, señor. I can tell from way back.'

'You think?'

'Yeah, man. When I first see you two together in Le Club Maritime du Soleil, I think – there's fire between these two. And the way she defend you in my office. The way she punch teeth out of my men's faces to keep you breathing. And the way she look at you – that's love, man. And I think she wanna show you the true meaning of "bon soir", if you catch my drift?'

Trabant flushed, and continued walking.

'There's no place better than La Casa de Amor,' added Gunboat.

'W-where's that?'

'In here,' smiled Gunboat, tapping his heart. 'The House of Love.'

Trabant paused at Gunboat's perceptiveness. Was it that obvious?

'I lucky. I already there. And we all need love, even criminal masterminds like me.'

Trabant suddenly felt lost again, in the enormity of what he desired more than anything. 'But I get so tongue-tied,' he replied, as if confiding in a best friend over a pint in the local pub. 'Because she's so—'

'Lovely?'

'Yes, exactly.'

Gunboat smiled. 'I the same when I first meet my wife.'

'Really?'

'Oh, yeah…' Gunboat's eyes drifted to a cherished memory. 'Long time ago I in this hotel in downtown Panama City, smashing the place up 'cos they no pay me protection. Anyway, something make me look across to the reception desk, and there she stand – my darling Antoinette – smiling back like an angel. We connect instantly.'

'Didn't all that violence put her off?'

'No, she say I have a muy lovely way with words,' beamed Gunboat. 'Anyway, I ask her out to dinner that very night. No hesitation. A week later we move in together, to La Casa de Amor. And now we add an extension 'cos we having a niño.'

'A what?'

'A child. A baby! Señor Trabant, La Casa de Amor now beckon to you. You wanna step inside?'

'Yes. More than anything.'

'Then go knock on the door.'

'I will. I mean, I am. But what do I say, you know… if she answers the door?'

'The words will come to guide you inside.'

'But I'm terrible at talking, and—'

'The words will come, señor. It time for you to close the deal.'

'I will,' replied Trabant, shuffling on to the door. He went to open it, but paused, thought deeply for a moment, then turned back to Gunboat. 'What does it look like, La Casa de Amor?'

'It different for everyone. Close your eyes and try to imagine. For me it a tall palace with big gates, marble statues, fountains, flamingos…'

Trabant closed his eyes and tried to imagine too. But for him, the House of Love was more like a small cottage set in a clearing, with quaint little windows, a thatched roof and smoking chimney. He'd seen it before, but had never dared to

341

step closer, as the forest always seemed so dark and cold. But today it was warmer, and the shadows had become light and airy. As he began to walk, rabbits and other animals scampered out from the trees to urge him onwards, to make sure he continued across the bridge that spanned the crystal river.

Safely on the other side, he stepped closer still. Already he could smell the delicious food wafting from the kitchen – penne pollo Avante, his favourite. He walked up to the window and peered through the gap in the curtains. Candles flickered to give the room a delightful illumination. To the right, a hearty fire burned brightly – the one he'd created on the desert island. And over by the far window stood a dinner table – the one from the flat in Biot? Yes, it was, *and* set for two.

And then she appeared – the most beautiful woman in the world – dressed in a stunning white summer dress, the one worn on the desert island, with her hair tied up as when they'd first met in Le Club Maritime du Soleil. She began to pour lemonade then checked her watch. Her guest must be late, but who was it? He hoped himself, but he'd never presume. Perhaps it *was* someone else and he'd lost her all over again? He looked closer at the table, and tried to read the names on the place cards. One was Eva's, but the other… he just couldn't make out.

Trabant jolted. 'I've got to go!'

'Bad dream, huh?' asked Gunboat.

'No, it was nice,' he replied, opening the door. 'I just need to know how it ends.'

'Well, go find out then. Time wait for no man, señor – no even me. And on your way, tell Prime Minister Hanlon he can come back to finish appeasing me.'

But Bristo Trabant had already gone.

342

32

Good Afternoon, Planet Earth

PRIME MINISTER CUTHBERT HANLON peered back inside Sickbay. 'Gunboat, request permission to show you the TV broadcast.'

'Granted.'

'Excellent.' As Hanlon took his seat, he said thoughtfully, 'You know, I've just passed Trabant in the corridor. He wasn't the slightest bit interested in seeing this news bulletin.'

Gunboat smiled. 'He got something w-a-y more important on his mind.'

Jones quickly switched on the wall-mounted television, picked up the remote control and scrolled through the countless channels until arriving at the image of a comfy television studio.

All three men watched intently.

The television studio was decorated blue and yellow, with a bright red sofa, upon which sat two presenters – one lady and one man – who both now looked directly into the camera, flashed their brilliant white teeth, and spoke.

'Welcome back, viewers, to KCMCC News Channel. I'm Ed Weinberg…'

'And I'm Pamela Martínez.'

'Good afternoon, Planet Earth!' they gushed.

Ed continued, 'And now, as promised, we're going straight to that breaking story in Panama City, Panama, where we join viewers' favourite – Tabitha Lansdowne. Tabitha, tell us, what news do you have?'

'Thanks, Ed. Well, yes, here I am on the rocky shores of Panama City, and if you look over my shoulder you can see the British Royal Navy's aircraft carrier HMS *Indomitable*, plus entourage. Now, why are they here, you ask? Well, a few hours ago the news agency Reuters received an anonymous tip-off that a British MI6 agent by the name of Bristo Trabant had been murdered.'

'That's an unusual name, Tabitha. Is that Trabant, as in—'

'... the car? Yes, Ed, that's right. Now, from what we can gather, and in response to this tip-off, the Navy deployed three boats of Royal Marines to attack the building directly in front of me – the Panama City Aquarium – where Agent Trabant had reportedly been held captive.'

'Isn't that a bit too coincidental?' asked Ed. 'The Royal Navy happening to be so close?'

Tabitha Lansdowne twirled a lock of golden hair around her finger and replied. 'Good question, Ed. Well, according to a Royal Navy spokesperson, the taskforce was already in Panamanian waters undergoing practice manoeuvres, a fact confirmed by the local authorities. Anyway, the aquarium is owned by local businessman and marine conservationist Charles Chávez, who is believed to be deeply traumatised by the whole episode. Eye-witnesses state that a huge battle broke out between the Royal Marines and señor Chávez's personal security staff, resulting in several injuries, including one man being shot dead while running away from the aquarium building, across these very rocks I'm standing on now, and on towards a waiting Royal Navy RIB. The British Government are refusing to confirm the identity of this man, except that it is not Bristo Trabant, who is confirmed as being alive, well and on board HMS *Indomitable* as we speak. They also state that Mister Trabant is not an intelligence operative, but merely a tourist caught in the wrong place and time.'

'That's extraordinary, Tabitha,' said Ed in the studio. 'And in this—'

'Oops, sorry to cut across you, Ed, but I've just been handed a statement from the Royal Navy's press office.' Tabitha Lansdowne began to read.

'We – the British Government, together with the Royal Navy – deeply regret the completely unjustified and categorically incorrect attack this morning on the Panama City Aquarium, and wish to apologise unreservedly to its owner, señor Chávez, for the mistake. We wish to make it clear we acted on information which later turned out to be incorrect. No charges will be made against señor Chávez' admittedly well-armed guards. And we also wish to stress that this error should in no way tarnish the squeaky-clean image of señor Chávez, who gives freely to charity, and has done more to help local businesses and extinction-threatened marine life than anyone else we know. That is all we have to say for now, except to point out that the Panama City Aquarium will be open again for business in next to no time, and will continue to offer unrivalled exhibits and a truly wonderful day out for all the family.'

Ed from the studio piped up. 'Tabitha, thank you for another accurate, cutting-edge report. Now, can I ask – señor Chávez must be fuming?'

'Yes, Ed, he must be. But getting any of the locals to elaborate is proving impossible. The one certainty is that this anonymous tip-off still hasn't been traced. Perhaps it was all a hoax. As soon as I hear more, I'll of course let you know. But for now, that's all from me – Tabitha Lansdowne, reporting from Panama City, Panama, for KCMCC News Channel. Ed, back to you in the studio.'

'Thanks, Tabitha. Well, viewers, extraordinary scenes going on in Panama. And as soon as we have any more news, we'll be straight back out there. In the meantime, if you have a cat and you're wondering how to translate its meowing, here's Douglas in Pontypridd with a very interesting story. Douglas…'

Prime Minister Cuthbert Hanlon flicked off the TV, then turned to Gunboat. 'Satisfied?'

'Nearly.'

Hanlon sat down, loosened his tie and settled in for a long night. 'Okay, what else will it take?'

'Well, while coming to this ship on helicopter, me and Enrique write this nice little list,' he said, reaching inside his other jacket pocket, 'to make sure I no forget no anything.'

'Little!?! It's five pages long!'

'I know,' beamed Gunboat. 'And here's the first thing: a nice big residence in Pimlico, London. You know, near where the Queen live.'

'Huh!?!'

'… with a garden too, 'cos my wife has her heart set on a Corgi.'

Hanlon buried his head in his hands.

'Next, I want… '

33

More, Much More…

BRISTO TRABANT WALKED ALONG the busy flight deck of HMS *Indomitable*; the sun was warm on his face, smiling down from a cloudless sky. It felt good to be alive. And there she stood, at the bow end of the flight deck, staring out to sea — the unmistakable outline of the most beautiful woman in the world.

Life had changed beyond all recognition. For the first time he had faced his mortality, lived under the threat that tomorrow might never come, only to cheat death and live on. And now, ironically, through that perilous journey a new perspective had dawned — a crystal-clear realisation of what really mattered in life. Yes, the lessons had been hard learnt, and a week ago he would have settled for simply coming out of this alive. But now he wanted more, much more.

The flight deck resembled a short stretch of motorway, with white lines marked out on the black tarmac, and red traffic lights blazing to confirm the end of military play. To the right, two mechanics wiped down a Harrier as it dozed in the shade, like stable-hands caressing a victorious stallion.

Trabant nodded in gratitude then hobbled onwards, together with his comprehensive selection of body bruises. Arms, stomach, face and ribs all screamed for attention, each insisting their own pain to be the worst, though clearly outdone by the walnut-sized bullet contusions on his chest. The pain was immense, yet at the same time a welcome reminder that he *was* still alive, in one piece, and perhaps in with a second chance for what he most truly desired.

'*Close the deal… close the deal.*'

Gunboat's words echoed as he drew ever closer.

ii

'Has Agent Avante found out yet that Trabant is alive?' asked Bravinger, looking down sheepishly from the bridge.

Jones turned and smiled. 'I think she's just about to, sir.'

iii

A cold wind blew through the soul of Eva Avante.

She stood at the very tip of the flight deck, as far away from Bravinger and the situation as she could get. Her thoughts ebbed and flowed out across the Pacific Ocean, twisted and torn amongst the rising swells. After everything that had happened, how could she carry on? Even begin to think about tomorrow? The horizon stared back, bereft of answers.

Another tear ran down her cheek, and though the late-afternoon sun did its best to dry her eyes, it could not stave off the deep, plunging chill of despair.

Eva wrapped her arms tighter around her body. If only she had—

Something caused her to turn, to look back down the flight deck to the hazy outline of the man who now approached, blurry like a mirage, walking uneasily, holding his side, dressed in a baggy blue medical gown. Maybe one of the Marines she'd met, hurt in the battle? Maybe Commodore Speed following up on his earlier offer of dinner? She could never love again, not now.

She wiped her wet eyes and peered closer.

Tall, slim, big ears…

Big ears?

It couldn't be…

It was.

'BRISTO!'

Eva ran forward and seized him in the tightest, warmest embrace ever known in Royal Naval history. 'I thought you were—'

'Ouch!'

'Oh, you're hurt?' she said, quickly releasing and searching his face, his body.

'Just bruising, where Bentley shot me,' he replied, pointing to his chest.

'He shot you?'

'It's a long story.'

'But… the rocks? The sniper? I saw you fall… and the radio message, and—'

Trabant shook his head. 'No, he shot Bentley, who was in my clothes. Bentley made us swap, then he ran outside.'

'But why swap?' replied Eva, baffled by the course of events.

'Another part of his plan.'

Eva shook her head in disgust, until something caught her eye. 'Your hand – it's all puffy.'

'Oh, yes. That's where I punched Bentley, before he shot me, that is.'

'You punched Bentley? Oh, mon chéri.'

'Well, he was saying some very unpleasant things.'

'About what?'

Trabant just smiled. It was so good to see her again, and the explanations could wait. Bentley had encroached enough on their lives already. 'I'll tell you some other time.'

She gently held his hands and smiled back. And her eyes sparkled again, as they had in Le Club Maritime du Soleil when

349

they'd very first met, when neither seemingly had a care in the world.

'Eva, I thought you were dead too, until Jones told me. I am *so* sorry for my behaviour in the beginning; for beating Gunboat at cards. I just got carried away.'

'You played well.'

'But you nearly died because of me. It's unforgivable, and I—'

'Ssshhhh,' she interrupted. 'I won't hear another word. You're a good man, Bristo Trabant, and that's all there is to it. Anyway, if I'd driven you to Paris in the first place, then none of this mess would have happened.'

'But how were you to know?'

'It's my job to anticipate.'

Trabant smiled to defuse her self-reproach, and it worked. 'How is your jaw?'

'Oh, fine,' she replied, waggling it side to side. 'A bit bruised, but it takes more than a size-twelve boot and an army of thugs to get the better of me.'

'I know it does.'

'Hey, I saw Gunboat flown aboard,' she said, with a hint of trepidation. 'Did you see him too?'

'Yes. He's downstairs right now, letting it be known what it will take to keep his black book of secrets closed.'

'With Bravinger, I bet?'

'No, he's been relieved of his duties, for sending me to Cannes in the first place.'

'Brilliant.'

'Prime Minister Hanlon is doing the talking.'

'I thought it was him I saw arriving,' Eva said. 'Honestly, it's been so busy on this flight deck.'

'It's busy round the world too. The press are going crazy, and a statement is being broadcast globally, apologising to Gunboat for all that's happened.'

'What about apologising to you?' exclaimed Eva.

'And you!' replied Trabant. 'Eva, surely something must happen to Gunboat?'

She lowered her head, then looked back up, deep into Trabant's eyes. 'Bristo, I am so very sorry. You are right, Gunboat should pay for all he has put you through, but with the hold he has over so many people, I know he will remain at liberty. It is a very unsatisfactory conclusion, but the way of the world right now. All I can say is that I have my own plans for him, and that one day – one day very soon – things will change.'

Trabant basked within the fire of Eva's passion. 'Perhaps I can help?' he said, meaning every word.

'Yes,' she replied, with a mixture of surprise and delight. 'I'd like that.'

'So would I. And to begin with, how about some valuable intelligence on a weekly delivery of arms, flown into the Central African Republic.'

'Really!?! One of Gunboat's?'

'Yes, masquerading as humanitarian aid, but diverting to Solomon Hurunguru.'

Eva's face lit up. 'Your father would be so proud of you.'

'You think?'

'I know. As I am, too.'

Trabant's eyes began to fill. 'Like you said, it's important to make a difference. Being a secret agent, well, I now see it's what I'm meant to be.'

'Are you sure?' asked Eva.

'Positive. My work has only just begun. And I'll try not to mess things up from here on, I promise.' He held that thought a moment longer, then continued. 'You know, we did speak – Gunboat and I.'

'Really? What about?'

His mind flashed to the horrors resulting from the lost piece of paper. 'Er, well… quite a few things actually. The best bit is he no longer wants to kill you, or me.'

'Oh, thank heavens,' she replied, with a momentous sigh of relief. 'But how come?'

'Hmmm, well... that's another thing to tell you later.'

'Okay. Anything else you discussed?'

'Nah, just boys' talk. Jones, however, told me the rematch was all *your* idea, and how you practically mobilised the world to find me.'

'It was just a few phone calls, nothing much.'

'Nothing much?' he exclaimed. 'Eva, you—'

She shrugged her shoulders. 'I just liked what I saw; what I see. Anything else you spoke about?'

Trabant smiled, recalling her words from the desert island.

'What?' she asked, intrigued.

'You women sure love to change the subject.'

Eva smiled too. 'Yes, sometimes, but women are allowed to. So, Monsieur Global Hero, anything else?'

'He also told me you resigned.'

'Ah, that! Yes, I did, because no one, including my own boss, was getting angry at Bravinger. But your Prime Minister has seemingly granted my wish.'

'So will you reapply?'

'There was nothing in writing, just a foul-mouthed outburst. But let's forget that for now. Tell me, how did you escape the shark enclosure?'

'You won't believe me,' replied Trabant.

'Try me.'

'Well, er... there was this talking shark, with a French accent, and it...'

Eva laughed. 'Aah – the wonders of the animal kingdom never cease. But what happened next? Were you taken to the Crow's Nest? And how did you get back here alive?' she continued, her mind beginning to race with the questions she thought could never be asked.

'*Close the deal... close the deal.*' Gunboat's words repeated, almost as if by command.

Trabant politely raised his hand. 'Eva, there's something I want to say, and I don't want to wait another moment.'

'Ooh, sounds serious.'

'It is. You see, the thing is...'

'Yes?'

'It's just that, well, what I wanted to say is that...' Oh, Lord, her beauty really was breathtaking... *and* incapacitating. 'Well, on my journey back from the dead, I did a lot of thinking... and, er... well, I wanted to say that, er... I really want to... (oh, jeez...) er... (gulp)... (help!) er...'

'It's okay,' she whispered. 'Take your time.'

'Thank you. I really want to, er... c-cook you my steak and kidney pie.'

NO! Cooking his stupid pie was *not* what he wanted to say at all. There was more, much more, but at the last moment he'd shied away like a horse facing a big, intimidating jump.

'I accept,' smiled Eva.

'Great,' replied Trabant, forcing a smile.

But his world stopped, and Eva waited...

... and his mind froze in a moment of crushing paralysis

... with the words stuck in his throat

... with the moment evaporating before his very eyes

... until Cupid flew down from the heavens, gently laid his bow and arrow down upon the flight deck, walked up and gave him the most almighty kick up the backside.

'OW!'

'Bristo, what is it?' asked Eva, searching his face with her eyes – her dark pools of milk chocolate ...

... and that was all it took – one more glance into those eyes, to know the time had come...

... to dive in headfirst and never resurface.

'Eva, there's more...'

353

'More what – food?'

'No. More I want to say.'

'Oh! Go on…'

Trabant smiled, took a deep breath, and continued. 'I am so sorry I rejected you on the desert island. I was stupid.'

'Bristo, it's okay, I underst—'

'No. No, you don't. You see, the thing is, I want more than to simply cook you my steak and kidney pie, and I want more than for us to be friends. Eva, what I'm trying to say, rather badly I know, is that, well… after everything we've been through, I know without doubt that I want us to be together – as boyfriend and girlfriend.'

There! He'd finally said it. And though his words echoed with kindergarten innocence, the satisfaction of having said them made him feel more alive than ever before.

'So, what do you say?' he asked nervously.

Eva's face blossomed like a harvest sunrise, basking in the warmth of the words she thought she'd never hear, from the man she thought she'd never see alive again.

She looked deep into his eyes and replied… with one word.

The word was heartfelt.

The word was everything.

The word was…

'Snap!'

THE END

354

'Paradise is defined not by where you are,
but by whom you are with'

BRISTO TRABANT
(on a desert island, somewhere in the Pacific Ocean)

Acknowledgements

This book would never have been possible without the passion, expertise, care, generosity of time, guidance and advice from the following truly wonderful people.

Foremost, I wish to thank my mother, Jill, without whom I may never have even started writing. It was you who suggested I enrol in a creative writing course, who encouraged me when I had doubts and who offered boundless support and enthusiasm as *Dead Men* built up its momentum. I can never thank you enough for opening the door to the wonderful world of fiction writing. I miss you so very much, but know that you continue to be with me, ready to share the many new adventures ahead. Love you masses, Mum.

Heather Steed, my creative writing teacher, for helping me find and develop my writing voice; my writing-group friends Josie and Steve for your invaluable feedback and encouragement; the people of Vienna, Cannes and Biot, especially the elderly lady whose stories of the French Resistance were hugely influential. The people of Panama City, in particular the guides at Ancon Expeditions; the officers and crew of HMS *Ark Royal*, who introduced me to the complex art of Royal Naval Carrier and Task Group operations, and in particular, Commander Rocky Salmon Royal Navy, Commander Air HMS *Ark Royal*, for your tireless proofreading, continued suggestions and insight; the Trabant IFA Club for the historical background;

Darren Harris for assistance with translation, and all the other people I have met along the way.

Lucy Ridout, my editor, who from day one embraced the essence of what I was trying to achieve, who encouraged and inspired, told me what I needed to know, answered my endless questions, raised the plot and characters to a different level, and helped me over the finish line.

Chris Duggan, whose artistic genius not only brought the visual aspect to life, but also perfectly reflected the soul of the book – thank you for your patience, willingness, counsel and likewise assistance with crossing the finish line.

Andrew and everyone at Hewer Text for your wonderful typesetting, design and care that gave each page its visual sparkle; Daphne Trotter, my brilliant proofreader; Rebecca Souster and everyone at Clays for being so helpful and accommodating; Nicky at Laurel Creative for your fantastic website design; Viel Richardson and Angela for the awesome photography; and the Society of Authors for end-of-the-phone advice whenever I needed it.

My sister, Susy, and all my friends for your belief, support and encouragement, especially Michelle, for your priceless input on various research trips.

Thank you all so very much.

And last but not least, thank you to you, the reader, for picking up this book. I hope you have enjoyed reading it as much as I have enjoyed writing it. And I hope we will meet again for the next instalment.

Best wishes

Dominic

Fear for our Sharks

The threats to sharks detailed in this book, particularly on pages 267–271, are sadly very real and alarming. The numbers killed each day are simply unsustainable. The threat of extinction for many species is immediate, and as sharks are a vital part of marine ecosystems, their loss will seriously affect the health of our oceans and many of their inhabitants.

Action must be taken to protect and preserve these wonderful, awe-inspiring animals. They urgently need our help – before it's too late.

For more information on sharks and conservation initiatives, please visit www.sharktrust.org.

Bristo Trabant will be back in
Dominic Canty's

KISS
OF
THE
BLACK
SOMBRERO

www.dominiccanty.com

TOP SECRET

AGENT CONTACT DETAILS

 www.facebook.com/
bristotrabant

 @bristotrabant
#bristotrabant

 www.pinterest/
bristotrabant

bristo@bristotrabant.com
www.bristotrabant.com

MEMORISE—
then tell everybody!